306.7662 Perry, Joel.
PER
That's why they're in cages, people!

$14.95

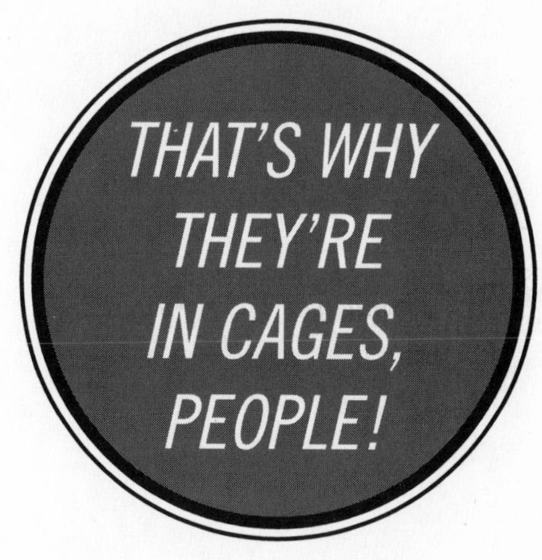
THAT'S WHY
THEY'RE
IN CAGES,
PEOPLE!

Joel Perry

alyson books
los angeles

Manufactured in the United States of America.

This trade paperback original is published by Alyson Publications,
P.O. Box 4371, Los Angeles, California 90078-4371.
Distribution in the United Kingdom by Turnaround Publisher Services Ltd.,
Unit 3, Olympia Trading Estate, Coburg Road, Wood Green,
London N22 6TZ England.

First edition: November 2003

03 04 05 06 07 a 10 9 8 7 6 5 4 3 2 1

ISBN 1-55583-742-5

Credits
Cover photography from Sterling Studio.
Cover design by Matt Sams.

To all who have shared their wisdom, support, encouragement, love, and other gifts, I thank you. To Fred for being all of those things and always being there—you have my undying love. And to God for a magical world. Oh, yeah, and to all our cats. Can't forget them!

Contents

Part Three: Food, Travel, & Sex

Part Four: Hollywood, Or Ready for the Dragon Cage

Part Five: Adventures in Publishing

Part Six: Getting Through It

Part Seven: Bitch, Bitch, Bitch

Part Eight: Telling Tales

A Final Thought

Part One: Living the Life

Stick a Needle in My I-Yi-Yi!

Around the seventh time I watched a steel needle go into a man's penis, I had to remind myself how I'd gotten into this position. During Long Beach Pride last year I had my nips pierced by a man named Mel. Since he was a friend of Corrine's, a coworker of mine, I got 'em done free. This year I paid for it.

In April, Corrine came into my office to say Mel was going to work the festival again this year and asked if I would be interested in helping them run his piercing booth. I agreed, mainly because I wanted to be able to tell everyone I knew I was working Pride in a piercing booth. Especially my friends. Especially my parents. Most especially my parents' friends.

I had met Mel, of course, but it was over a 14-gauge surgical needle with dozens of strangers watching, so other things were on my mind at the time. Like screaming. Or rather, trying not to and failing. This year I got to know a little bit more about Mel. He's short, thick, has thinning hair and is New York–abrasive, which, since I've lived in Manhattan, doesn't faze me. As he drove Corrine and myself to the festival painfully early on Saturday morning, he told me about his hustling days in New York. Once, while Mel was hawking incense on the street dressed like a bum, director Spike Lee came up to him. "How much for the incense, man?" "Five dollars a pack," Mel told him. Spike bought two and asked how he was doing. "Aw, I'm just tryin' to make a living," Mel said, shuffling his ragged feet. "You know how it is, man, just tryin' to make an honest wage, support a family and get by, you know, and stay off the drugs and booze, you know what I'm sayin'?" Spike nodded, moved by Mel's earnest personal struggle against poverty. "I understand," Spike said, thrusting a fresh $20 bill into Mel's hand. "Take this and good luck to you." At that moment, Mel's cell phone went off. Spike's mouth dropped open. "Damn!" Spike shouted, "New York hustler!" This was my boss for two days.

When we arrived at the site, Mel put out his secret weapon, a sign that read ALL PIERCINGS $30 INCLUDING JEWELRY, drastically undercutting the other piercers. Of course it was cash-only because, as Mel said, "There's no need to involve the IRS." Corrine and I laid out the jewelry and went to work. Corrine is an outgoing, often loud, always buxom New Yawk gal with a big heart, big mascara, big glitter eye shadow, and an accent so thick it was converting me. I would hear myself saying, "Gimme ya money, take a numbah, an' as soon da chaih is free, youse c'n siddown." At $30 we soon had a crowd. "Do you really mean *all* piercings?" people would ask. Mel would answer, "Ay, you point, I poke."

Our area became jammed with groups of supportive, if queasy, friends, looky-loos who were horrified but unable to turn away, and those who wanted a piercing but still needed a couple more beers to get it. For a large part of both days the wait was upward of 20 minutes. At peak times, those desperate for new holes but broke from earlier purchases were forced to wait in the ATM line for an hour, push their way through the crowd surrounding our booth, plunk down their fresh money, then go stand in line for another half hour. I spent my time hawking jewelry and entertaining people so they wouldn't get irritable. It was part business, street theater, freak show, sometimes even peep show because, true to his sign, for $30 Mel pierced *anything*.

Soon Mel had his shirt off, exposing major tattoos and thick gold nipple rings. In addition, he had no problem showing off his other piercings, which included a thick Prince Albert, three hafadas (scrotum piercings), one guiche, and a partridge in a pear tree. In fact, showing his dick was such a crowd pleaser, it became a regular show every quarter hour. Customers naturally wanted to know if Corrine and I were pierced too. Corrine changed into a very open-mesh beaded top to show her nipple rings and navel jewelry. She was extremely popular with the lesbians, go fig. She encouraged me to take off my shirt, which I was sure would be bad for business. I look like a shag carpet that needs to back off on the Big Macs, but having my beginner nipple rings exposed gave me credibility. I had also forgotten that there is a moderate-size fetish for my look these days (something for which I will always be grateful to the bear movement). A large group of bears—and a group of bears can be quite large at only three or four—were persuaded to get their own itty-bitty titty rings. They even gave me tips. It wasn't anything I could spend, but rather a generous mauling I intend to remember and use the next time I'm alone and Fred is out of town.

I also met Larry the leather guy, who said he had a lizard tongue. And he did. I had kissed him in a manner I had intended to be merely friendly and came away feeling like I'd just had my uvula jerked off. He insisted on sucking my armpit. I demurred, for I had liberally applied deodorant in anticipation of the heat. But he didn't seem to mind. He lifted my arm and attached himself like a lamprey. I had to tell him I'd be forced to call for security if he didn't stop in exactly 15 or 20 minutes. I ended up taking the other customers' money with my free hand.

As the evening came it got chilly, so I could put my shirt back on and stop sucking in my gut. I was returning from the much-abused Porta-Pottis, the use of which by that time could only be described as a growth experience. Suddenly I was grabbed by an earlier customer, now shirtless and smelling of beer, who dry-humped me with such force that his new navel ring bled all over my shirt. Now, I love a good grope, but I couldn't enjoy this one because (a) he was drunk, and that hardly makes a girl feel special; and (b) I kept trying to remember if cold water removes a bloodstain or sets it. Mercifully, his burst of activity made him nauseous. At least I prefer to think it was the activity. Anyway, he excused himself, saying he wished he had something to make him throw up, and lurched toward the Porta-Pottis. I was confident that once he opened the door he'd get his wish.

We got home on Saturday around midnight. After a fitful sleep (dreams of being trapped in a honey wagon with lizards licking my armpits with their forked, pierced tongues) I was back over at Corrine and Mel's in Burbank, already exhausted, for the early morning drive down to Long Beach. On the way, Mel told me how when he was 15 he'd robbed a Citibank on Long Island with duct tape and a Hefty bag. It was in the early '80s, before video surveillance was everywhere. He opened the night deposit box with a "borrowed" key, put the Hefty bag inside, and taped it all around the opening with duct tape. All night long, people made their deposits. The next morning he took the Hefty bag out and went home with $7,000 cash. My God, I was working with a character straight out of a Woody Allen movie. I felt like I was riding with the Barrow gang. But hey, I was getting paid in cash and figured the odds were good I'd get hit on some more.

And I was. On Sunday I had a burly polar bear daddy willing to take me on. He was so hot I was actually glad I only had time for a quick nuzzle of white chest fur. Otherwise I could just see me explaining to Fred how I got those bite marks there, there, *and* there—or worse, explaining to Mel, who insisted I give him the "take" in neatly folded $100 increments like a drug dealer, why I'd disappeared for an hour during his busiest time. Still, it was a good stroke for the ego, and I felt good about myself for the rest of the day. Until I thought about it. As big a thrill as it was to be pawed and felt up by studly strangers, it was depressing to think that it took tens of thousands of men to produce three who would do it. And one had to be drunk. Shit.

When the festival finally closed that evening I was ready to collapse. I had been paid primarily in single bills, which Mel regarded as pocket lint, and had lived for two days on chicken quesadillas and Gatorade. Mostly Gatorade. I had avoided eating anything that might make me visit a Porta-Potti for longer than I could hold my breath.

Corrine and I broke down the booth and threw all Mel's stuff into the car. As he drove us home Mel told us his latest scam. He had taken photos of a bunch of different dildos to use as an ad in various skin rags touting, "This entire assortment only $15!" After hundreds of people had sent their money in for such a great deal, he would wait six weeks. Then he'd send a letter back explaining that, regretfully, the distributor had gone out of business, and enclose a $15 check as a refund. Of course, emblazoned across the top of the check would be GIANT ASS-REAMING DILDO COMPANY. He floored the gas pedal and laughed at all the people who would eat the 15 bucks rather than take that check to their bank.

Hungry, covered with dust and boxes of piercing paraphernalia, sitting uncomfortably on my wad of $1 bills, and so exhausted I wouldn't be able to go to work the next day, I kept thinking one of us was in the wrong business. As Mel raced the car down the freeway at Indianapolis 500 speeds while cackling at the suckers-to-be, I wondered which one of us it was.

Are We Not Men? We Are TiVo!

My partner, Fred, and I were visiting some rich friends of ours, something we like to do as often as possible because, being wealthy, they pay for whatever we do. Anyway, we were admiring their latest art acquisition and pretending we cared because we were going to ask them later if they'd let us bubble in their Jacuzzi, when Rick said, "Have we showed you our latest TV toy?" On an earlier visit, we had seen their flat-screen, four-inch-thick yet-stunning liquid crystal television the size of a small billboard. What could they possibly have now? Satellite laservision? A holodeck? They had TiVo.

Now, I'm hopelessly inept when it comes to technology. I mean, I work in radio and have no idea how it works. I can tell AM and FM from S/M, but that's about it. That said, I will try to explain TiVo as I understand it: TiVo is a box that records everything on every channel every moment of every day forever. I couldn't live with such a thing. I already have movies on DVD I will never watch, but at least I can shut them in the cabinet. Having a glowing box in plain view next to the TV avidly recording that much stuff for me would only make me feel guilty every time I passed it.

Like I should maybe quit my job and watch the programs it stored for me. Even then, while I was watching old shows, new shows would be airing that TiVo would be recording for me in a hopeless unending cycle. I could never catch up; I could only despair and self-medicate. I was glad our apartment was TiVo-free.

Well, our evening out with our stinking-rich friends turned out even better than we'd hoped. Not only did we have drinks at a club so trendy we'd never heard of it and dinner at a place we couldn't pronounce, but they asked us to house-sit for them while they spent a week at some spa we'll never afford. Free Jacuzzi all week and a giant TV! Woo-hoo!

So during that week, between soaks in the hot tub, Fred and I became acquainted with TiVo. One of the cool features is that you can be watching a program, the doorbell can ring, and you can put the show on "pause" while you prove to the private security that someone who drives a '95 Neon actually does have business in this neighborhood after dark. Then, when that's settled, you can come back and watch the rest of the TV program, which it automatically recorded for you while you were trying to come up with a believable photo ID. You don't miss a thing!

It's such a fabulous feature that I wish people came with TiVo. For instance, the other day I was talking with an idiot about Mariah Carey. I voiced the opinion that it was time she landed another sugar daddy and this guy got all bent out of shape over that. "She earned success with her talent," he huffed, "*not* through her first husband, Tommy Mioto." *Mioto?* All right, I couldn't think of her meal ticket's last name either, but it sure as hell wasn't Japanese. "I don't think his name's Mioto," I said. "Oh, I think it is," he responded condescendingly, "After all, I am in the business." I so wanted to put this jerk on "pause" while I found the real name so I could come back to the conversation with an immediate and scathing, "Wrong, Sparky, it's Mottola. She married Tommy Mottola, who bought her airplay and a Grammy, and if the bitch hadn't gotten tired of the taste of doughy Italian dick, she'd have a career today."

A similar feature is "replay." When you miss a line, you can go back 10 seconds in time and replay it. Boy, would that come in handy on visits to my parents. There's never a day I'm there that something doesn't fall out of their mouths that makes me go, "What the fuck?" Like the time my mom asked me, "In your relationship, are you the 'receptive' one?" Or another time, when she said, "I hope you never had unprotected sex with Rock Hudson."

Another attribute of TiVo is that it can learn what you like to watch, and record that for you every time it's on. It was a telling experience coming in every day to find it had already stored *Pop-Up Video, Wheel of Fortune,* and *SpongeBob SquarePants.* I was horrified. It was like an intervention for the stupid. I realized I desperately needed intellectual stimulation and forced myself to watch CNN's *Larry King Live.* His guest was Pamela Anderson.

TiVo will also examine what you told it to record and go looking for similar material. Sometimes, though, it just doesn't get what the draw was for you. We recorded an episode of the HBO prison drama, *Oz.* TiVo said, "Oh, OK!" and went out and recorded *Birdman of Alcatraz* and a week's worth of *Hogan's Heroes.* I didn't know how to tell it we weren't interested in the prison theme so much as the full-frontal male nudity. Other times, however, it knew exactly what to go for. We recorded *Rosie* one afternoon and the next day TiVo came back with *Desert Hearts* and *Personal Best.*

As we neared the end of the week we realized our friends were going to come back from Baden-Baden or wherever to a visual record of our stupid viewing habits as well as every show TiVo found that was similar. We couldn't have them learning we spent the week gawking at the shirtless men in *Temptation Island* reruns and Bowflex infomercials. So we set the TV on the Learning Channel for the last two days while we lounged out back in the Jacuzzi. That way our friends could check what TiVo had recorded and see we had spent our time bettering ourselves with educational documentaries.

Unfortunately, the Learning Channel had aired a series of shows on psychosis, inbreeding, incest, and head trauma. Remember that feature where it goes after similar programs? It turned out we left our friends' TiVo filled with wall-to-wall *Jerry Springer.*

I'm much happier back at our own apartment with our simple TV. I may not know how to program our VCR, but at least I can't be judged by shows I didn't watch. I just wish it came with a Jacuzzi.

The Best Money I Ever Spent

I don't understand money. Some say it's like water, flowing right through their fingers. For me, it's more like alcohol, evaporating before it even touches my hands. In 25 years I will be the person at the grocery store buying cat food with pennies. Only I will own no cat.

The concept of investment is lost on me. When Prudential sends me my IRA statements, they may as well be in Chinese. The only thing I can glean from them is that it ain't gonna be enough. Fortunately I have made other kinds of investments that, over the years, have paid great dividends no bank could hold.

Around 1980, when I lived in Florida, I paid something like $75 to take my parents with me to Disney World. Dad was open to it, but my mother was grim the entire trip down to Orlando. "You're not going to force me to watch singing dolls, are you?" she asked.

"Mom," I said, "you will only be forced to hear the dolls if you are bad, die, and go to hell." She frowned, sure she was being railroaded into a Disney Day of the Damned. In every photo I have of her in the park, though, she's grinning like a joyous 10-year-old fool. She even went on the doll ride—her idea. It was too small a world for me, so I waited outside. She came out of it still smiling. "Whoever you are," I told her, "I want my real mom back."

And my dad? On the back of the last float at the end of one of the many Parades for No Reason, Jiminy Cricket was waving and "conducting" the taped music. I watched openmouthed as my father literally skipped down Main Street after a cartoon insect. To this day I would have paid 10 times what I spent on their entry tickets and still counted it a bargain.

In my time I have shelled out for some very expensive meals in some very hoity-toity places, but I can't tell you what I ate. Yet I remember a gyro I bought at a hole-in-the-wall for the equivalent of 78 cents on Mykonos at 4 in the morning with a fondness most people reserve for loved ones. I recall a fish taco I bought from a street vendor in Ensenada for less than a dollar that was so good, it changed my mind about NAFTA. Once, through a series of totally unexpected circumstances, I found myself in Paris, which is the most beautiful city I've ever seen. I sat down at a tiny outdoor café in the Marais District and ordered a cup of coffee. This was before Starbucks had conned us into paying sirloin prices for a cuppa joe, so when it came with a bill for around $7.50, I was taken aback. But I paid it, and paid it happily, because it came hot and strong with a beautiful silver service which included two cubes of brownish sugar, a tiny pitcher of very hot milk, a perfect little decanter of cold water with a glass, and, the height of *civilité,* a small square of deep, dark chocolate. Plus, I was drinking it *in Paris,* y'all. That alone made it the best cup of coffee I've ever had at any price.

I bought a meal for a homeless man in Times Square who said he was Mr. Barnes & Noble. While he ate he told me that, yes, ampersand was his middle name, and how he had been swindled out of his rightful ownership of the bookstore chain. Mr. Noble said it happened because he knew about the drugs we were all being given. You see, doctors want to help people, but they don't really have the power they think they do, so when they cut people open, well, the people naturally die. The doctors are in agony about killing people, so they give themselves drugs to feel better. But they have to keep everyone else from noticing how bad and doped-up the doctors are, so they give the population at large massive amounts of drugs in our food and water. Barnes (by now we were on a first name basis) was going to publish a book exposing all this, but the doctors found out and took away his bookstores. A story like that is well worth the grilled cheese, fries, and Coke it cost me. I'd have joined him, but I don't do drugs.

Similarly, I bought a song for a dollar at Venice Beach from an African-American man with blue eyes, a guitar, a turban, and roller skates. For my buck he composed a pretty darn good ditty pointing out man's absurdity and hubris for wanting to go to Mars while the Earth is so fucked up. Did I mention he did this while skating backward?

On Santa Monica Boulevard in West Hollywood I once gave some money to a homeless woman who said she was a composer who had had her songs stolen by famous singers. Because I hadn't run away yet, she offered me one. The chorus had the line, "The richest man in the world is just a poor man with money." Wow. That's the kind of thing that should be done in needlepoint and framed. People pay hundreds of dollars at seminars to learn that lesson. I got it for a buck.

In an entirely different vein, I was in a Los Angeles sex shop when the clerk, for no apparent reason, loudly declared I needed a stretchable Masturbating Sleeve. Curious as to why I appeared to him to be a man who needed to masturbate more—or at any rate, a man who needed help doing it—I engaged him in conversation. He showed me a cylindrical, ribbed sleeve made of some kind of pink gel material that does not occur in nature. It had a tunnel down its length about the size of a pencil, but keep in mind it was highly stretchable. He put a drop of lube on my finger and had me stick my finger in it. Holy shit—sold! Now, you may be wondering why I include this very adult little item in a warm-and-fuzzy list like this. How many times have you spent big bucks in the sex shop only to get home and shout in angry frustration, "This isn't what was on the box!" Well, darlin', for only $20 this little jelly puppy is the real do-it-yourself deal. Other toys may come and go, but this one's here to stay.

But if it's highbrow stuff you want, I can give you plenty more examples. I have bought countless books that affected my life, from bringing beauty and humanity into it to altering my view of the universe in ways that set me free and, more important, pissed off my parents. I have paid for plays and musicals that have made my spirit soar, that broke my heart open only to fill it again to overflowing. This is why I don't pay that much attention to my sad little IRA. No matter how much money you make, there are other things at least as important. I count every cent I have spent talking long distance to friends as a bargain. I am perfectly content with zero financial gain on dinners with loved ones, trips to the beach, or checks to charities. And I regret not one penny of what I have ever paid for ice cream, amusement park rides, parties, the good champagne, cotton candy, songs on the jukebox, lube, or glitter. I recommend all of those in any combination. Well, except for the lube and glitter. It's pretty, but it really kills the mood.

Pissin' 'Em Off Good

Don't you love the look on their faces when you shock the shit out of people who deserve it? My friend Trey couldn't get out of going to his family's Fourth of July gathering, so he took me along for moral support. The poor guy had just been dumped by his boyfriend of two years and let go from his job in the same week. At the family do, his homophobic right-wing cousin Linda was using this as an excuse to tell him how wrong his life was.

"Your lifestyle keeps you from maintaining either a relationship or a job. I mean, what do you see yourself doing in 10 years?" Trey ignored her for the better part of the day because she was saddled with an abusive, philandering husband, and he felt sorry for her. But after about the fifth time she demanded, "What do you see yourself doing in 10 years?" he snapped and let her have it.

"In 10 years I see myself doing gay porn, Linda, making a film called *Barely Legal,*" he said much louder than strictly necessary. "Which means in 10 years I see myself doing someone who's 8 years old today."

All conversation stopped, spoonfuls of potato salad midway to mouths. "That's my awful fate, Linda. Now tell me about your happy heterosexual marriage."

We didn't stay for dessert.

Few things feel quite so good as the well-deserved shutdown. An African-American friend of mine named C.C. used to drive limousines. He picked up a handsome young white passenger at the airport and drove him to the address given. It turned out to be the home of his hated former high school coach, now retired, who came out to take care of the fare.

"If it isn't C.C. 'Sissy' Robbins!" the ex-coach exclaimed. C.C. decided he wasn't going to rise to the bait. The older man pointed at my friend's freedom ring, mistaking it for a wedding band. "Well, looka there. And I was sure you'd turn out a big ol' queer," he said paying with a $50 bill. "Hey, that was my son you picked up. Whadja think of him, boy?"

C.C. narrowed his eyes. That word "boy" had finally done it.

"I think he could use more practice," he said.

"What do you mean?" shot back the coach, angry that any fault could be found with the man's man who had sprung manfully from his manly loins.

"Well, his teeth get in the way, but he's enthusiastic and he swallows, so I'm sure he'll be very popular."

And he drove away, not bothering to make change.

The only drawback to deliberately pissing people off like this is having to be ready. You wish you knew these things were coming, so you could have a great response. Well, guess what? You do.

Every four years you get a great chance to do just that. It's the biggest and best opportunity for pissing off the most people possible. It's voting. Merely by filling out your ballot you can cast votes that'll completely void your parents' vote. And that's just for starters. All those red-faced homophobic assholes ("major-league" and otherwise) want nothing more than for you to be a good little abomination and stay home. But you can fuck up their day and piss them off with one little visit to your polling place. And it's so fast, it's practically a drive-by pissing.

It's so easy, how can you resist? They send you ballot stuff in the mail that's just like the ballot you'll see in the voting booth. It's like getting a copy of the test a week before the exam! Simply flip through it, figure out which candidate would cause the gay-baiters the most acid-reflux, and mark it down. Take it with you on election day and refer to it as a cheat sheet in the voting booth.

The great part is that since homophobes are the majority, it's mostly their money paying for you to do this. OK, some of it is your tax money too, but that should be even more incentive. I don't know about you, but if I'm shelling out for something, I want to get all I can out of it. Not voting is like paying for your McNuggets at the first window and driving past the second without getting 'em.

Most businesses allow you to come in late on Election Day too. You know how coming in late pisses off your boss—but there's nothing he or she can say this time, is there? "Don't you yell at me, Miss Thang. I was being a good citizen, so you just shut your cake hole and get me some coffee." Well, you may not want to push it that far. Nevertheless, if it's an excuse to come in late, take advantage of it. Meet your friends for early morning lattes and troop over for a party in the polling place.

And your little vote counts too. My friend Brenda, who didn't use to care about any kind of voting, now has a button that says I'M A BITCH AND I VOTE. It all changed for her one Sunday afternoon at her church's congregational meeting. One of the two major items on the agenda was whether to allow the Boy Scouts to continue meeting in their Fellowship Hall. The preacher was for it for all the standard hypocritical reasons. Gathering her courage, Brenda argued against it, using the occasion to come out as a lesbian to her church. It was an emotional vote, and when the tally was taken, it was a tie. The preacher cast his vote to allow it, and several people left in protest. But not Brenda. See, the other item on the agenda was whether to increase the preacher's salary or use the money to renovate the Fellowship Hall. Guess who did *not* get a raise by one very loud vote? "Maybe there's something to straight sex after all," Brenda told me later. "I never felt so good as when I fucked that man."

Oh, and the weeks of renovations rendered the Fellowship Hall unusable. The Boy Scouts are now at the Armory where they have to pay to meet.

So take your own opportunity for revenge every Election Day. Don't think of it as voting, think of it as pissing off all the people who ever made your life miserable. It's so delicious. It's so satisfying. It's so *Survivor.*

Make your plans to get out there and rip someone's 'roids. Fuck "civic duty." It's getting even, girlfriend.

Written in the Stars

I share an office with Matt, a man who writes part time for the *Weekly World News.* He comes up with stories for them like "Three-Legged Skater Banned From Competition," and "How to Renegotiate Your Deal With the Devil." It's a bizarre niche in the humor world, and I envy his abilities. He gave me his contact there and I pitched them some headlines. They ranged from stories like "Anal Penetration Key to World Peace" to op-ed pieces like "Gays in the Military: Is Giving Them Guns Really a Good Idea?" I guess it just wasn't what they were looking for. Matt suggested I try something a little less gay-specific, so I sent them "Man Eats Clay, Shits Brick." Nothing.

I was forced to admit I'm not cut out for crafting material for housewives from Wichita who think cereal is a viable option for dinner. In giving me the brush off, the woman at *Weekly World News* said, "Sorry, but it's just not in the stars," and hung up. Stars? Damn! Why didn't I think of that? Astrology is where I know I could contribute! So, in the fervent hope that some gay boy at *Weekly World News* has read this far, I offer the following as a writing sample for the astrology section:

Written in the Stars

ARIES (March 21–April 19)

There are amazing things in you. Fortunately, a skilled intern will be able to remove them without surgery.

You will find the perfect lover who is quiet, receptive, won't bring up your faults, and travels well. He will also be inflatable.

Avoid shaving what you cannot see.

TAURUS (April 20–May 20)

You're ready for a new experience. Practice on a carrot.

An abusive behavior is getting out of hand. Tell Mom to go home.

Your best friend is lubricant.

You will be loved, but it will cost you by the hour.

Remember beads—they're not just for wearing anymore.

GEMINI (May 21–June 21)

You'll be much happier if you quit Weight Watchers and join your local bear chapter.

Your lucky animal is the ferret.

You will discover the perfect way in which to express yourself but will be stymied by that 10-day waiting period and background check.

CANCER (June 22–July 22)

Someone in the stall next to you will tap his foot. Do not tap back.

You know that flavored lube makes a decent dessert topping.

You will hurt someone you love. They will really, really dig it.

You will meet a rich, good looking doctor. He will tell you that you have polyps.

LEO (July 23–August 22)

If you're wondering why you haven't healed since your last affair, it's because herpes is a recurring virus.

Whatever you have been doing supine, try prone.

You will meet the man of your dreams. Unfortunately, it'll be that dream with all those snakes and Jesus.

VIRGO (August 23–September 22)

Learn to appreciate your body for what it is. Humor helps.

A coworker will reveal she has a crush on you. Turn her into a fag hag.

Your lucky color is dung.

Occasional alcohol in moderation will not do the trick.

You are in a wonderful, loving relationship. Don't worry, you'll think of a way to fuck it up.

LIBRA (September 23–October 23)

You make friends as easily as your friends make you.

You're not a chubby chaser, you just live in a small town with few options.

Antonio Banderas is hard and thinking about you right now, but he doesn't have your number, so Melanie gets it in the back door. Again.

SCORPIO (October 24–November 21)

Whatever you pretend, you are still all about sex.

Nobody likes you, but if they did, you'd lose your edge.

Chunky Monkey is not only your favorite flavor, it's your type.

Try not to worry; the sun will go nova one day and everyone's lives will be as meaningless as yours.

SAGITTARIUS (November 22–December 21)

Now is a good time to attempt the previously impossible. Try fitting in another finger.

You may be a size queen, but try being more discreet. Leave the ruler at home.

Someone wearing a yellow hankie will hand you a full, warm beer can.

Hang up and drive.

CAPRICORN (December 22–January 19)

Open yourself up to love as much as possible. Poppers can help.

A major decision is weighing on you. Dump him.
Your lucky color is glitter. Wear it everywhere, even if it makes you chafe.
You will be surrounded by men with nothing but sex on their minds. It will be in a clinic.
And remember, paddles aren't just for canoes.

AQUARIUS (January 20–February 18)
The key to freedom is with a partner. And until he comes back, you're never getting out of those handcuffs.
Dating a ruminant doesn't count.
You will be surprised to find yourself excited by a man in a dress. It will be right after Mass.
Get used to that burning sensation.

PISCES (February 19–March 20)
A trip is imminent in your future, especially if you don't start picking up your feet when you walk.
You think your newest boyfriend is much better than all those others you had, but he's not part of your life, he's just part of your pattern.
You will meet a new friend…through a hole in a stall wall.

OK, so you may wonder how a person with such obvious ignorance of astrology could hope to be hired as an astrologer. I figure if multimillionaires who know nothing about real life keep getting elected to tell us how to run our lives, if tits but no talent can make the pop charts for years, and *Just Shoot Me* can be called Must-See TV, then I should fit right in with "journalists" who consider my friend Matt's headline "Tooth Fairy Accidentally Flies Into Electric Bug Zapper" news. So, again, if you're an editor at *Weekly World News,* I ask you to consider my application seriously, because if you don't, I'll spread a story that'll put you out of business: "Nostradamus Revealed: 'I Was Just Fucking With You.' "

Bring Your Own Pride

It was my first summer in L.A. I knew almost nothing about the place, so I was still completely in love with it. My straight writing partner, John, and I were driving down Mulholland Drive for the sheer beauty of the valley lights. As we came over a crest on the city side, we saw dozens of glaring searchlights clustered in one location below. John said it looked like aliens had landed from the planet Disco. We had to investigate. Whatever was going on, it could only be awesome. We sped down Coldwater Canyon, headed east on Sunset, turned south on San Vicente and arrived at Santa Monica Boulevard with our mouths open. John had been right.

It was the pride fair, my first, and I had never seen so many gays and lesbians in one place. The music, the festivity, the open delight people took in outrageous display was overwhelming and thrilling. I saw thousands of gays, none of whom I'd ever seen, and one word filled my mind: *family.*

"Pull over!" I yelled, "I'm getting out!"

"Wait!" he shouted back as I slammed the door. "How will you get home?"

I laughed. "John, I *am* home!" And I ran into the crowd, never looking back.

That's how the pride festival feels to me every time. It's too crowded, too hot, too commercial, too expensive, too hard to get to, a giant sprawling pain in a nonlubed ass, and you couldn't keep me away. Reverend Nancy Wilson, in her book *Our Tribe,* says that gays and lesbians are the only people who have to search to find their tribe. Well, every June we here in L.A. hold one hell of a reunion. Grab your dancing shoes and get your wig on straight, 'cause it's party time again!

I come each year to immerse myself in the miracle. Well, that and to drool over the shirtless eye candy. The miracle I see is that despite enemies who labor tirelessly to strip us of our basic rights, deny us our love and spirituality, and impede any action that might stop the plague ravaging us, we still can come together in joy on San Vicente Boulevard in both massive numbers and bare-ass chaps. It's a miracle that even though laws we are forced to support through our taxes regularly discriminate against us, we can dress up, oil down, and show a great glittering middle finger to the world as we party down Santa Monica. It's a miracle that, as outraged as we have a right to be, we haven't turned violent. Yet. Who knows, maybe we will one day. Sometimes I think the only reason we haven't had an all-out riot is that we'd take far too long looting Barneys and get arrested. "But I *had* to go back—I stole the wrong formula clarifying lotion."

God knows there's plenty wrong with the festival. Nobody finds pride in dropping $15 just to get through the gate where you then have the privilege of overpaying for crap you don't need. You can do that at Disneyland, and there are almost as many homos. But at least the festival has better rides. You just have to take them home.

Another thing to hate is the crass commercialism of straight companies trying to squeeze queer cash out of a targeted, localized market. (Did anyone say "beer?") I for one am not impressed with what amounts to two days of product placement. You want my money? Impress me. Advertise with same-sex couples in *Ladies' Home Journal* or during *Touched by an Angel.* Show you're willing to take the same flak we've been taking all our lives, and we'll talk. Till then, I'll keep the bank and long-distance service I have, thank you.

That said, there are also plenty of great things about the festival. Where else can you fight AIDS by kissing porn stars for a dollar? Where else can you transparently grope strangers while putting a GOD THINKS I'M FA-A-ABULOUS! sticker on them? And who could quibble with hundreds of sweating people jammed under the dance tents all rhythmically rubbing their naughty bits against each other? OK, so that may not be pride, but as my friend Fernando says, "It's getting hard enough to find pride at the festival, but it's also enough at the pride festival to find yourself getting hard." I agree. Damn it, I want *some* kind of satisfaction for my $15.

Maybe now would be a good time to talk about what pride is not. Pride is not free condoms everywhere you go. It's a handy perk, especially if you're looking for balloons that'll make that homophobic sales manager's office birthday party memorable, but it's not pride. Pride is not dishing everyone who walks by. That's just bitchy and, I've learned, marks one as bitter fruit, so I'll try to refrain this year. Pride also is not about going broke buying anything and everything rainbow. That's just sucker marketing. I mean, do I really need a rainbow pet dish symbolizing gay sexuality for a cat who no longer has his balls?

Pride is not something you buy or attend. No, not even the festival itself is pride. Let's be very clear on this. It's a party. *You* carry the pride. And when enough of us get together with the pride we have in the lives we lead, critical mass is achieved and a party naturally occurs. It's a scientific fact. The quantum definition of "festive" is 10 or more gays + music. Get enough of us moving in one direction and it's a parade. That or a sale at Fred Segal. Either way, you know you'll spend way too much money and parking will be a bitch, but ultimately it's still worth it.

Bring Your Own Pride

So if you're searching for pride, don't look at the festival, look in the mirror. It's in you, honey. Yes, it is. Whether it's going to the festival or anywhere else, always remember it's BYO pride. Cherish it. Honor it. Then decorate it with leather, spandex, feathers, or just some SPF 15 and bring it on down to the party and work it!

You Do the Math

I am so bad at anything involving numbers that I'd have to call myself an arithmaphobe. I cannot add or subtract. I am against division on principle, and being gay, I certainly don't multiply. God invented calculators for people like me. The only numbers I like come with a Broadway show wrapped around them. I have a friend, though, who teaches—I shudder to say—higher math. I believe the fact that he remains a friend speaks highly of my open-mindedness and tolerance. He tells me he likes math because questions have only one answer—a definite fixed value, inflexible and inviolate.

Not in my world. I see numbers the way Dali saw clocks. Math would be much easier if everybody felt as I, although it does tend to confound creditors:

"Mr. Perry, your most recent minimum payment should have been for $300."

"Colt Video? But I wrote you a check for that."

"No, you wrote it for $30."

"Well, just move the little dot thing over one and stop bothering me with insignificant details! And when are you coming out with a DVD of Steve Kelso and Carl Hardwick doing each other?"

You Do the Math

Last week I took my checkbook in to the bank because I had bounced some checks and was furious. I mean, how dare my bank run out of money? A very nice lady named Liz tried to explain it all to me, and it was a real learning experience. Did you know "rounding up" to the nearest dollar is frowned upon? Why did they teach us that in school? Did you know ATM withdrawals count? Even if they're not at your bank? Liz called my checkbook a surreal experience. She suggested I close my account and start from scratch with a nice new one. I agreed and asked if I could choose it myself because I wanted one with lots of money in it. Then I asked if it was really wise for her to be taking four aspirin at once. She told me to leave the counting to her and call if I ever needed help again. Not because she was eager to help; she wanted fair warning I was on my way in so she could be out of town.

I pity those like my math teacher friend, creditors, and Liz, who actually believe numbers are incapable of altering. They are desperate to cling to something hard and rigid. No, wait, that's me. Try again: Math is for people with small minds who need to believe things do not change. In real life, however, numbers cavort, shift, and ooze into other values and columns. The truth is, there are no absolutes or fixed answers in math, and I can prove it with the following five examples:

1. Bob is traveling from San Francisco to Los Angeles to meet friends for Club Spit at the Faultline leather bar on a Friday. If Bob leaves after work, drives 60 mph, and stops only to cruise the at Buttonwillow rest stop, will he arrive in time for last call?

2. You're dining alone and the bill comes to $37.50. The food was mediocre and the service was spotty. The waiter, however, was really cute and flirted with you shamelessly. How much do you tip?

3. That $98 linen shirt to die for at Banana Republic is on sale but still pricey at $69. Next week it'll be marked down to $35. What are the odds of it still being there when you go back?

4. Mel Gibson is offered the lead in *The Harvey Milk Story.* He tells his agent they'd have to pay him a shitload of money to play some fag. His agent wonders, *What is 15% of a shitload?*

5. Lawrence sent out invitations for a dinner party "beginning promptly at 8 P.M." Given Gay Standard Time, how long past 8 will he have to keep the food warm?

Maybe it's because I'm gay. As in every other aspect of my upbringing, nothing worked like I was told, and I had to make up my own rules. For example, remember all those confusing properties of math we learned in school, like the commutative property of multiplication? (And what the hell was that about anyway?) Well, I believe gay life shows that there are more properties to numbers than any straight board of education is capable of teaching. Here are a few concepts I've learned on my own:

The Feline/Lesbo Theorem: When lesbians move in together, the number of cats automatically doubles.

The Ellen Consequence: Any evening spent with straight friends who want to show you how "hip" they are will result in at least one tired reference to toaster ovens. Followed by, "How nice it was they gave her another show, even if it flopped."

The Inaccurate Property of Addition: Four towels outside the steam room do not necessarily equal four men inside. Or that you would want to do any one of them.

The Associative Property of Drag Queens: Nobody will associate with drag queens—until Halloween. Then everybody wants to *be* one.

The Inequality Property of Division: You and Bill bought that entertainment system together paying 50-50. But when you split up, Bill came over while you were at work and took the TV, the DVD player, and the stereo, leaving you the broken cassette deck.

The Commutative Property of Property: He also took all your Barbra CDs.

You Do the Math

Math is a lot like gay folk. People think they know the subject but don't. We are too varied and wonderfully indefinable, and how do you compute that? How do you subtract us from the population at large? How do you add up so much humor in the face of bigotry? How do you solve a problem like Maria? (I warned you I liked Broadway numbers.)

I say we show the world a thing or two about so-called standard arithmetic. I believe it's high time homos took back math and made it our own. So, in closing, I would like to start this work by offering new queer definitions for certain mathematical terms:

- *acute angle:* whatever, as long as it's not just hanging there
- *right angle:* getting where it's at least possible, if not comfortable
- *Abscissa:* my math friend's name if he were a drag queen
- *significant digits:* anything displayed in *Inches* magazine
- *prime number:* Alec Baldwin
- *irrational number:* Alec Baldwin with a photographer
- *periodic function:* The White Party
- *y coordinate:* because we're gay and it's expected—duh
- And finally... *standard deviation:* Well, now... that would be us, wouldn't it?

Big Boy

I just got the family holiday photos back and they upset me worse than the pictures of Carnie Wilson's surgery. These new Christmas pics are distressing not because family members are exchanging cash as a tacit admission we don't know each other anymore, not because we're uncomfortably posed with all the spontaneity of a Sears underwear ad, and not just because we have red eyes like guest demons even Buffy couldn't defeat. It's because in these photos I'm a full-color, fill-flashed big fat load.

My father took individual pictures of us. Everybody else was framed in portrait. Me? I was landscape. Even then he had to step back to get it all in. There I am, worry all over my face that he's going to step backward into the box of Whitman's Sampler candies rendering them, if not inedible, certainly more difficult to distinguish between. I look like a Christmas sausage in Eddie Bauer casing. Something must be done.

My spouse, Fred, who loves me unconditionally, says I'm in perfect shape. I would agree, but only if I were a potato. I've fought this weight thing all my life, going up and down like out-of-sequence reruns of *Roseanne*. Still, this bout of the bulges took me by surprise.

Big Boy

You'd think I'd have noticed that one, then two, and now three boxes in the corner full of clothes I can't wear anymore. Or how salads went out of my life once Krispy Kreme became a major food group. Or I'd have heard what I was saying when I told friends I was quitting the gym because the parking was too far away.

Ugh, the gym. Well, damn it, it's time to bite the bullet. And try not to swallow it because of the calories. Like millions each January after holiday bingeing, I decided to join a gym and actually stick with it. But it had to be the right gym.

I toured the one on Santa Monica Boulevard in WeHo and quickly saw that my main workouts would not be in the gym area. Besides, I was overly intimidated by too many already-ripped abs belonging to boys approximately the same age as my cat. Also, everyone there shaves areas I believe should be celebrated for masculine hairiness. What is that about? Who convinced these people razor bumps were hot? When I go down, I don't want to come up with whisker burn. And for the record, Aqua Velva is a major teabagging turn-off. Whatever. This gym was not for me.

I enjoy drinking $8 lattes at the coffeehouse across from another gym, at the corner of Sunset and Crescent Heights, and ogling the buff bodies going up to their workouts. They never take the stairs but use the escalators, going up and down in a motorized parade of spandex. It's like being at one of those sushi bars where the food comes by on a conveyor belt—except grabbing what you want can sometimes cause a scene. I decided to stop watching all these shiny preppy people and check out their gym, so I went up. Inside it was gleaming, sleek, and steamy with waterfalls and muscles, like something out of *Spartacus*, only with chrome and CNN instead of Tony Curtis and oysters. I was put off by so many industry people working out with cell phones on their weight belts. I never want to be that important. Plus, heaven forbid I should get between them and an urgent E-mail. "What happened here?" "Don't blame me, officer. This fat-ass was using the treadmill when I got a page from CAA and dove for my laptop." Still, my gym salesman said all this high-level sweat and snobbery could be mine for the monthly equivalent of another car payment. That's a tad pricey for someone with my book sales, so I pried him off my wallet and left.

I went next to a more gritty gym on Beverly Boulevard with a line of busy StairMasters facing away from the large front window. It's locally knows as Butts on Beverly. There were far fewer TV stars here, and the ones I did see were less Kevin Sorbo and more Kevin Pollak, which is a big plus in my book (are you listening, Mr. Pollak?). Anyway, I liked the locker room because it looked like a locker room and not something out of a George Michael video. I liked the staff too, because when I showed them the Christmas photos they politely suggested hiring a trainer instead of joining the circus. The monthly cost was affordable if I just gave up my maple-nut oat scones. ("That one in back, please, with all the icing.")

I had my gym, now I needed an incentive; otherwise I knew I'd cop out at the first opportunity. "Joey and Chandler are finally going to kiss? How could I possibly work out now? I have to go home and prepare!" I needed something that would (1) give me a goal date so I wouldn't think I had to do this forever; (2) be covered with sex appeal for stimulation as well as motivation; (3) offer a prospect of embarrassment if I failed, but (4) come with a safety net if I wasn't as buff as I hoped to be by my goal date. So I'm entering the Mr. Southern California Bear Contest. It's in June, which gives me six months to slim, tone, and discover if I have a waist. The sex appeal quotient is obvious; in fact, Fred says this whole thing is just so I can have an excuse in six months to walk around in skimpy little shorts with other hairy men in skimpy little shorts. My indignant reply was, "Yes, *and...?*" Embarrassment would take the form of not meeting my personal goals, but the safety net is, hey, they're bears. With these boys, bulkage is not a bad thing, God love 'em. And anyway, it's not about being thin but being happy with the body you've got. Hell, it was the bears who taught me that—as well as that Lane Bryant is the place to shop for Halloween.

So I've made the commitment to get into shape, or at least a shape that fits in a standard photo. And I'm making that commitment here in print, so if I don't follow through, I'll hear about it from everyone I know. If I'm forced to move to Tonga, you may assume I gave up.

If I stick with it and still fall short of my goals, I can always join a club called Girth and Mirth, both of which I have in abundance. My new trainer says that kind of thinking is copping out on my commitment. Fred says I'm just covering my ample ass. They may be right, but I prefer to think of it as niche marketing.

You Lying Sack of Shit

You've heard the lies. You've used the lies. Some of us *are* the lies. They're the falsehoods we foist on each other whenever one of us wants to get out of a boring relationship or an unpleasant situation, or just the hell away from you. But isn't it time someone gave you that snappy comeback you wished you had when the lie was dropped on your smarting ego? I say, "Yes, yes, it is," and not only that but, "Here you are." So memorize these puppies, because it's only a matter of time before someone lays another one on you.

The Lie: "You're not my type."
Translation: "I'm so shallow, I can't be bothered with being open to new things or growth." It means there's some perceived physical flaw keeping you from falling into the tiny pool of possible sex partners. You could respond with, "You mean a decent, caring, honest, loving, understanding, humorous, empathetic, imaginative, sincere, intelligent, witty, supportive man who can cook is not your type? Thanks, I'd hate to have wasted my time with you." But that assumes he's actually looking for those things. Move on.

Response: "Your type? Oh, I'm sorry, I didn't realize this was a hustler bar."

The Lie: "I love you, but I'm not *in* love with you."
Translation: "I don't love you, I never loved you, nothing could make me love you, it was just that thing you do with your tongue." This is what they say when they don't have the spine to tell you they're only there for the sex. True, a caring person with a healthy self-esteem would have realized after six months of dating that you both deserved more than just good sex and would have had the decency to tell you that. But you don't date that kind of man, do you? So you need a good comeback handy.
Response: "Oh, good, then that'll make this easy: You were a mercy fuck."

The Lie: "It's not you, it's me."
Translation: "It's you, man. You, you, and you. It is so you, it's not even partly me." He wants to get away from you so badly, he's willing to make the grand gesture of taking the blame. Of course, saying "It's me" shuts down all possible dialogue, but for him that's the beauty of this passive-aggressive cliché. The funny thing is that in using this hackneyed, transparent lie, he demonstrates that the problem really *is* him.
Response: "Oh, good, I thought I might be the asshole here, but thank you for owning up to it and corroborating what everyone else has been saying."

The Lie: "I don't think of you that way. You're more like a brother."
Translation: "You're a walking wood-kill. But you laugh at my jokes and you have a car and you don't mind driving, so I don't what to piss you off." Oh, please. A sizable portion of gay porn is alleged relatives shooting vastly similar DNA on each other.
Response: "Hey, my uncle fucked me since I was 7—I'm OK with the incest thing."

The Lie: "This doesn't mean we can't be friends."
Translation: "That's exactly what it means. Why would I want you hanging around? I already have friends, and boy, am I going to tell them all kinds of shit about you!" The good thing about this one is that this is a lie that comes at the end of a relationship (or after a really bad date), so by the time he lays this one on you, you at least have his phone number.
Response: Say, "You're right," give him the obligatory chaste hug, then write his name and phone number (home *and* work) on every public bathroom wall within a 10-mile radius. He can "be friends" with all of them too.

The Lie: "I have to get up early in the morning."
Translation: "Nothing you could do is worth my going in to work sleepy." As if by looking at you he has any idea of your special skills and talents. That "*I* have to get up early" part is also nasty for assuming that *you* don't have anything to get up early for in the morning, like maybe a life.
Response: "Not a problem. You're not worth making love to. You're such an uptight asshole I just thought you needed a quick fuck."

The Lie: "I was only out drinking with my best friend, Betty."
Translation: "I bought my best friend, Betty, drinks while I was on my knees in the back room." God made fag hags so we could lie about what we did and they would swear to it. In return we tell them what outfits make them look fat. It's a circle of life kind of thing. But going out with a female friend doesn't mean squat. Everybody knows that. Hell, my born-again Baptist *grandmother* knows that.
Response: Your patented bitch slap. After all, how fucking stupid does he think you are?

The Lie: "I love you, but I'm not happy in the relationship."
Translation: "You're nice enough, but I've found someone with a bigger dick." And we all know "dick" is a metaphor for more money, a better car, a house in France, or a blind eye to philandering. It all

screams "Shallow!" Because if he really did love you he'd be willing to stay and work it out, but you're not that lucky, are you? This lie also has a vague insinuation that you are the problem while maintaining plausible deniability if you call him on that. It's passive aggressive at best, and at its worst it's a power trip to make you feel like shit. Don't buy into it. Let him go. Anything more is time wasted and you've got those *Sex and the City* DVDs to catch up on.
Response: Clap hands twice and say, "Begone! You have no power here!"

The Lie: "It's just not going to happen."
Translation: "I'd rather fuck my dead mother where I shot her than fuck you." He let you chat him up for 20 minutes just so he could drop that line and watch you twist in the wind. That's why we never go up to people without something handy that leaves a stain. "Oops! So sorry I spilled my Bloody Mary on your Versace." Why not? If it's not going to happen with you, why should it happen with anybody else?
Response: "Fine. *Next!*"

The Lie: "I jacked off earlier today."
Translation: "I so don't want to be with you that I'll not only pretend I masturbated, but I'll let you think I'm only good for one shot." Of course, if that were true, what's he doing cruising the biggest meat rack in town? That "only good for one shot" part really adds insult to injury. It says he thinks so little of you that he doesn't give a damn what you think of him. But you can use that to your advantage.
Response: "Oh, well. Don't feel bad; my ex was only a one-a-day guy when he got to be your age too."

The Lie: "Your birthday/anniversary/whatever gift hasn't arrived yet."
Translation: "Duh, me stoopid, me forgot." Then he'll tear out and buy you the first thing he sees and give it to you the next day, saying, "It came!" I'm so sure. Then, every time you look at whatever

hideous Pier 1 or Spencer Gifts abortion he came up with, you stew with rage. Better to avoid the whole scene.
Response: "Look, we both know (a) you forgot because you have the IQ of fish bait; and (b) you haven't ordered jack, so just give me $$$ so I can buy myself something decent and you're off the hook. This time."

The Lie: "I'm just waiting for a friend."
Translation: This one's not so easy. In fact, it's that openness to interpretation that makes it so popular. It could mean, "No, thanks, just looking," or "I have superpowers that enable me to assess your abilities as a potential element in my life and you don't even rate," or even, "Ugh, shouldn't you be back home under your bridge, you big troll?" In that case, you may respond, "I only came over because you smelled like a goat," sniff at him, and then continue, "OK, *Aramis.* Same thing." Then again, there are those times one wants merely to hang out with the tribe but have one's own thoughts. It could, despite the brush-off, mean he really is just waiting for a friend.
Response: "Well, you just missed one."

The Lie: "I'm here with someone."
Translation: This one's a toughie too. It's probably "I'm here with a friend I can claim as a lover when losers like you get too close to the merchandise." Or else "I'm not here with anyone, but I'm certainly not going to be here with you." Or it could mean he's actually there with his lover. But isn't there an annoying smugness in that? An attitude that just reeks of "I have someone, you don't, so I win?" And even though you really want to say, "Really? How the hell did *that* happen?" you don't because you're better and healthier than that. So you lovingly use the mature response below:
Response: Find out who he is there with and then go fuck that person in the bathroom. That'll show the little pissant.

The Lie: "I'm not used to anything that big."
Translation: "I've become bored, but I'll flatter you so much with

this consummate crock of shit that you'll have to let me go home." This is the lie we actually love hearing, because we're just that fucked up. We're so insecure that the mere intimation, no matter how bald-faced a lie it is, that our small-side-of-normal cock could possibly be considered "too big" is pounced upon by an overneedy ego without any question whatsoever. Oh, my God, I must have been transported to the Planet of the Pencil Dicks! Why, I'm huge! Odd I never realized it before. But *I rule*!
Response: None. Nada. Zilch. Even though we lost out on sex with the hunky guy we brought home, this lie has made our entire evening worthwhile.

OK, now it's time to take what you've learned here and get back out there in the trenches. Just remember who gave you the ammunition you've needed for so long. I did it because dishonesty hurts because it's wrong, and I'm sensitive to that. I am. Really. Would I lie to you?

Part Two: Holy Cowhide!

The Religious Left

The religious right was named wrongly. They should be called the religious left, because once they've sucked all the love and inclusiveness of God's spirit out of things, what they've got is what's left. But then I've always thought them a joke.

One of the funniest aspects of the religious right is how any kind of sexuality, even hetero, is denied by so many claiming to be people of God. Get this—God gives us all a great gift called sex and somebody comes scurrying down the aisle screaming, "Don't open that!" What is that about? I mean, what if they arbitrarily decided to ban some other intrinsic part of our humanity, say, rational thought? Oh, wait. They did.

You don't believe me when I say sex is a gift? Then why do we say a guy has a "package" and a gal has a "box"? Tie either one up in a bow and it's a present. Tie it tight and it's kinky. And as far as I'm concerned, that's all you need to be well-dressed for any party I'd want to attend.

I know a lot of us have trouble getting past all that Christo-biz damage of being told the body is corrupt and evil. I suppose your body could be, if you're doing it right, but certainly not in the way they would have you think. True, there is such a thing as abuse, but only then does sex enter the moral arena. Are you hurting yourself or someone else? This could be a problem. Unless, of course, that's what you signed up for and have established safewords. For anyone who's interested—and I'm hoping you are—mine is "pudding."

With all this church-inflicted baggage, what is the spiritual queer to do? Unfortunately, many of us are now uncomfortable with any religious practice at all, the only exception being us Christmas queens during the holidays. The result of that is: (a) far too many overpriced Christopher Radko ornaments in storage; and (b) an impish bent for "sacrilegious" holiday presents. You know, like giving your friend a quart of lube with pump dispenser to commemorate the birth of Christ. I'm here to tell you that's not sacrilegious. How can it be, especially when God gave you the gift of all those delicious nerve endings between your legs? It is, however subversive. Not to God, but to the religious right. How dare you claim your body in the name of Joy? Or Steve or Russell or Wanda or whomever.

This is what pisses them off so much. We don't buy into the power trip the leaders of the religious right put on their believers to keep them in control. Not only that, but we're getting laid.

Oh, but it says in the Bible that our brand of sexuality is an "abomination." Well, blah, blah, blah. Not only is this a purely literal translation of Leviticus, but it's a *selective* interpretation. You don't notice any Christians getting upset at the Two Fat Ladies on the Food Channel for whipping up rabbit stew or hamhocks (Leviticus 11:6-7) or shouting "Unclean!" at menstruating women (15:19). Why? Because selecting those passages wields no power over people. But if you can stand there in your nice linen-wool blend suit (prohibited by 19:19) after a lunch of oysters Rockefeller (a no-no according to 11:10) and scare people into believing there's only one thing they can do with their "nasties" and it better not be fun, *then* you've got some power. Stand back and let the money roll in.

We upset the hell out of the leaders of the religious right because we don't accept their power over us. What if everybody did that? What if everyone claimed their right to spirituality, to their hotline to the divine, to a power within that was wholly separate from and independent of the organized religion biz? A lot of homophobes in robes would be out of work. We're a job threat, like Eve Harrington on steroids. That's why we homos must be demonized. We are used by the religious right's leaders to scare their followers away from thought *as well as their own connection to God,* which every person already has.

Yes, darling, even you. If you thought you had a connection to Diana Ross, line dancing, or anything bigger than 9 by 6 inches, it's nothing compared to the direct line you have to whatever you consider your higher power. You were born with it, just like you were born with a perfectly worthy soul and a penchant for lip synching. Do not ever think that the Religious Right—or anyone else—can separate you from God. Especially over something as ridiculous as sex.

By defining us by our sexuality, they forced us to look at it, consider it, and talk about it. A *lot.* Like Kathie Lee yammers on about Cody. We can tell you about sex like Imelda can tell you about shoes. Most nongays still can't do that. Can you see them handling something like "Daddy, why does Missy wet her seat every time k.d. lang is on VH1?" Or "Is eating precome a high-risk behavior, Reverend Wilkins?" For them, sex remains a dark secret and a shame-based thing, sort of like what I do with Hershey's Syrup and pie filling after midnight. Any 12-step program will tell you you're only as sick as your secrets. Ironically, those who would silence us have instead made us healthier by forcing us to talk about sex. Hell, just try shutting us up. This openness, this incorporation of sexuality and spirituality into a whole, ultimately is our gift to the rest of the world. We are witnesses to repressed heterosexuals (and homos) everywhere, proving that claiming your sexuality is healthy. As Martha would say, "It's a good thing."

A Noisy Church

At the Metropolitan Community Church in Los Angeles there is a hymn we sing called "Enter, Rejoice, and Come In," and in verse 4 is the repeated line "Don't be afraid of some change." This ought to be required singing for any new member. You will encounter many changes in this church. One of the reasons I love MCC-LA is that it constantly challenges me. The first thing to hit me—and the first challenge—was that this is a noisy church.

Growing up in a Southern cracker Methodist congregation, I was taught to sit quietly in my pew, hands folded, with my attention directed toward the front so that like everyone else's, my eyes could glaze over during the sermon. Sometimes we'd stand to sing—not too loudly, please, and not too well, thank you. Sometimes we stood to speak aloud for the responsive reading or the Affirmation of Faith, both of which we preferred low and mumbled. We certainly didn't have any of that "Amen!" stuff going on like they had at those "heathen" churches. We had a guest preacher from a black Methodist church one time, and during his sermon he had to ask repeatedly, "Can I get an amen? Please? Can I? Somebody?" I think the organist finally said it, not out of the spirit of the thing, but more out of a feeling of "if we give him one, maybe he'll go away." He didn't. But he did learn not to ask for any more "amens." Our loss.

I believe I saw a tambourine only once in my entire Methodist career. It was in a Sunday School text showing musical instruments of the Bible. I never saw one actually used until *The Monkees* came on the air and it was the safest thing to give Davy Jones. Tambourines were for hippies and other lawless, drugged-up, dirty, disrespectful hedonists who were going to hell in high-speed handbaskets. One time, the Baptists had a traveling preacher come through who pitched a revival tent. I had gone with some Baptist neighbors and was surprised that the sermon was titled "My Green Tambourine." It was about passing a tambourine through the congregation—repeatedly—and having it come back filled with green. When I got home and told my parents, they looked at each other and said, "Baptists." So you can understand how difficult it is for me to accept a simple, joyful shaking of the tambourine. That was nothing, though, compared to dancing, clapping, holding hands up to receive the Spirit, and other expressions of worship my upbringing deemed undignified.

When I was a child, my parents encouraged me to experience the services of other churches: Pentecostal, Presbyterian, Catholic, Church of Christ, Assembly of God, Lutheran, Baptist, Episcopalian, Maranatha, and Moravian. I went to a Unitarian church once, but where I'm from that didn't count as church. Anyway, I recall the more noise, both from the pulpit and from the congregation, the more condemning the church seemed to be. Even now, it's the loud churches, not just in their sanctuaries but through the media, that cause gays and lesbians such grief. Therefore, I only ever wanted to be far, far away from anything like that. Then along came MCC, founded by an ex-Pentecostal preacher, thank you. The Pentecostals are a sect not known for being low-key and retiring. They're folks who frequently have difficulty remaining in their seats. They also have one or two issues about gays. These Pentecostal roots naturally raised my hackles, and believe me, I have lots of hackles.

Joel Perry

When the service started my first time at MCC-LA, I wanted to flee. There was clapping and people shouting, "Amen!" and hands held up and not just tambourines but drums and bass guitar. My first prayer was very nearly, "God, get me outta here." The only thing that kept me from lurching out the door was that the congregation was obviously mostly gay, and several of the members were really, really cute. I stayed to hear the sermon because that would decide whether I ever came back.

I don't have a clue what that sermon was about. I'm pretty sure I was supposed to learn something specific, but whatever it was, it went right past me. I was too busy crying. I may have missed the sermon, but I got the general message. I stayed. And I'm staying.

At MCC-LA we all come from different backgrounds, and what a rich blessing that is. It's an opportunity to learn other points of view, other customs, other means of worship. I had never heard the Invitation to Communion in Zulu before. It gave me chills. I'd never seen a Bible story acted out very seriously—and very effectively—by someone in full leather drag. For that matter, I'd never seen a male deacon dressed as the Good Fairy, complete with tutu and wand, tossing glitter during a service in order to promote a church fair. (Fair, fair-y, get it? Hey, we're a church, not an ad agency.) All this, and I have a problem with a tambourine?

I am getting over it. But for the time being, if you come to MCC-LA and see me just sitting in my chair instead of clapping, or looking sheepish when we're asked to hold our hands out toward someone for a prayer, or if you hand me the tambourine and I pass it to the next person, be patient with me. I may not dance in the aisle—in fact, the only time I have ever danced in the aisle of a church was when, as a boy, I forgot to go to the bathroom before putting on my acolyte robes—but I am just as glad as anyone to be there. I am learning to be less afraid of noise. I'm learning not to be afraid of some change.

Can I get an amen?

Halloween in Leather

"You gonna be in the Halloween contest?" chirped gratingly perky Becky, our office "Do-Bee" from hell. I loathe participating in company-sponsored anything, from softball games to Secret Santas. Hell, I avoid the Christmas party, thumb my nose at dress-down Fridays by dressing as far down as I can get away with *every* day, and participate in the 401(k) program only at Fred's insistence. The thought of cavorting with accountants, programmers, and people like Becky in some $9 costume from Party City was making my lunchtime panini upwardly mobile. Straight people just don't get Halloween. Don't misunderstand me, I love straight people. It takes two of them to make one of us. But the Halloween heteros I've seen in no way compare with what I'm used to seeing on Santa Monica Boulevard come October 31. Dull people in duller costumes having punch and pumpkin-shaped sugar cookies do not a celebration make.

"Golly, Becky," I told her after my stony silence had failed to make its point, "I'd love to, but I'm getting on the phone right now and scheduling some root canal work for that day."

"Oh, you! You're so funny!"

"Not necessarily."

"You know you want to," she said, poking me with a stubby finger and wrongly assumed camaraderie. "We've got super prizes this year!" She handed me the sign-up form with all the information and skittered down the hall to intrude elsewhere. Our firm does all kinds of barter business, so the prizes for some of the categories were actually pretty good, including the grand prize: a cruise for two. So I decided to enter. Not that I had a costume or anything. But I did have something I thought might grab a bit of attention.

I got up early Halloween morning and shaved my head. I put on my black jeans, studded belt, leather harness with chains, bar vest, leather hat, and black work boots. Fred woke up and saw me and thought he'd slept all day and it was evening. I eased his panic, but not his curiosity.

"Where's your shirt?" he asked me.

"In the drawer," I said defiantly. "Where it's staying."

He rolled his eyes. "Why can't you just get a rainbow mug like the rest of us?"

I left in a huff. Actually I left in my creaky Dodge Neon, which barely made it over the hill into the Valley that morning. By the time I hit Ventura Boulevard, the "check engine" light was blinking madly and the car wasn't going much farther. I coasted into a garage on Van Nuys. I would like to say that when I got out of the car dressed like Glenn Hughes killing time until the Faultline bar opened, it excited comment. In truth, the opposite occurred. The whole place stopped dead.

I may be a big fat newbie to leather, but I know better than to apologize to anyone, anywhere, anytime for wearing cowhide. Still, I like to dress for the occasion as much as possible. If it's underwear night at the local bar, I feel uncomfortable wearing jeans, and a pressure to take them off and blend in. If it's team cap night at the stadium and I don't have one, I want to leave. So I hope the community will forgive me when I say I would not have chosen to wear fetish gear while taking my car to a garage in the San Fernando Valley. Years of theater, though, have taught me two things: (1) play the part; and (2) commit. I strode over to a stray mechanic with

"Tom" on his shirt and demanded, "Can I get some service here, or what?" He hesitated, looking around in distress. "For my car, service for my car."

"Oh!" You could see him relax. "OK, sure. What's wrong?

I explained, and he said they'd have to look at it. Naturally, I had just missed the guy who took customers to their jobs, so I'd have to take the bus. Standing at the corner was actually a relief. As I boarded the bus with a homeless man in thermal underwear and a woman's hat, a guy in an El Pollo Loco uniform, and a nun, I felt much less conspicuous.

At work, though, it caused tongues to wag. People I've never had a reason to speak to found cause to drop by my office and gawk. Becky heard I was "in costume," so she came bounding into my office to show off her predictable getup. "What do you think?" she warbled. "I'm a sexy pirate!"

"Well, you're a pirate."

"Oh, you! And what are you?"

"A top."

"I don't get it. Do you spin?"

As I rolled my eyes, Tony, one of the salespeople from downstairs, walked by for his gawk and did a full-on double take. "Oh, my God," he whispered. Then, recovering, he said, "I'm sorry. For a second I thought you were someone else."

"Who, Tony?" I asked with arched eyebrow.

"Someone...I used to know." He still stared without moving.

Nobody was paying attention to Becky, so she had to say something. "You know, Joel, technically this isn't a costume. I mean, if you have this stuff at home regularly, what makes it special?"

"Today the armband is on my left arm."

"What difference does that make?"

"O-o-oh," Tony said, "a lot."

Becky looked at him, annoyed to be outside this subcultural loop. *Hmm,* I thought. "Hey, Tony," I said, "let's do lunch next week."

"Uh, I gotta go," he said and scurried away.

Oh, well. At least his reaction convinced Becky to let me compete. At 1 o'clock the entire company was summoned to the 24th floor for enforced frolic. All the contestants lined up and paraded by for voting. Becky had concocted about a dozen categories to ensure prizes would be spread among many departments—Most Elaborate, Most Disgusting, etc. If there had been a Most Cliché category, it would have been the most hotly contested. We had 1920s flappers, a Church Lady played (yawn) by an actual lady, a Marilyn Monroe (ditto), a Cher (again, ditto, what is with straight people?), a caveman with plastic club and his subservient cave woman, a *South Park* Brian Boitano, about seven Draculas, a toilet-paper Mummy, and one guy dressed as a female cheerleader (who was much more enthusiastic about it than the role called for).

While the votes were being tallied we had Halloween treats. My boss came over and said, "Impressive."

"Impressive, *what*?"

He needed a moment to figure it out. "Impressive…sir?"

I patted his head and moved on. I wanted to find Tony and order him to feed me. He may have suspected something like that because he was nowhere to be found.

As it turned out, I didn't win first in any category. I came in fifth in Most Politically Incorrect, which I didn't understand because I'm so PC and liberal, I think Tipper Gore's a fascist. I'm sure she'd want to slap a warning label on me and my leather and chains.

I came in third for Most Scary, an award that went to our corporate law officer, who was one of the Draculas. I lodged an official protest. He's a lawyer, which means he's already a bloodsucker. We were just seeing his true self.

And I was awarded fourth place in Best Costume Made From Materials Around the House. I still don't know what to think about that.

I was annoyed that the grand prize went to an enormous woman dressed as E-mail. If your reaction to that is "Huh?" you're not alone. That's what I thought when she announced what she was. In my book, if you have to tell people what you are, the costume ain't working. But she came with a little recording that said, "You've got mail," so she won the freakin' cruise.

Fuck it, I had my car to deal with. This miserable mandatory merriment put me so far behind in my work that I wasn't going to be able to leave until late. I called the garage. Tom, my mechanic guy, said they closed at 6 but he'd wait for me. I've had dates that wouldn't do as much. Of course, most dates don't cost what a new fuel pump does.

When I got there, I had to knock on the locked door. Tom opened it and let me in to the office. I was getting a weird feeling from him as I wrote him the check. He led me into the garage where he shut the door behind him and looked around furtively. *Oh, hell, this is how I die,* I thought, *fag-bashed by a Pep Boy.*

Suddenly he went down on both knees, put his hands behind his back and bowed his head. "Sir!" was all he said. Oh, my God, he was presenting. What do I say? What do I do? Where the hell is Emily Post in a situation like this? I'm just a newbie! And a bottom, at that. I was out of my league. Damn it, I knew I should have gone to that S/M training weekend at Butchman's in Palm Springs! Think, Joel, think. You've hung around Master Skip and Slavemaster; what would they do?

I put my hand on his head. "Arise," I said, hoping it didn't sound too *Camelot.* He stood, still keeping his eyes down. "Keys, Tom." He looked hurt. "Keys, slave Tom."

That made him happy. "Sir, your keys, sir!"

Coming back over the hill home, I looked forward to Halloween among my own kind that night, people who understand the seriousness of absurdity and the need for outrageous display. Still, I hoped it wouldn't be a letdown after the events of the day. Although I hadn't won any prizes, I had made a blatant statement at my workplace (a company that owns the Dr. Laura radio show, thank you), had my coworker Tony come out to me, got to order my boss around, and am currently reconsidering my status as a bottom.

And best of all, if my car acts up again, I now have a mechanic that truly understands the word "service."

Holy Cowhide!

Here's a leather piece that starts at church: The Metropolitan Community Church recently held its 30th Anniversary World Jubilee General Conference in downtown L.A. Over 3,000 people, the vast majority of whom were gay, came from six continents to attend. We turned the Bonaventure into the world's biggest gay resort for an entire week. From the constant screaming and hugging, I'm sure the hotel staff thought everyone was named Mary. Well, except for the lesbians. It was a stitch seeing "normal" guests deal with a lobby overrun with same-sex hand holding, kissing, and what have you—lots and lots of what have you. You'd see tourists from Nebraska looking over the roster of events posted for the day trying to figure out where the hell all the homos came from. "Oh, it's so disrespectful," I heard one woman say to her friend, "especially with a church trying to hold a world conference here."

Each night there were open worship services, and on Thursday night the service was to include an acknowledgment honoring the leather community. The regular hotel guests had just gotten used to vanilla queers all over creation, and then, boom, here came scary, hulking leatherfolk. The poor dears were simply not ready for gays, dykes, and everything in between showing up in the lobby wearing chaps, chains, vests, harnesses, and lots and lots of skin, most of it tattooed or pierced. Elevators opened to pour forth overt sexuality and studded cowhide like a Fred Phelps vision of hell. I saw one shaken family of four cringing in a corner with fresh Disneyland T-shirts. "Oh, please," I wanted to say, "you just got back from seeing a giant mouse and a duck with no pants. Get over it!"

At the service we were honored with a special seating area front and center. It was jam-packed with leather from cows around the world. It smelled like a fetish shop and rattled like a dungeon—which of course it wasn't, because just try getting that equipment past Customs.

After worship there was a meeting of the leatherfolk in the hotel's Santa Barbara Room to discuss church acceptance issues. It seems even some MCC churches have a problem with leather, which is ironic when you consider MCC was started by a big ol' leather queen. It was heartening, though, to see pastors there trying to learn. As one femme lesbian said, looking at a room full of people sporting bar vests and tit clamps, "There are some things they just don't teach in seminary."

I understand how she feels. I'm still new to all this myself and just learning the ropes, no pun intended. I don't purport to speak for the whole community, only for me, but it seems there's a lot of misunderstanding about the leather world even among gays. Wearing a simple studded armband conjures up all kinds of murky sexual fears in noninitiates, although it does keep those visits from Seventh-Day Adventists remarkably brief. For those who insist upon focusing on the sex (and who could blame you), let me state that there are negotiations as to what will be done to whom. There are other safeguards too, but mainly you use common sense. If you go home with just anyone, you deserve what you get. Go rent *Looking for Mr. Goodbar.*

Leatherfolk often get asked by other gays, "Do you have to be so open about it? Can't you just keep what you do behind closed doors? Do you have to flaunt it?" Hello? Do any of these sound like questions your family asked you when you told them you were gay? Relax, we won't hurt you. Unless, of course, you really, really beg for it.

I'll warn you, though, you might be surprised to find out you like it. That's what happened to me. The whole S/M thing used to repulse me. *Those sad, sick people with their need to be denigrated, hurt, and highly accessorized for sex*, I used to think as a teenager. *I'm so much healthier whacking off to photos of my Methodist Youth Fellowship pool party.* Then the Village People came along with hairy Glenn Hughes in leather on the cover and I no longer needed my pool party pics. Since I didn't know any other boys who liked boys, let alone boys who liked boys who liked leather, I remained simultaneously aroused by and deathly frightened of Glenn and his ilk. Like a good American, I was raised to disdain what I was afraid of or didn't understand, so I avoided looking at Glenn and tried to concentrate on Bruce Jenner in that hot tub on the *Can't Stop the Music* soundtrack cover. Fat chance.

OK, 2½ decades go by. Suddenly one Sunday here in L.A., I met genuine leathermen—not in a back room but in my *church.* I panicked. They were so scary and sexy and confusing and upsetting and worst of all, most inexcusably…really, really hot. They were also very sweet to me, and the more I heard and saw of them, the more I was drawn to leather. Finally, one day in Payless, the smell of the shoes gave me an in-store chubby and I knew I was hooked.

Getting to know these leathermen was a series of surprises for me. The first was discovering they were a family of three slaves and a master. You should have seen me trying to carry on a conversation not knowing the slave had to have permission to talk. The second was how easy it was to discuss spirituality with them. Well, once permission was granted. You may be saying, "How the hell does all this fit in with any kind of church?"

Most churches I've been to want you to make babies, but they don't want to know how it's done. They divorce sexuality from the person and make it a shameful thing, like bearing false witness or eating communion wafers with garlic dip. MCC tries to teach, and a few other churches are learning, that whatever your sexuality is and however you express it among mutually consenting adults is a part of the wonderful creation that you are and the entire package should be celebrated. Love me, love my slave. Or my master. I still haven't figured it out. I've got too many issues of masculinity, attractiveness, and being finished in time for *South Park* to work out. But I know whatever I decide, I'm welcome at my church.

Which brings us back to the meeting in the Santa Barbara Room at the Bonaventure. When the participants broke up, about half went off to the Faultline while the other opted to go to the hotel bar. I had too good a parking place to give up just yet, so I joined the group at the hotel. When half a hundred big, dangerous-looking sexual outlaws descended on the bar, the regular patrons leaped to their feet in terror. They took one look at this large group of severe men and women in black leather wearing more hardware in their skin than they had in their kitchen cabinets and fled, spilling drinks in their panic. We sat and ordered umbrella drinks. I don't know what those people were afraid of. Hell, we'd just come from church.

Fat Fag

Among the last places I expected to be called a fag was at the theater. I mean, that's our turf, right? Well, Fred and I were at the Ahmanson in Los Angeles, next to a family of five: mother, father, young teenage son, older teenage daughter, and—what were they thinking?—a 4-year-old boy. Bringing a 4-year-old to an evening performance is like bringing Pat Robertson to a circuit party—it is not going to be pleasant for anyone. Naturally, the 4-year-old got cranky and started whining. The mother picked him up but made no attempt to shush him.

I'd had enough and leaned over for a pointed "Shh!" at her followed by a glare I'd learned from my mother. Having made my angry case, I retreated. Where? Why, into fear, of course. Fear of what? I don't know. Her glare back? The family hating me? It hardly mattered. When you're raised as white-bread as I, you'd rather hack off a limb than confront someone. Besides, my mother had also taught me that feelings aren't for expressing, they're for stewing in.

When the play was over, I dove into my program. The family got up, and according to Fred (because I was too craven to look at them), one said, "Fuck you." Fred shrugged it off and asked me if I was ever going to get up and go home. Shame, my one motivator bigger than fear, got me moving toward the car.

In the depths of the hot, smelly parking garage below the theater, we were driving around and around through ever-rising levels, hopefully toward a street exit. I remember thinking, *I didn't know Dante worked in concrete.* Just then, the upward traffic halted and we were right beside that family as they walked in front of us headed for their car. The teenage girl stopped, pointed at us with a sneer, and said, "Oh, look, it's the fat *fags.*"

I lost it.

It wasn't cute, and it wasn't funny. The word "fag" in her mouth threw me into an instant irrational rage. I dared not step out of the car, but I would show her! Yes, indeed, I blew the car horn as loudly as I could. Did you know no matter how hard you press on the horn, it does not affect the loudness? Further angered by that, I roared my engine out of there. Then I slammed to an echo-enhanced screeching stop on the next level because we were only able to move about 20 feet.

Fred looked over and said, "You handled that well."

I remember being scathingly sarcastic back. There's nothing like dumping inappropriate anger on a loved one.

I was ashamed of how I'd behaved in the theater, to say nothing of how I acted in the parking garage and to Fred. I was outraged that I was in the right but that this fact simply didn't matter. I was furious I had given them my display of impotence and pathetic horn-blowing. But I was most shocked that it took so very little to turn me into what I most oppose.

Because of the power of those words in her mouth, I wanted to jerk the steering wheel over, gun the gas, and run her and her hateful family down, thereby ridding the world of these intolerant, hate-filled people. That, of course, makes *me* an intolerant and hate-filled person, but I was in no condition even to begin dealing with this, especially since running them over was only the beginning of my revenge fantasy. Once they lay twitching and quivering on the concrete, I would kick their ribs in with my steel-toed Prada shoes (hey, it's a fantasy, remember?), then remove my flawless DKNY pants, sit on their faces one by one and shit, grinding it in with my smeared ass. Then I'd get down on my hands and knees, the better to scream directly into their now-bleeding ears, "*Tha-a-at* is what it feels like!"

And the fact that it did feel so awful infuriated me even more. Here I am, writing articles about pride, self-respect, rising above the crap, moving past our wounds, and all that noise, and it only took a three-letter word to make me certifiably insane. Damn it, hadn't I done the soul work? Hadn't I gone to overpriced workshops? Paid thousands to my therapist? Read all the healing books? Done the meditations, affirmations, and self-congratulations? Still, here was my hurt exposed, gaping, and shockingly vulnerable.

At that moment, I had wanted to kill an entire family. And they weren't even named Phelps. Where were all my pretty ethics then? My dainty ideals of turning the other cheek and not returning hate with hate? My credo of not feeding that which I do not wish to grow? My resolve never to engage with people in Crest-colored eye shadow? Gone. Wiped out in two words: "fat fag."

A friend who is much more spiritual than I could hope to be said I must now learn to love that teenage girl for what she said. I listened, nodded my head, and replied, "Fuck you!" The bastard smiled and said, "Good, you know I'm right." I loathe people like that. I wasn't asking for guidance, I just wanted to wallow in my drama. Where the hell does he get off telling me what I need to hear? Asshole.

So I did an inventory of myself to see what I had learned thus far. Boy, did *that* suck. I've learned that I am not as mentally or spiritually healthy as I had thought. It's a big reminder that I need to keep on working on my woundedness in this area. I can't sit back, smug in my current state of spiritual evolution. The two words "fat fag" stripped away my narcissistic complacency. They are forcing me to grow and I hate, hate, *hate* that. Growth is a pain in the ass. It's work. It's letting go of stuff for which I've already worked so hard but that is no longer serving me. This bitch is bludgeoning me onto being a better person, whether I want to be or not. And frankly, right now, I'd rather not. I'd rather call friends who'll tell me how perfectly evolved I already am and stuff myself with Oreos.

But sooner or later I know I'm going to have to stretch and move beyond my anger and hurt into wisdom and forgiveness. For one thing, Fred and I have season tickets to the Ahmanson, and we may end up sitting next to the little shit bags all miserable year. I need to get my feces together so I can meet them with a rebuttal that will be dazzlingly brilliant, and most importantly, heard.

I'm thinking of something like, "Yes, I'm a fag, and I thank God for it, because it makes me different from the stupefying numbers of people trapped in your normalcy. You fear me because I am a living, loving, laughing trickster god. I am a triumphant symbol of freedom from gender assignment, unthinking patriarchy, sexual roles, and your softer side of Sears. I have been tested in fire and emerged like tempered steel, stronger and more brilliant than ever. How else could I take your hate and fucking *dance* with it? I stand before you as proof that no one, not even you, has to be A or B or even Z. You can be 5 or Orange, and my God, how you *need* that. I am the Book of Other Learning. I am your window into astonishment. Don't just stand there looking at me. *See* me! And be free. Yes, I'm a faggot, and you know what? You're welcome!"

OK, it's a little over-the-top, but it beats leaning on my horn. What the hell, I think I'll rehearse that just to have it at the ready. Because the next time I'm called a fat fag—and we all know it will happen—I can't afford to give over that amount of power again. That alone is motivation. I will come out of this a better, stronger, and—provided my spiritual friend doesn't piss me off again—a more loving person. And that couldn't have happened except for this incident, which has taught me three things. One: I can learn to love what being called "fat fag" has done for me. Two: I can even learn to love her for showing me this by calling me "fat fag."

And three: Maybe it wouldn't hurt to diet.

Older, Yes, But Wiser?

My birthday is this month, and I always like to see what, if anything, I've learned since the last one. Of course doing this forces me to admit is how little I know, period. For instance, I just don't "get" loyalty to a professional sports team. Why should anyone care about a group of people who are not from your town, engaged in the business of making more money for already rich white men, many of whom are also not from your hometown? "Oh, but it's the players," you say. Oh, please. If some other city offered those players 10 cents more than they're making playing for your town, they'd drop your precious team like a day-old Dodger dog. And don't tell me it's the skill, beauty, and grace of the game. If that were true, the American Ballet would sell out the Rose Bowl.

I don't get the popularity of those millionaire shows, either. Why would I care about someone I don't know winning money I'll never see?

I know there are some things we do not need. For instance, we do not need any more of those tiresome "Got Milk?" ads in magazines. Unless, of course, it's the Sisters of Perpetual Indulgence appearing in *Catholic Digest.*

Older, Yes, But Wiser?

We do not need any more interpretations of the Absolut Vodka bottle. I mean, I love them for being homo-friendly hooch, but I think what we really need is a better interpretation of the Constitution. Especially about that justice and equality thing.

I was going to say we don't need any more bumper stickers, but there are three I'd like to see: "My Child Was Named Nihilist of the Month at Some School, But Who Cares?" "The Truth Can Set You Free (But I Could Be Lying)" and "Road Rage Kills, You Fucking Moron."

Perhaps I'd do better if I stuck to things I believe: You cannot be called a "boy band" unless you actually play instruments in that band. Otherwise you are just "twinkies who sing."

I believe talking on cell phones causes brain tumors. Maybe not to the person on the phone, but for those of us driving behind them, definitely.

I believe no one should be allowed to wear overalls unless they own a tractor.

I am absolutely certain artificial intelligence is already here and it is evil. The proof is that the copier knows when you are in a hurry.

I believe the word *melba,* as in melba toast, is an adjective meaning squashed flat and dried. Used in a sentence: Kitty was missing for days; when we found her by the freeway, she was melba.

Speaking of words, I love the expression "woof" in the bear vernacular and believe it should be encouraged. "Woof" is fun because it can be used as an interjection, as in, "Did you see that guy? Woof!" Goofy, yes, but a lot shorter than, "Ohmigod, he is, like, so-o-o way beefy big and H-O-T hot!" Not to mention more butch. It can be an adjective, as in, "Everyone looks woofy in red plaid flannel," although some lesbians might disagree with the example itself. "Woof" can be a noun, as in, "Jack Radcliffe is one giant woof," an indication that Mr. Radcliffe embodies many if not most of the elements of woofoidosity and therefore is a paragon of highest wooferiFciousness and supreme woofitude. And trust me, he is. It can be used as a verb, as in, "When Hank Hightower grabbed my ass last night at Faultline, I woofed." I'm not quite sure what it means in that context, but if anyone as hot as Hank grabbed my ass, it would involve dry cleaning later.

Even though I go to them, I believe there are too many Starbucks. My day job is on Ventura Boulevard in Sherman Oaks. The other day I was giving directions to a place in North Hollywood and heard myself refer to it as "just 5½ Starbucks down the street." I have learned a few things in that store, though. If you can afford coffee at Starbucks, you can afford to give a homeless person a buck. I think that's in the Bible. The book of Joe. And even if it isn't, it's better to risk giving a dollar to panhandlers who don't need it than to miss the ones who truly do. Another thing is, if you're using a credit card to buy your coffee, that's God's way of telling you you don't have enough money to be buying it.

I believe gay people are far more different from nongays than we're giving ourselves credit for. There is no way straight people could have reinvented Halloween or come up with the Pacific Design Center. Nongays *need* us. Never forget that.

I believe gay people have a far greater lack of respect for authority than straights. Gee, go figure, huh? Maybe that's because in most cases, straights *are* the authority. And if somehow it is a gay authority, heaven help them. Can you imagine how hard it is to appear authoritative when your name is George and angry fellow gays stand up in your town meetings and start with, "Now listen, Mary..." On the other hand, it would make C-SPAN a lot more fun.

Why do we have such a problem with authority? I believe it's because you can only put up with being treated like shit for so long before you finally get sick of it, stand up and say, "*What* is your problem, bitch?" If we figured out that being gay is not a bad thing—a realization that runs counter to what some people would have you believe is the cornerstone of creation—then maybe we would realize the people who told us that are so full of crap that there doesn't exist a suppository big enough to clear 'em out. Then again, ramming something else up their ass might do them a world of good.

In her book *Another Mother Tongue*, lesbian author Judy Grahn says, "Authority is a sham—it *does not even exist* except as our beliefs and our fears give it credence, form, and power over us." Did you get that? Not only does the emperor have no clothes, but *there is no emperor.* So enjoy your disrespect of authority. I do. In fact, before the Supreme Court ruling, I arranged a trip to every state that still had antisodomy laws, just so I could hit every one of them and be an aggressive bottom. Hey, Louisiana, up mine!

I also believe we have a much more developed sense of joy and play than nongays. Even in the teeth of hatred toward us, we are still able to be funny and laugh. A lot. Humor is our *refusal* to suffer.

And play is our spirituality. Yes, it is. If you are doing something 100%, you are fully present in the moment, and that is play. We have evolved a spirituality that is joyous and fun. Tell that to serious people and watch 'em sputter.

People who believe homosexuality is wrong should not engage in it—end of story. I believe canned shrimp is wrong, but you don't see me calling on God to help me smite those who enjoy it. So let it go. Besides, if homophobic men don't want us sucking their dicks, they should quit sneaking off to truck stops.

OK, all that's well and good, but it doesn't get to the point of what I actually have learned. I've been avoiding it because it's a sad, short list. It's time I faced up to it and admitted that this is all I've learned:

Always warm up first.

Use sunblock.

If there is pool or lawn-mowing equipment sticking out of the pickup in front of you, your way through the canyon road will not be swift.

All morality can be summed up in three words: Don't. Hurt. People.

Now, despite your best efforts, you will inevitably hurt some people, and that's why you need to do something that balances the scale by actively working to help people. You know, walk for breast cancer, organize a porn benefit for AIDS, read to the blind. Reading to the blind is great; you can wear anything, and if they're not grateful, you can make faces at them.

Joel Perry

When the cat gets in your lap, sitting there is occupation enough.

It's not enough to use or even wear glitter. It is vastly more important that you *be* glitter.

And always keep a bathing suit and battery cables in the car. That way you're prepared for anything, be it joy or helping others. And don't worry, you almost never have occasion to use both at the same time. "Mommy, mommy, look at the fat, hairy man in a Speedo by the freeway, tangled in battery cables!" Well, in 45 years it only happened once. I'm just glad I didn't end up melba.

Coming to Church

I come from a traditional Methodist church background. That means that we traditionally didn't want to upset anyone, the result of which is that there is not a single sermon I remember. It was our function to sit in the pews and feign attention. Church demanded a displayed reverence to God, so my brother and I had to dress in suit and tie. Reverence was expressed in discomfort. Although the shirt was small enough to fit my stubby arms, the collar was not big enough to fit my thick neck; plus my Sunday suit was black wool. We lived in the South, and the church's air conditioning was negligible. I was a fat little boy, choking in an unforgiving shirt, sweating in my scratchy husky-size pants and coat. I learned to loathe neckties and resent God for them. But we went almost every Sunday. If we didn't go, we were expected to sit home and be reverent, which meant gloomy. Forget Bullwinkle cartoons—we couldn't watch TV at all unless it was a sermon. What was the point of staying home?

I'm telling a lie about the sermons; I do remember one. We had a preacher who had been in the military before entering the profession. One Easter weekend he had gotten drunk and ended up in a tattoo parlor. Because it was Easter he chose Bugs Bunny to be tattooed on his arm. That meant that every Easter that preacher rolled up his left sleeve to gave the Bugs Bunny sermon. It was about how he had been so sinful, drunken and godless that Bugs Bunny had been all Easter meant to him. I was 10 or 11 at the time, and I knew Easter was not about Bugs Bunny. It was about chocolate.

Once, during a painting party in the nursery, I saw that that preacher had Yosemite Sam on the other arm. I wondered what religious holiday had inspired that one. I decided I didn't care as long as we didn't get another annual sermon out of it.

In another town, although I don't recall any sermon, I do remember a lovely service. It was Maundy Thursday, the commemoration of the Last Supper, not a day Methodists particularly observed then. It was an evening communion service, and the church was dark except for a large table in front of the pulpit. The preacher had positioned 13 chairs at the table. Each setting had a place card to represent each of the apostles present at the Last Supper. There was no music or singing, only readings that echoed in the sparsely filled sanctuary. We took communion by coming to the table in groups of 11. The 12th chair, at one end, was draped in white to represent Christ. The 13th chair, at the other end, was draped in black because it was Judas Iscariot's. It was a deeply moving service that brought home the meaning of this heretofore obscure day. Sadly, it was never repeated, because the Altar Guild threw an ugly fit over the fact that the front two sets of pews had been removed to accommodate the table—and then replaced. Thus I was taught exactly what was important.

My father was a member of that church's board. One meeting, the board decided to make everyone sign a total abstinence pledge. My father liked having a beer during the Saturday football games on TV and, perhaps once a week, had a seven-and-seven after a hard day at the bank. We were also allowed a tiny amount of scuppernong wine when we had Wednesday night spaghetti. My father didn't feel any of this was particularly evil, so he refused to sign even though every other board member had. After a fractious meeting, the other members, three of whom were known alcoholics, threw my father off the church board. In my imagination I see these men going home and having a stiff drink or six to steady their nerves so they can get down to some real boozing.

A prime irritation I had with my particular church came every Mother's Day. Our church gave a dozen red roses to the mother who had the most children. The mother of the next largest brood got 10 roses, the next largest got eight, and so on. Father's Day was the same thing, only with carnations, I guess because carnations are the more butch flower. I wondered, why stop there? Why not honor the woman with the biggest birthing hips or the man with the highest sperm count? Secondary awards could focus on ovary production or motility. It was a thinly veiled fertility rite, yet there was never, ever any talk of sex or what to do with it. The entire subject of sex was taboo, dirty, and shameful, yet we were honoring those deemed most successful at it. What is wrong with this picture?

Actually, I pretty much filled in that gap myself. Whenever I was bored, which is to say *always*, I would look at married couples and imagine them "doing it." Somehow, I tended to focus only on the men. Go fig.

One of the reasons I had such anger at church was that it seemed an unspoken function of religion to teach us whom to hate and how. The preferred method being with a smile on the face and the word "love" on the lips. I credit my parents with mitigating most of the messages I learned, but they still came through loud and clear. For instance, "Pity the poor sad Jews. There they are, looking for the Messiah to come any day, and here he came and went 2,000 years ago!" Laugh, laugh, laugh, then, "You wanna freshen this drink?" The attitude was the Jews had missed the boat, which was kinda sad, them being so smart and all.

Catholics were as "other" as Jews because they worshiped Mary and the pope. Worshiping the pope was idolatry, and idolatry in Catholicism ran rampant; just look at all that claptrap in the Vatican. As for Mary, well, Catholics just overshot the target, worshipping the mother and not the son, as if it were a spiritual dart game where it was easier to hit Mary because she was a larger adult as opposed to the tiny infant. Maybe if they'd aimed a little more to the right or left. We Protestants didn't need an emissary such as Mary to take our prayers to God for us; being non-Catholics, we were good enough to pray directly to God, His Mighty Male Self. Mary seemed rather like a postmistress with appointed rounds and a halo. And beautiful fabric. Lots and lots of fabric.

My understanding of Catholicism was woeful. When I was in elementary school there was a school bus marked "Catechism" that some kids got on. I thought it was labeled the way the Trailways buses were labeled for other local out-of-town destinations like Pumpkin Center or Sneads Ferry, out on the edge of the county. Since I'd never heard of Catechism I figured it had to be way, *way* out there. From some of the stories ex-Catholics tell me today, I wasn't so far wrong.

It wasn't till high school when I learned how many of my friends were Catholic and I began to sort through it all. It could be drawn as a vertical organizational chart. The Episcopalians were practically Catholic and looked down on the Presbyterians and Lutherans, who looked down on the Methodists. We looked down on the Baptists and all other "lesser" denominations. Looking in the other direction, each church thought the one above it on this ladder was too stuck-up and highfalutin for its own good. An example of just how ridiculous this was is the time my father was ushering at our church one Sunday. The preacher went to the water fountain just before the service only to find it out of order. My father, who was standing by it, joked that the Assembly of God next door had turned off our water. During the announcement portion of the service, the preacher reported this as news, causing great upset in the congregation. After the service my father tried to tell everyone he had been kidding, but no one listened. One of the members, a county supervisor, promised an investigation.

As far as "the coloreds" were concerned, once a year there was a joint service with the black Methodist church from the other side of town. Several families attended, and a big deal was made about seating them up front. Nevertheless, you could just feel our members gritting their teeth. When the visiting preacher invited us to their church the next month, our family were the only representatives. I remember thinking, *So this is what it feels like.* I was young; what did I know?

Not all memories are unpleasant. At another church we attended, there was a man named Jack Pindell who was leader of the choir and the Methodist Youth Fellowship. He was a sincere and devout man who reached out to me to join the MYF. I attended a couple of times but no more because it was full of the obnoxious, jeering jocks I avoided the other days of the week at my high school. They also mercilessly mocked Mr. Pindell, who was the band teacher, behind his back. But Mr. Pindell is very important to me. He changed my life.

As part of his outreach to me, he and his wife invited my family to go with them to see a local summer stock performance of *Man of La Mancha.* I had never seen live theater before, and it exploded my world into a wonder of never-before-imagined possibilities. That evening I experienced primeval magic and awe. I was moved by powers of poetry, beauty, and wonder I never knew existed. I have ever since been in some form of entertainment.

Wherever you are, Mr. Pindell, thank you for setting me on that journey, and God bless you. In only a few years I would leave the church for what I swore would be forever. It would be your introduction of culture into my life that would save me in many ways.

Even though I no longer attended, the church's fondness for telling congregants whom to hate would become particularly pointed once I accepted myself as a big ol' fag in my early 20s. Without this apostate interference, I know I would have been able to accept myself years earlier, gotten on with my life and not spent nearly so long in a self-loathing torment of denial, self-recrimination, destructive behavior, and fear I'm still sorting through. It makes for interesting "and how were *you* fucked up?" conversation, and I've learned to tell it so it gets a laugh or two, but I really could have done without it. How could religion, which was purportedly based on love, be so vehemently *un*loving and condemning?

Joel Perry

There was a week during September in my early 20s that was shattering. It occurred when I finally realized I was the best person I knew how to be at that time. I was not the monster I'd been taught I was, not the abomination I assumed I must have been. But I struggled with this new realization that I might just be OK for days because it meant everything, *everything* I had been taught about myself was a lie. If such a basic, primal, fundamental thing could be false, then everything else was up for grabs too. I was such a wreck that entire week that I remember going to the grocery store once and coming back with a bag full of nothing but Oreos, Kleenex, and Vaseline. (OK, so how do *you* handle stress?) During that week I finally managed to put things back together—albeit a little differently than before—but every message I have received since that revelation has remained suspect. High on that list was religion. If religion didn't want me, fine; I didn't want it either.

Away from church, I founded my own religion: art. I looked for humanity and truth and was able to find it in literature, music, art museums, and the theater. There are, after all, worse places to look for these things. Sister Wendy of the PBS series on art says, "So many people live in a prison of daily life with no one to tell them to look out or look up. If you don't know about God, art is the only thing that can set you free. It satisfies and challenges the human spirit to accept a deeper reality."

When I saw a painting that moved me, I felt the connection I needed. The more tortured the artist, the more I related. In the Musée D'Orsay there is a room where there are seven Van Gogh paintings. When I walked in, it literally took my breath away. I sat on the floor and wept.

In every city I visit I still make a point of going to the art museums. On return visits the sculptures and paintings are like old friends who got me through some rough times. How could I be in town and not drop in on my *Madonna of the Rock* by Leonardo, my *Floorscrapers* by Caillebotte, my *Napoleon* by David? How could I resist spending time with *The Burghers of Calais* when they had more to teach me about pain, selfless sacrifice, and redemption than ever got through to me in a pew? I saw devils remade into angels in Caravaggios and miracles of light and truth in *Water Lilies.* From literature I received excellent sermons from *The Screwtape Letters,* lessons in humanity and hope from Mark Twain, Alice Walker, Toni Morrison, and Maya Angelou. My soul was moved by Stephen Sondheim, Terrence McNally, Tennessee Williams, and the like. Joy was found in Red Skelton, Mel Brooks, *Mad* magazine, and Monty Python. I saw the divine in any nature special on television and, when I would take the time, in sunsets, trees and stars. All of this without God. Right.

Imagine my shock, after I had come back to church, to learn I had not been walking proudly without God all those years as I had thought. I had not been alone at all, merely unable to recognize God right beside me or, often, in front of me.

When one is moved by a piece of creation—and that includes all art—one gets a hint of a breath of a promise of an infinitesimal glimpse of the face of God. The glory of God being so powerful, this tiny inkling is all this human form can handle and still I could be left reeling and weak. That *something* that touches you, that connection to the artist and, through the artist, all humanity is, for me, God witnessed and at work. It is the connection we all share that reveals the divine.

The coming back to church itself was a surprise too. As I entered the door, something removed the resentment I was carrying; something loosened my bag of anger and bile that, though heavy and difficult, I had grown to accommodate, even treasure. Something made me forget my heartbreak at being taught self-hate in the name of love—and it all happened in an instant without my knowing it. I found myself with nothing to gnaw on in bitterness during the service. I was naked. I had no means to defend myself, nothing with which to block the message. And I heard the message.

The particular message that day was "We are holy people." In the past, statements like that infuriated me. I would think, *Who are you to claim for yourself special favor from God? How dare you wear this self-bestowed presumption like a badge of heavenly privilege, making you smug in your certainty of salvation over others?* Instead, at that service what I heard in the phrase "We are holy people" was that piety is practiced, not paraded. We do not claim holiness because we deem ourselves special, but because we—all people—are of God and therefore can only be holy. This state does not make us better than anyone, for we are all, each of us, equally of God. It does, however, make us responsible to God, which is to say each other, to live our lives as would most honor God. I finally got that. God loves us all, just as we are. All. Even me. Just as I am. I got it. Finally.

And so now my real journey has begun.

Things Mother Never Told You About Leather

There are several books that do a good job of covering S/M basics and leather protocol, but I wish they talked about some of the more mundane practical things to expect so a newbie like myself can be ready. For instance, I was standing in a long line at the grocery when my weighted cock ring slipped down my pant leg and rolled past everyone, coming to a ringing rest at the bag boy's feet. Nobody told me that could happen. And "I have a hole in my pocket" didn't cover it. So in hopes of helping other newcomers, I offer some tales of experienced buddies as well as discoveries I've made on my own.

My first education came as I was selecting leatherwear, when the big, hot, butch clerk at Mr. S. Leathers in Los Angeles educated me in "How to Wear Leather Pants." Rule 1, no underwear. Rule 2, you had to sit down to put the pants on. I didn't understand what that meant. The clerk immediately dropped his pants down to his ankles and sat on a stool to demonstrate how you have to pull them over your knees as much as possible, then stand and pull them the rest of the way up. I didn't hear a thing he said the first time because I was too agog of his following rule 1. Wow. You don't get sales help like that at Penney's.

A pair of good leather pants does not come cheap, a fact that bothered me as I was struggling into a pair, dutifully following rule 1. I told my clerk waiting outside the fitting booth that I didn't know if I was really ready for leather pants. He roughly pushed the curtain aside, saw my hard-on, and said, "Looks to me like you're ready."

The day after I got my new leather pants, I was so jazzed I had to wear them to work. I held them up with my big badass double-studded belt that weighs about four pounds, and naturally I was following rule 1. After three cups of coffee I really needed to pee. I hurried to a men's room urinal and barely had time to undo my belt and open my pants before whizzing mightily. I wasn't ready for the weight of my belt to make my pants fall down to my knees, exposing everything from my waist down. It was of course at that moment that my boss entered the men's room—and stopped cold. I had too much bladder pressure to stop so all I could do was go, "Um, hi!" Whatever he had come in there to do, he decided could wait. He turned on his heel and fled.

After wearing my pants for a few months, they began to feel loose—that's the leather stretching to fit your body. I took them back for alterations, getting them cut nice and snug. I loved them even more. But did you know that when you fart in tight leather pants, it doesn't go anywhere? It's like an air bubble trapped under a surgical glove. You have to kind of move around to let it out, at which point it emerges with all its pungency intact. One time I was riding with a friend on a hot day, so he had the A/C on and the windows up tight. I desperately needed to cut one. I was able to use this little known fact about tight leather pants to my advantage, but I had to remain perfectly still to keep it contained in the pants until we arrived. When we turned down Mulholland Drive with its hairpin curves, I knew we were both in trouble.

I'm not the only one to have suffered the indignities of black leather boo-boos. A leather master friend of mine sadly told me that expensive car seats and his S/M family's heavily studded leather/fetish wear do *not* mix well, as the numerous punctures in the black leather back seats of his Infinity attest. I can just see the person he eventually sells it to wondering what the hell went on back there. And not even coming close.

He also tells the story of how he had attached the Seven Gates of Hell to one of his slaves—that's a cock-and-ball device consisting of seven steel rings of diminishing size attached to a leather strap, as if you didn't know—and taken him to his weekly leather bowling league. "During one throw of the ball," he says, "it worked its way free, fell down his pant leg and dropped with a thud on the lane floor for all the world to see as he finished his follow-through. I think he got a split."

Sometimes the leather thing's kind of a hoot. Fred and I were meeting Sue, a woman we hadn't seen in years, at her birthday party she had organized at that same bowling alley. When we arrived, it was league night and I saw my friend's four slaves in a nearby lane. Being very friendly, they came jingling over like studded, chained, cowhide-covered puppies to hug us and say hello. Just then Sue came up, and we were thrilled to see her after so long. I was further delighted to be in the position of introducing them saying, what else, "Sue, slaves. Slaves, Sue."

And sometimes it's less than a hoot. One night those same four slaves and their master, all proudly dressed in their full leathers, came swaggering out of the movies, the butchest S/M family you'd ever hope to see. A woman came up and asked if they were in a rock band. Fortunately, it helps to have humor no matter how you're dressed.

When that family travels by air, they've learned to allow an extra 45 minutes to get through the metal detectors, what with steel-toed boots, chain collars, piercings, cock rings, studded belts, jackets, and whatnot. One time they got stopped for a bag search after something looked suspicious going through the X-ray machine. As soon as the inspector saw the chastity device, she immediately stuffed everything back in the bag and said, "OK, you can go. Now. *Please.*"

One helpful piece of advice no one bothers to tell you is that it's good to have backup equipment for your backup equipment.

Another friend was telling me how during the '70s in San Francisco he had been handcuffed to a sling in a public dungeon for an all-night scene. When it was over about dawn, the key to the cuffs broke off in the lock, trapping him in the sling. His partner had to go down to reception to get someone to come up with bolt cutters and free him. This was not an unusual predicament for this establishment. In fact, the bolt cutters the manager brought up had been used so often they could no longer cut. The search for something to free my friend took hours as he started panicking. What if there was a fire or earthquake? And even worse, what if he was stuck there and missed his sister's wedding, which was only a couple of hours away? They finally found a metal file that took forever getting through the chains on the handcuffs. By this time it was mid morning and he raced out of there, jumped in the shower, threw on his tux, and arrived just in time, artfully keeping his handcuffs shoved up his jacket sleeves. That is, until the reception, when he reached over for a piece of cake and they both slid down in plain view. The groom's mother raised an eyebrow but said only, "Nice cuffs."

And of course it's always good to pay attention to what you're doing. One of the fiercest-looking men I know told me of being at the Spike in New York circa 1982, across from the piers. His pickup's motorcycle was parked at the curb, where there were about 250 leathermen on the sidewalk. Going for the great butch gesture, he mounted the backseat and threw on his helmet to make a grand exit. But he put the helmet on backward, which made it look like an enormous hair dryer as the driver took off. He rode into the sunset with it like this, arm in the air and, what the hell, wrist bent back slightly.

Which I think puts it all in perspective. I guess what no one told me is that along with all the cowhide and attendant paraphernalia, I'd need a sense of humor. But what else should I expect from a fetish that requires so much role playing, production, drama, and drag? In saying that, it's not my intention to offend anyone in the leather community. But then again, if I have, well, I need to be punished, don't I?

Part Three:
Food, Travel,
& Sex

When Bad Food Happens to Good People

I recently flew back east to visit my parents in North Carolina. I was seated in the rear of the plane as the dinner cart came down the aisle.

"Salisbury steak or chicken?" the perky flight attendant asked me.

"Chicken," I said.

She shook her head sadly. "No."

"No?"

"That's right. We're out of chicken. We only have Salisbury steak."

"If you only have Salisbury steak, why did you offer me the chicken?"

"Because if you had wanted Salisbury steak you would have gotten your wish." She turned her attention to the passenger beside me. "Salisbury steak or chicken?"

The man next to me squirmed like this was a test. "Um, Salisbury steak?"

The flight attendant beamed. "Correct; here you go." And she continued chicken-and-steaking her way down the aisle.

I can handle the irritation of being offered a choice when there is no choice. I mean, who hasn't voted in an election? But this seemed a new height in some form of procedural idiocy. No wonder air rage is so fashionable.

I let it go. If therapy could teach me to let go of junior high gym class, I could get over this. I settled down to a nasty compartmentalized meal that was a marvel of individually wrapped and sealed components, an anal retentive's wet dream. *Oh, well,* I thought, *when I get to my parents' the food will be better.*

The burden of being an optimist is not merely the frequency but the severity of disappointment.

My father has become an Omaha Steak junkie. He ordered from them once and the frozen meat arrived in a chest packed full of mystically swirling dry ice and free offers for his next order. Dinner my first night at my parents' house consisted of marvelous cuts of meat from perfect cows, lovingly defrosted over two days in our fridge, transported with care to the oven, and then burned to a cinder. That's how we eat meat in the South. One has to order steak "blood rare" in restaurants there for it to arrive well done. If you order it "well," your plate will come with anthracite and a side of fries.

Accompanying our charred flesh was prepackaged iceberg lettuce salad mix, combined with expensive on-the-vine tomatoes, carefully selected and brought home in their bright redness and promptly ruined by my mother putting them in the fridge to turn mealy. That was easily overlooked, though, because of the hideous fat-free allegedly Italian dressing. If the Italians ever learn of this bottled abomination, we will once again be at war. I grabbed the store-brand can of grated Parmesan cheese in an attempt to mitigate it. My mother saw me reading the label and assured me, "It's the good stuff." Indeed. There were three ingredients listed before the actual cheese.

I have no desire to make my parents feel bad about what they eat, but there was no way I could choke this down for another five days and not report it to the authorities. Therefore, the next night I offered to take them out to dinner. Their choice was the Golden Corral, a buffet-style steakhouse. There we had our choice of more overcooked cuts of gray beef, this time from imperfect and deeply depressed cows. It came with a baked potato not only wrapped in, but tasting of, aluminum foil. The big draw was the all-you-can-eat buffet featuring everything from iridescent meat to highly processed desserts. My dad explored the pasta/soup/salad/potato/bread/condiment/Jell-O bar with the joy of a child at FAO Schwarz. I made a quick salad, got my mother situated at the only available table, and had just negotiated iced tea with the bus boy as my dad arrived,

"I like it here because you can make your own balanced meal," he said, setting down his plate of baked potato, corn, peas, beans, hush puppies, and white bread, a symphony of starch. He had been impressed by the selection and bounty. "Did you know they even have meat loaf over there?"

"Mmm, meat loaf," I said before I could filter out the sarcasm. My father took umbrage and another pat of butter.

"Well, maybe you're used to that in Los Angeles, but they don't have it a lot here." He buttered his hush puppy in the ensuing silence. I needed to make it better.

"Actually, it's a rare sight in Los Angeles too," I admitted, careful not to add, "Thank God."

That did the trick. The rest of the meal was pleasant as only a meal topped with three varieties of cobbler, two kinds of cookie, and a brownie and ice cream with sprinkles and caramel can be. Yes, I too had been sucked into all-you-can-eat hell, the black hole of bloat, and I hated myself. As we prepared to leave, my dad asked if I wanted anything else. I decided not to say, "A good purge."

The following day I knew better than to tempt them with their next favorite dining experience. On a previous visit, they had taken me to S&W Cafeteria. The food looked like the clientele: tired, gray, overdone, and fatty. So that night I announced that I would cook.

"That's real nice, son," said my dad, "but you don't have to do that."

"Oh, yes, I do," I replied as I left for the grocery.

I came back with a beautiful roasting hen, fresh herbs for the bird, and a *bouquet garni* for the side dish of wild rice with cranberries. Instead of a salad I bought fresh spinach, which I steamed, then seared in a saucepan with olive oil, lemon, and crispy pancetta. I called them in to the table and they were duly impressed. The blessing was said, and I tucked into a delicious meal, reveling in the subtlety of the herbs with the chicken, the tartness of the cranberries in the rice, and the interplay of the bitter spinach, lemon juice, and smoky pancetta. Then I heard my father.

"Son, I don't believe this chicken's done."

"Sure it is," I said. "What's wrong with it?"

"It's awful…moist."

"Daddy, chicken is supposed to be moist. Meat is supposed to be moist. In fact, *food* is supposed to be moist."

"Did you mean for cranberries to get in the dirty rice?" asked my mom.

"Yes. And it's wild, not dirty."

My father was picking the pancetta out of the spinach. From the cruet on the table my mother was pouring vinegar on her heretofore lovely spinach. Neither would touch their chicken. I realized they felt about my meal like I had about theirs. Roles reversed, they were doing their best to choke down what to them was the worst food they had eaten in months.

"Mama, Daddy, I thank you for giving it a shot. If you don't like it, though, don't force yourselves." They were visibly relieved. "I'll put it up, and for the rest of the time I'm here, I'll eat it." That seemed a good plan all around. "Is there something I can whip up for you quick for dinner?" I asked.

"We like that Top Ramen mixed with a can of Veg-All."

I shuddered violently, but I got up and made it for them.

My experience had taught me that I needed to approach all food in a different light, something that came in handy on the flight back to L.A. The trick was to look at the unpleasant food the same way one considers the in-flight magazine crossword puzzle. Like the puzzle, the meal is only a distraction that helps pass the time, only not as tasty or full of fiber. This time, a handsome flight attendant stopped his meal cart by me.

"Chicken or Salisbury steak?"

"That depends," I said. "Which do you have?"

"Salisbury steak," he beamed.

"In that case I'll have the Salisbury steak."

"Correct; here you go."

You already know it was dreadful. But when faced with a culinary comedown, I had learned to make the best of it and, through sheer determination, I had found a reason to love it. All my life I have wanted secretly to be really big, 6 foot 7 and 250 pounds. As I sat there with a Salisbury steak the size of a Post-it note, I felt absolutely huge!

My Not-So-Fair Lady

Fred and I had never been out of the country and were therefore nervous about it. Even though we were only going to England, I think we had visions of being waylaid in some alley and sold into white slavery. Or perhaps they were fantasies. At any rate, we had provided our cats with only two weeks of pet-sitting, so we decided to play it very safe. We bought one of those all-inclusive package deals that included airfare, hotel, and various tours. Yep, we were suckers.

On our first morning, we had to be downstairs for breakfast at 6 so we'd be ready to board the bus by 7. When breakfast turned out to be grilled tomatoes and tiny, mangled, oily fish, we were ready to board by 6:01. Unfortunately the bus didn't arrive until almost 8. Our guide, an intense, intimidating woman, arrived promptly at 7 and was livid that the bus was not there. Our tour group heard her on the phone in the lobby tearing the tour company a new one for being late with the bus. She was booked to do another tour for some French tourists at 2 and swore she was going to do "whatever it bloody well takes to be done with this idiot lot to be ready for the filthy frogs by 2."

Once the bus did arrive, her first move was to throw the fear of God into the driver. Consequently, our London tour was a blur: Boom!—Parliament! Bam!—Buckingham Palace! Bang!—the Tower! All pictures were from the speeding bus. As our relentless guide shouted out, "On your left..." everyone pressed to that the left of the bus for a fuzzy photo. "And on your right..." the same thing occurred on the other side. Whatever historic site we passed, our bus listed alarmingly toward it. The only place she allowed us to stop was Westminster Abbey, which was apparently by law as every tour bus in the country had already stopped there. We were hustled off the bus and admonished severely by our dominatrix in tweed to keep our eyes on her black umbrella and "do not *dare* lag behind." She raised it over her head and charged inside. We scampered after her, confident we could follow an upraised umbrella.

Inside there was a forest of umbrellas. The cathedral was a solid jam of noisy massed humanity, with dozens of tour groups. Each was struggling to follow behind a determined guide bellowing rote facts in one of God's many tongues and holding a black umbrella aloft. Above the heads of the many-hued throng were arms waving umbrellas from the entry all the way back into the darkness. Someone shouted, "There she is!" and we pushed our way into the mob. In the tight quarters of the Lady Chapel in the rear, it was so crowded that we became far more familiar with a group of Japanese men than most of us desired, although there were a few who had hard evidence of enjoying it. When Fred and I did at last emerge back into the sunlight, our bus was gone, which neatly resolved our concern about what we would tip our ruthless guide.

The next morning was to be our excursion to Stonehenge and Bath. The bus wheezed up to our hotel and when the door opened, there stood the Wicked Witch of the West End. "Aha," she said pointing at us, "the stragglers. Fall behind today and you'll be hitchhiking back from the Home Counties."

I sighed and climbed into the doorway. Turning around, I saw Fred looking at me like I was nuts. "I *really* want to see Stonehenge,"

I said to him. I knew I'd need to entice him aboard. "And I'll need someone to hold my hand when she yells at me." Fred wasn't falling for it. "Plus I have the room key and your passport." He got on and cursed me all the way to Salisbury Plain.

This trip being more leisurely, our tyrannical tour guide filled the time en route by testing our scant knowledge of English history. It was like shooting fish in a barrel. We were Americans. Hell, we don't know our own history past last Tuesday.

"Can anyone tell me when Stonehenge was built? Can they? Anyone?"

"I thought that was *her* job," I whispered to Fred. "I hate being made to feel stupid."

"You'll show her who's boss," he whispered back, "just as soon as she asks us about musicals."

At Stonehenge black clouds threatened to pour any moment, so only a few of us got off the bus. We practically had the prehistoric site to ourselves. and it was magical. I was so excited to be there that I felt a Druid fire in my belly. Or maybe it was just the hotel breakfast. After a fleeting stop at nearby Salisbury Cathedral, we were on our way to Bath.

"Can anyone tell me who built the Roman baths? Can they? Oh, come now, I'm practically giving you that one." Fred had had enough and raised his hand. "Yes?"

"Do you know any other games?" he asked pointedly.

"Sorry, no," she said with a smug smile, "but if you don't care to learn anything, feel free to play what you like."

"I spy, with my little eye," he said, looking directly at her, "something that begins with C." I elbowed Fred. She ignored him and went on with her agenda of proving colonists pinheads.

At Bath we had only an hour and a half. Just time enough to fall in love with it, but not enough to really explore beyond beautiful Bath Abbey and the obligatory Roman baths. This was the town of William Wordsworth, Oliver Goldsmith, Thomas Gainsborough, and Jane Austen, but there was no time to seek out their homes and enjoy the history. We were too concerned about missing the bus back to London. I had visions of being forced to make train fare by selling my body. And with what I figured I could get for this body, that would have taken many months.

On the return trip to London, our guide was by now openly reveling in how little Americans knew. "Surely you know something about us. Britain was your mother country after all. I know—what happened in 1776?" I knew that one! I proudly thrust my hand in the air.

Fred whispered, "I don't think she means the musical." I withdrew my hand and sulked through another 20 minutes of cruel quizzing.

Between the passengers' dislike of her and her contempt for us, the tension became palpable. At last she asked, "Does anyone know who assumed the throne after the Glorious Revolution? Anyone? Think really, really hard. Anyone at all?"

An older man's voice came from the back of the bus. "Who cares, lady? Ask us who saved your limey ass in the last two World Wars."

Fred and I led the applause and cheers. She scowled indignantly, sat down, and fumed all the way back to London. It was our favorite leg of the tour.

So Fred and I learned to steer clear of the package tours. On our next visit to London, we managed to visit—on our own, thank you—most of the places we had only seen from the road at 40 mph earlier. We even spent five delightful days in the charming town of Bath. You have to love a place where you can meet at the corner of Queen and Gay.

Oh, and as for our tour guide, she's got a new job now. I'm pretty certain she went on to host *The Weakest Link*. Yeah, *that* lasted a long time.

Goodbye.

Love Me Tonight—Then Get the Fuck Out

By now you've got to be sick to death of me yammering on about my life partner/spouse/soul mate/significant what have you. You are one of the proudly single. You are open for anything. You are alone. All you're doing right now with this book is killing time until the bars open and you can find a tawdry new sex partner—not that there's anything wrong with that. I know how you feel, and I want to help. Since I'm not physically there I can't fuck you myself, so I thought I'd do it in the form of a quiz!

How can you tell whether or not Hot Stud #2,943, whom you will soon be chatting up over a beer and dish of pretzels hundreds have fingered, is sexually compatible for you *right now*? Take the following quiz by circling the appropriate response to each question to see if you should blow him or just blow him off.

The A answers = Oh, yes! The B answers = No, no, no! And the C answers = M-m-maybe. So the more A's and C's you have, the better your chances.

All you want is a blow job in the car—*now.* He says he:
(a) wants your dick in his mouth—*now.*
(b) needs to meet your parents first.
(c) is a priest.

You want to fuck him. He wants to:
(a) get fucked.
(b) fuck you.
(c) fuck around.

He says he wants to eat out your hot ass. You:
(a) bend over.
(b) just had those warts burned off.
(c) tell him you came directly from the gym without showering and monitor his expression.

Tonight you're in the mood for vanilla sex. He:
(a) has an easygoing attitude, a smile, and a condom.
(b) is wearing rubber pants, a leash, and a ball gag.
(c) lives with his parents.

You are an atheist. He is a:
(a) howling-at-the-moon pagan.
(b) foaming-at-the-mouth fundamentalist.
(c) priest.

You're looking for a guy who looks like Tom Cruise. He looks like:
(a) Tom.
(b) Nicole.
(c) a divorce lawyer.

You're a stretched-out pig. He:
(a) is nicknamed "Beer Can."
(b) can't find his cock with a magnifying glass.
(c) has a so-so dick but great hands and a can of Crisco.

You want a man with lots of muscles. He has them:
(a) in abundance.
(b) in another life.
(c) in his head.

You're looking for a night of great sex, and thus far he:
(a) makes you wild with desire.
(b) makes you heave.
(c) makes you pay.

You're looking for someone who finds you sexually attractive. He has:
(a) a big hard-on
(b) his eye on the bartender.
(c) a gold Rolex.

You need to feel loved before committing to sex. He:
(a) already adores you.
(b) keeps calling you "The Mouth."
(c) is willing to lie.

You want him to chain you to a wall, flog you senseless, and fuck you silly. He is a:
(a) known leather master with his own dungeon.
(b) snuff film producer.
(c) priest.

SCORING: Give yourself 10 points for every A answer and 5 points for every C answer. Forget those B answers; they indicate incompatibility, so they don't count for shit.

100–60 points: Bingo! Let the shtupping begin. You match well enough to get it on at least for tonight and maybe even a couple of times more. You know, until you start finding out too much about each other and all the baggage gets in the way. But what do you care? You're single! You can drop his sorry ass and go find another fuck partner tomorrow night. Then go on to the next. And the next. Like you've been doing for years. And years. But, hey, no judgment here! Just try not to think about things like life patterns and why you don't know what a two-week anniversary is like.

55–25 points: OK, you might need to do a little more negotiating, but it doesn't mean tonight's deal is off. With this kind of compromised compatibility, though, don't expect to hook up again. But that's not necessarily a bad thing. What the hell, while you've got him naked and prone, do that filthy thing you've been dying to try. The worst that could happen is he gets up, leaves, and you never see him again. Like that wasn't going to happen in another 20 minutes anyway.

20 points and under: It ain't gonna happen. Forget it. Move on. Go home and come back to this book of alleged humor with its aforementioned yammering about being in a long-term committed couple with all its attendant glories and joy. Then jerk off and go to sleep. After all, that's what we usually do.

Instant Sex Palace

OK, you've just spent 30 valuable seconds on the Internet and Mr. Perfect (at least according to his JPEG) is on his way over. Quick! You've got to turn your pigsty into the Love Shack. Ready? Go!

T MINUS 15 MINUTES AND COUNTING…

Dash into your bedroom and dive into your cleanest dirty jeans and a T-shirt. Just do it! You don't have time to stress over the perfect outfit. You can't be bothered with accessories like belts or underwear. Now, stop dithering over Calvin Klein versus Old Navy and throw something on! You've got work to do!

T MINUS 14 MINUTES…

Starting with the living room, grab anything that could be viewed as unsavory. Stuff it wherever it'll fit. Cram it in the armoire. Toss it into the linen chest. Jam it into the microwave, whatever it is. Dirty laundry. Last Sunday's half-eaten Sara Lee. Your new butt plug in the shape of a fist. Just get it the hell outta sight. If the place looks like sleaze, that's what he'll think you are.

Never mind that you met five minutes ago in the chat room at Mandrinker.com, you don't want to look like a slut.

T MINUS 12 MINUTES…

We both know you live in filth, so overhead lighting is out of the question. You need something with a golden glow that conceals dust bunnies. You need something that warms the room but hides the caked-on dirt. You need about eight dozen candles. Start setting them out, pronto. Light 'em later, just get 'em out, all right? Make sure they're non–holiday specific and—most especially—nonreligious. Nothing goes from romance to wood kill like burning Santas or, worse, an array of *yarzheit* candles. Now move it! Your candles should be clustered tastefully about the edges of the room. Yeah, it's New Agey and kumbaya and all that crap, but screw it. You're a charming romantic, you frantic fuck, and more important, you'll be softly lit. Now let's see some hustle with those candles!

With this many contained flames, there are precautions you're going to need to take. If you wear a lot of hair spray or cheap Halloween costumes, stay in the center of the room. If you have excitable pets, put them outside. If they're strictly indoor animals, kill them.

T MINUS 9…

Race to that kitchen! Put out more candles and *no other wine but red.* Got that? White wine has to be kept cold. That means opening the fridge. *That must not happen!* He'll see you have take-out from '98 in there worthy of a hazmat team. Plus, stains on the floor that have been there since the bicentennial will be revealed by that fucking lightbulb inside. Damn you, Thomas Edison! OK, focus, focus. Find two glasses. Shit. There's only jelly glasses. OK, you're gonna have to sell the romance here. Practice saying, "I like to drink it like I did when I was a student in Geneva." Suddenly it isn't tacky, it's bohemian. God, you're a genius. Hmm. Let's make it two bottles of red. The drunker he is, the easier it'll be to pull off this romantic crap and get your dick up his ass.

Gotta have food out. Wrap a couple of baskets in something that'll pass as bistro towels. Come on, *think*! You've probably got a checked shirt or striped pillowcase that'll work if the lighting's dark enough. Throw bread and a hunk of cheese in one basket, and sling a buncha grapes in the other. Forget plates, feed each other. It's not only passionate, it saves on cleanup.

7...

Scurry into that bathroom! You're stuck with him using the overhead in here, so drop to your knees, you harried bitch, and start wiping. Throw five or six Ty-D-Bol tablets in the tank. If the water's blue enough he'll never see the rust and scum. Dust whatever he'd be looking at when taking a piss. Now, sit on the crapper and wipe everything you can see in front of you. If he takes a dump, he's going to have time to notice that stuff. You want him to notice how clean things are so he'll think you're clean too. The fool.

Throw open that medicine cabinet. Hurl anything questionable into a drawer. Prozac, Xenical, Outgro, Cruex, Rid, just lose it. Now jam the drawer. You want him finding only Band-Aids and condoms. And not a gross of Trojans either. Any more than a dozen says "whore." Keep the rest of your condoms elsewhere. That's why you bought luggage.

Into the shower, chop, chop! Not to bathe, you don't have time. Just hope he's into smells. Meanwhile, scoop up everything in the shower and dump it under the sink. Leave behind one (1) bar of soap, one (1) shampoo, and one (1) conditioner. You want him to think you're well-groomed, not high-maintenance.

5...

Bounding into the bedroom, you see your white sheets are now slate-gray. At this point there's nothing to do but get more candles. Now make that bed, soldier! And while you're doing it, kick everything on the floor underneath the bed.

4...

Dash to the dresser and yank open the top drawer. Scoop

everything on top of the dresser into the drawer. Leave one premium cologne out in view. No, wait. He'll think you're straight. Make it five or six. But no more.

3...

Slap some Luis Miguel album on the CD player. If your date knows Spanish, he'll know what to do when he hears *Besame Mucho.* If he doesn't know Spanish, who cares, it's Luis Miguel. That man could sing the Guadalajara phone book and I'd be sporting *el woody.*

2...

He's almost here! Don't just stand there; *go light all those fucking candles you just put out.* Oh, my God! How do you explain those damn photos you never took down of your ex-lover? No time to replace them. What to do, what to do? Nothing! Yes! If your trick asks, just say he's your *late* lover. He died, um, uh, in a shipwreck, yes. After insisting that you climb up on the floating headboard where you each promised never to let go. Keep lighting. Must light candles.

1...

You never noticed you had so much embarrassing shit out. That Colt Model ad the size of a billboard. The coffee-table book of *Treasures of the Liberace Museum.* Your Mormon family tree. Blame it on the deceased. That's what he gets for screwing the gas man. On your anniversary. Fuck him. Lighting candles, lighting candles, how many damn candles did you put out anyway? Good grief. OK, almost done. Just tell him you're sentimental. That's why you haven't chucked all that tacky crap you're blaming on your cheating bastard shit of an ex. It's touching, really.

ZERO!

You did it! In only 15 minutes you turned your dump into a love nest. You're not only a stud but a conniving, lying, manipulative romantic love god. As the doorbell rings, take a deep breath and run your fingers through your hair. Striding through the glowing room toward the door, you wonder if you'll be able to lay your hands on any of the sex toys you shoveled under the bed in your frenzied "cleaning." Oh, well. If you can't find them, at least you've got a whole houseful of hot wax to play with.

Let Them Eat Cake

Oh, do we love muffins. Muffins are healthy and therefore acceptable for breakfast. Yeah, right. The muffins we know today came about because baby boomers wanted to have cake for breakfast but our mothers forced us to eat healthy stuff like raisin bran or those horrid old-style muffins made out of twigs. We may have grown up, but we never grew out of wanting cake for breakfast. Torn between our desires and what our mothers told us, we made cakes the size of your fist and called them muffins. It was only natural this phenomenon would spread. Take bagels, for instance.

Growing up in North Carolina, bagels were unknown to me. As a kid I read the word once, probably in *The Hardy Boys and the Mystery of the Missing Foreskin,* and asked my teacher what a bagel was. She said, "That's Jew food, honey." When I finally got to visit New York as an adult and had a bagel, I was ready to convert. My idea of heaven was a deli on every corner and men who wanted to touch me. Between Bagel Nosh and the David Theater on 54th Street, it's a wonder I ever came home.

When I did, I came laden with bagels. I lived off bagel sandwiches for lunch, piled high with sliced ham and slathered with mayonnaise. When I got through with a bagel it certainly wasn't "Jew food" anymore.

But now breakfast bagels have proven prone to muffinization. They've mushroomed in size and now come in muffiny flavors like blueberry and cinnamon raisin swirl. I know it was some Jewish baby boomer who really wanted to eat cake for breakfast who came up with cranberry delight and pumpkin spice bagels. I'm not complaining. I eat them with joy and cream cheese. I'm not even that fond of cream cheese, I just love saying "shmear." But just how did Judeo-Christian breakfast turn into dessert? Two words: Pop-Tarts.

When Pop-Tarts were introduced in 1964 they were instantly on the cutting edge of unabashed garbage for breakfast, and it's high time they were celebrated for it. The chutzpah of Kellogg's! There was never so much as a nod to nutrition because they knew we didn't care. They would have sold just as well if they'd called them Crap-Tarts. They were nothing but crust and jam, and I thought them the most perfect of foods. Then one day, in the grocery with Mom, I saw that someone had had a divine vision of how to improve them. Frosting. With sprinkles. I wet myself.

As a 7-year-old I saw Pop-Tarts advertised on Saturday morning TV and was rabid for my mom to buy them. She refused, saying they were expensive, pretentious, unnecessary, and a gross indulgence, to which I replied, "Yes, and?" If she'd been paying attention, she'd have known I was gay right there. Instead, she merely declared that Pop-Tarts were not proper breakfast food. "Sure, they are Mom," I whined. "It's just like jelly toast, only made by professionals." "Pop-Tarts are not good for you," she said, playing the health card. "Now have some more bacon." I wish I could have told her I'd grow up to eat cake for breakfast.

Our house was a constant breakfast battleground. On school days I would lie in bed until the last possible moment. For a while my mom compensated for the shortened time at the breakfast table with instant oatmeal, as if oatmeal in an instant was a good thing. What towering nerd woke up one day and said, "I'm going to improve the world by making oatmeal available in 30 seconds?"

Ugh. There could only be six people in the world who would find that a good thing, and they're all Amish, so they can't have it. Instant oatmeal remains with us today, though, so how did this product survive? Sugar. Lots and lots of sugar. The folks at Quaker Oats caught on and added maple flavoring, blueberries, cinnamon and raisins, strawberries, vanilla, are you getting the picture? They made the oatmeal taste like lumpy cake batter. Muffins as we know them today were only the next logical step.

In my senior high years I would bolt out of the house in the morning because eating at home was, like, so-o-o uncool. Concerned I wasn't keeping up my strength, Mom would block me at the door and force Carnation Instant Breakfast on me. I gulped it down to get her off my back, then I'd stop off at Hardee's on the way to school and buy sausage biscuits. I'd be sitting in homeroom processing milkshake and cured pork and wondering why I had gas.

All sugared cereals were considered the work of the devil in our house. No Sugar Pops, Frosted Flakes, or Cap'n Crunch crossed our threshold. We had Skinners Raisin Bran and Winn-Dixie store brand cornflakes, both of which had to be bales of hay in their natural state. Now they make cereals out of cookies, for crying out loud. Witness Cookie Crisps and Oreo O's cunningly displayed in your grocery at eye level. The latest, most blatant devolution of morning nutrition is a cereal called Reese's Puffs. At long last, we have achieved that which my generation could only dream of: candy for breakfast.

I for one am completely comfortable with this. I have no problem starting my day with processed sugar and refined flour covered with frosting. In fact, I'm so used to the simple sugar buzz that I now need to top off my breakfast with another, more jolting stimulant from my neighborhood drug dealer: Starbucks. Yet even there I find myself getting my grande drip ("And leave room for sugar!") with a double shot of almond, hazelnut, or maple cinnamon. Yes, it's gotten to where even my coffee tastes like a muffin.

Now, if I could only figure out how to butter it.

Greek Active

The trouble with being a tourist is that you're constantly surrounded by other tourists all glaring at each other, pissed that the tourist site they're touring is overrun with stinkin' tourists. On the plane headed to Athens, I had been told it would be impossible to get pictures of landmarks without hordes of snot-nosed children and braying Americans standing around in Day-Glo tank tops and ill-considered shorts. At the hotel I heard that sightseeing could be perilous. "Ruins are nothing but broken rocks," I was told by a sausage-limbed lawyer, "and then they let people walk through 'em. I tell you, it's a lawsuit waiting to happen." I paid him little attention as I set out to view the Parthenon. After all, he was already wearing his scary tank top and shorts—with Hush Puppies and black socks, no less—so what could he know? As it turned out, a lot.

Scaling the Acropolis was like rock climbing for beginners. Instead of U.S. National Park Service–style stairs with sturdy banister, we had to scrabble up slanted, irregular stone, some of it broken, all of it worn smooth by millennia of erosion and tourists. Added to that, it had rained, making all of this marble slick as spilled lube. Ahead of me, tottering their way upwards, was a convention of the Oldest People in the World on a land excursion from the cruise ship *Osteoporosis.* They were all retirees who appeared rich and brittle. Some of them looked vaguely familiar; I remember wondering if I'd chosen any of them in that year's death pool. They were doing fine, though, until their leader, who looked for all the world like your cruise director Julie McCoy, slipped and crashed into the alpha geriatric. Suddenly we had dowager dominoes tumbling down the steep, zigzagging path toward me. A strapping young woman behind me came up and barked something in German at me. She braced herself against the elderly lady in front of me and I understood. I braced against her and a handy rock so when the falling action reached us, we were able to stop it. Miraculously, no one was hurt. International intervention had saved the day. I felt so U.N.

Once atop the Acropolis, I found it covered with restoration projects and tourists, some of whom could have used restoration themselves. Everybody wanted everyone else to move out of the way so they could get a decent picture of ancient edifices under ugly scaffolding. People were waving their arms and shouting in languages incomprehensible to those at whom they were shouting to move. Nobody did, and since the sun had come out, making the Acropolis a giant hot rock, tempers flared among God's many-hued children. A Japanese group had intruded on a trio of German couples, and a fistfight appeared imminent. I wanted to rush over and say, "Shame on you! You should be getting along better than that. Doesn't anyone remember World War II?" but I had my own problems. Everywhere I went I was overrun by a group of nuns whose leader seemed to be telling them, "See that fat, bald queer? Whatever he does, get in his way." Here I was in Athens, home of Socrates, Plato, and Pericles, birthplace of democracy and reason, whose very streets were trod by the holy apostle Paul, and all I wanted to do was to punch out a pushy nun and suck back a bottle of ouzo. I was determined to take my photos but, short of sparking an international incident, what's a traveling queen to do?

Show tunes, darling, show tunes. I decided on the particular shot of the temple I wanted, then stood in front of it and started singing:

O-o-o-o-o-o-o-o-klahoma,
Where the wind comes sweeping down the plain!

You know that commercial where they put a drop of dishwashing liquid in a sink full of greasy water and in a single spasm the grease instantly shrinks away? That was the reaction Rodgers and Hammerstein had in front of the Parthenon. People of every creed and color backed away, clutching their children. As soon as they were clear, I ran to my spot and snapped my photo. I proceeded to the Erechthion with its famous porch of caryatids.

One! Singular sensation,
Every little step she takes!

I couldn't resist adding choreography. It was the only time that damned jazz class ever came in handy, and it made for a great tourist-free photo. On to the temple of Athena Nike!

I am what I am!
And what I am needs no excuses!

By now people were taking photos of me, but as long as they gave me a wide berth for my pictures I didn't care. I think people were beginning to catch on to what I was doing because as I left I saw an Asian man in front of the propylaeum singing "Masquerade" from *Phantom*. We are everywhere.

When I took a bus trip to the oracle of Delphi the next day, I decided I would do "Rose's Turn" from *Gypsy*. I'd be making a lot of noise there, because this time I had a panoramic camera.

Sing out, Louise!

Carnivores in Florida

God, I love visiting the South. Fred and I had just picked up our friends Don and Tim at the Jacksonville, Fla., airport. It was past 1 o'clock and we were all hungry, so we stopped for lunch at Sonny's Barbecue. Where else but the South can you find banana pudding made with Nilla Wafers, chocolate pudding too, baked beans in molasses, one bowl of shredded cheddar plus two other heaping bowls of cubed cheese all on the *salad bar*?

And oh, my God, the sugar! We were served giant tumblers of the sweetest tea ever. I thought there could be nothing sweeter. Then I had the coleslaw. This slaw was all about mayonnaise and sucrose. Not surprisingly, the waitress who came to take our order was so large it was tragic, but we tried not to notice.

"What's the best barbecue?" Don asked trying to ignore her enormity.

"Well, I don't eat the pork," she said.

"*Really?*" Don blurted. "I mean, I'll have the chicken."

After lunch we drove to the condo we had rented on the beach and turned the air conditioning down to 65 degrees. If Disney can bring back the Electrical Parade during an energy crisis, I'm gonna crank the

A/C till I can see my breath. I spent my delightfully frigid week perusing the local paper of record, *The Times Union.* I felt Southern familiarity sink in with the daily stories such as the one headlined, "10 of Tallahassee's Kudzu-Eating Sheep Disappear." Did I mention this was on the front page? Kudzu is a vine that grows at a rate that makes triffids seem like slackers, so keeping it at bay is important business. Still I questioned whether the lead line really needed to be, "Something ba-a-ad has happened to Tallahassee's kudzu-eating sheep." Someone with a taste for mutton stole 10% of the state's herd of sheep. Given the intellectual capacity of Florida's politicians, I'm sure they're looking for Wile E. Coyote in connection with the crime.

Another story was of an 85-year-old woman who slipped on wet grass outside her canal-front home and fell. She "lay there immobilized, hollering." The good news is that she was heard. The bad news is that she was heard by a nearby 10-foot alligator, her cries of "Help! Help!" translating roughly as "Dinner! Dinner!" The only thing that kept her from becoming reptile chow was her dog who engaged the gator in battle, sustaining several bites. The alligator gave up, and both dog and octogenarian are recovering nicely.

In Winter Haven a three-foot alligator crawled into a sleeping family's home one night via the pet door. And you thought you had problems with your dog chewing on things. The father stumbled into the kitchen for breakfast the next morning only to find something that sent him scrambling up on the countertops and waking him faster than any coffee could. His wife and little girl huddled in the nearby bedroom, shouting for him to call animal control. He did, but not before dialing a local radio station for his drive-time moment of dubious reptilian glory. I hope his boss gave him shit for being late. And I hope his wife gave him nothing for weeks for calling the radio station first. See, this is why I hate radio. It has devolved into such a moronic morass that a meathead with no more than six words to say gets airplay. I mean, after "there's an alligator in my kitchen," what could he possibly have to relate that would be of interest to anyone? "Oh, it's moving over here. Oh, it's moving over there. Oh, my tiny brain fell out."

Carnivores in Florida

Getting beyond gators, there was some other news. In Tampa, a judge threw out almost 40 cases against lap dancers. These working gals had violated the lap dance law prohibiting them from dancing within six feet of customers, a law designed by good Christians to impoverish their sexually powerful, therefore sinful, sisters. Now the repressed straight men of Tampa can once again entertain out-of-town clients with full-body-contact lap dances in the traditional business manner. Poor guys. I almost feel sorry for them for not having the hetero equivalent of a bathhouse. Almost.

In West Palm Beach a botched bank robbery sent thousands of dollars in cash flying down the street. *The Times Union* didn't say exactly how that happened, although I can only imagine it involved an alligator. But fly, the money did, and among the cars that screeched to a halt so the drivers could grab fistfuls of it were Mercedes, BMWs, and a Rolls-Royce. Those rich old bats may be too stupid and weak to punch a simple ballot, but they can fight over flying $50 bills like WWF all-stars.

By this time it was the end of the week and we wanted to end our stay as we had begun it, with a gustatory gorging on Southern soul food. We went to the Homestead, a family-style restaurant where the meal started with giant, fluffy, hot biscuits with butter and honey. We had the choice of chicken wings "breaded or naked," which we ordered breaded to get the maximum amount of grease. And once I spotted it on the menu, how could I resist an order of actual gator tail? It tasted like a chicken that died angry. But after so many stories in that week's paper, it seemed only appropriate to finish with all the news that's fit to eat. I also had chicken and dumplings smothered in such rich, thick sauce that, by rights, I should be dead of cardio-fricassee. The table was made complete with communal bowls of creamed peas, fried okra, yams, mashed potatoes, gravy, and collard greens in fatback. It was a meal that was going to take years off our lives, but who cared? All I know is that, provided my arteries don't clog like an ad for Roto-Rooter, I'll be back for more next year.

Till then, see ya later, alligator.

Food, TV, and Me

The fourth Thursday in November was intended as a holiday devoted to giving humble thanks. Instead, over the years it has become an expression of gluttony and sloth. Proof enough that things do get better with age.

I love gluttony and sloth. Lust is up there too, but I keep finding myself overcommitted and having to pass. Sloth, however, is kind enough to wait for when you're ready. When it strikes, you're not doing anything but lying around being slothful anyway, so you may as well eat stuff. Is this a great holiday or what?

The only problem with a day like this is that someone has to cook. Two hundred cooking shows a week (most of them featuring Emeril Lagasse) have lured me into the false belief that I'm capable, and so holiday food prep becomes an enticing adventure. Recipes that for 10 months of the year were just harmless fantasies become irresistible temptations and guides to holiday havoc. And I become a big fat sap, because every year I fall for this.

I don't know why. When it comes to day-to-day cooking, I can keep myself alive, but that's about it. Fred comes home, inspects what I'm making, then heads for the phone. Sometimes I'll call

Fred to tell him I'll be late leaving work but not to worry because there's stew in the fridge he can eat. When I get home, the stew is untouched and there's a Domino's box in the trash. I feel guilty about it, but there are very few things I can cook that he likes. Not that I don't try. Once I heard Fred say he missed his mom's mashed potatoes. That, I decided, would be my quest. The first batch was too lumpy. The second needed butter and cream whipped in and was still lumpy. For the third batch, I dumped major butter and cream in the potato bowl, set the mixer on whip and went into the living room to watch *Jeopardy!* and *Wheel of Fortune*. Did you know potatoes can double in volume? And having done that, fly across the kitchen if unattended? It may have been on the wall, but by damn it wasn't lumpy.

One problem I have is a bad tendency to get overly exuberant and stray from the recipe. For instance I know the general model is beef + celery + onion + carrot + potato = stew. But if there are packets from Taco Bell, curry paste, and some gorgonzola lying about, in it goes. I try to tell Fred it's piquant, not "stinky." I get nothing for my troubles except more Domino's boxes in the trash.

I hold the Food Channel responsible for my errant belief that I can concoct a delicious dinner from whatever dregs are in the fridge. Specifically I blame *Gordon Elliott's Door Knock Dinners* where Aussie has-been talk-show host Gordon Elliott drops in on some unsuspecting household, dragging along a chef who actually can whip up amazing things from whatever he finds in their kitchen. If his chef can do it, why can't I? So I attempt the same thing, only the TV guy creates "fusion dining" while I create "what-were-you-thinking garbage." Green peppers, onion dip, and oil of peppermint. This is why Fred has PDQuick food delivery on speed dial.

That isn't real world stuff anyway. You know if they found everything for a soufflé except, say, flour, butter, cocoa, sugar, eggs, milk, cornstarch, and a soufflé set, they'd send some intern scurrying off to Safeway to get it. Who eats soufflés anyway? I'd like to see this fancy chef deal with regular food. I mean, can he fry a peanut butter and banana sandwich? I can. Hell, in college I could make a spaghetti dinner in a popcorn popper. Of course, back then I could also swig 151 rum, which may have been what lead to the spaghetti in a popcorn popper. But my point remains. If you served that chef fish sticks and ketchup, he would run screaming from the room, which I say is reason enough to do it.

Those darned Food Channel chefs have invaded my life in ways I never thought possible. I find myself gripping my armrest because I truly want to smack Sissy Biggers with a mackerel. I have nightmares of the dead Fat Lady forcing me to eat butter so I can join her. I have another one from *Melting Pot* where the banter between Aaron and Pilar Sanchez turns ugly, they reach for the knife block and everything goes red. I must admit to one pleasant dream I have where I'm able to beat the Iron Chef because the challenge ingredient is mayonnaise. (I have another dream too, where chefs Bobby Flay and Ming Tsai make a sandwich and I'm it, but that's another story.)

And two of these people have got to be stopped. I mean, that damned Emeril is evil. No one can do that many shows and TV appearances without powers of bilocation, a known attribute of the devil. And Martha has gotten completely out of control. Her shows and products have spread across this country like scabies in a dorm. Enough!

So as the holidays approach, I'm thinking: dining out. That eliminates the whole home-cooking catastrophe and, more important, allows me to concentrate on gluttony and get back to sloth a lot faster. If you go this route, remember to order too much so you can take it home for sprawling on the sofa later. That way you can continue the orgy by cramming food in your face as you lounge. Yeah! Stuffing: It's not just a noun.

To make the picture complete, the universe knew we'd need something stupid to look at during this quality couch time, so we wouldn't have to actually talk to anyone present. That's why God gave us football. And then gave us those locker room interviews. Mmm. Talk about meat and potatoes.

Christmas in the Air

If you're going to be flying during the holidays, you're probably already dreading the journey. You have no control over who sits next to you and nowhere to run if it turns ugly. Some years back, my partner, Fred, was bound for Christmas in Florida. Shortly after takeoff, the tipsy man next to him requested a blanket. He arranged it over himself, then pulled his pants down. Apparently that's how he liked to sleep because in no time he was snoring—loudly. He shifted in his seat and the blanket fell, revealing mesh underwear and three testicles. Not knowing what else to do, Fred lowered the man's tray table to block the sight from innocent passersby and removed himself to the galley, where he spent the rest of flight. We now get Christmas cards from four flight attendants.

Two Christmases ago I was flying from Atlanta to Raleigh and ended up next to an extra out of *Deliverance* named Floyd. He showed me his carry-on, packed with Mason jars full of moonshine. "Want some in your Coke'cola?" I declined. "I'm takin' it to my brother Wilbur," he told me, sipping from the jar. "He cain't make it no more since he went blind and all. It's his own fault, though. He oughta know you gotta flush the radiator good first."

Floyd and his homemade hooch didn't even faze me. Earlier that day, on the flight to Atlanta, I'd sat next to a woman who showed me the Christmas present she was bringing to her nephew. From a Macy's shopping bag she pulled out a largish clear plastic box filled with live snakes. "Aren't they beautiful?" she asked, dropping the box in my lap. "The poisonous ones are always the prettiest." I rang the flight attendant for a double vodka anything, STAT. By the time I got to Floyd on my connecting flight, I was already as full of ethanol as his Mason jars. I arrived home quite festive. Plus I had a sealed jar from Floyd that I gave to my dad. He uses it to strip leather.

Another December I was flying standby. When they let me on the plane there were only two seats available. The first seat was next to a man who was practicing singing with a ventriloquist's dummy. *Oh, please,* I thought. *Somebody tell this man* The Gong Show *was canceled.* I moved on. The remaining seat was next to a hunky-looking Navy man in the back. How could I resist? I plopped myself down next to him with a coy "Hi, sailor, new in town?" He laughed. I fell in love. *Who knows what can happen in a situation like this?* I said to myself.

As the flight attendant was going through her routine, my man in blue nudged me. *Ooh,* I thought, enjoying the need to adjust myself, *it's already starting.* That's when I looked over and noticed his eyes were open far too wide.

"You don't have to wear your seat belt," he told me.

"Oh, really?" I asked. "Why?"

"Because I have special powers."

"Do you, now?" I said, blood leaving my groin. "And what would they be?"

"I can make sure nothing happens to this airplane." He must have seen the light from the sign flashing "Freak!" behind my eyes, because he scowled and added, "You don't believe me do you?"

"On the contrary," I said, "since you told me about your special powers I can say with certainty that nothing is going to happen on this flight."

After takeoff I changed to the other seat and learned how to sing "Mary Had a Little Lamb" without moving my mouth.

Not every travel situation is a nightmare, though. I was waiting for my plane at LAX last Christmas when a man rushed up to me, thrilled to tell me he was wearing the exact same hat as I had on. "Oh, dear," I said cautiously, "does this mean we're going to friends?" "Friends?" he asked. "Darling, we're family." I thought, *How dare this man assume anything about my sexuality.* Followed quickly by, *Oh, wait, I am traveling in a bar vest.* I decided to open up.

He told me he had spent several days at a compound in Palm Springs learning to be a slave. He was very excited about it and, of course, I was instantly eager to learn. His name was Rudy, or rather, slave rudy, in all small letters. slave rudy (yes, even at the beginning of a sentence) told me about the various disciplines demonstrated at the compound, such as gags, mummification, role definition, tit clamps, and piercings. You should have seen the reactions of the other passengers. "No, no, the Apadrava pierces the head of the penis from top to bottom," randy explained, somewhat louder than necessary. "The Ampellang goes through it side to side." On cue, every man within earshot crossed his legs.

The weekend-long workshop was conducted by an acknowledged dungeon master with the experience to ensure all activities were done properly, safely, and especially, on time. slave rudy showed me the schedule, which read something like:

8–9 Breakfast.
9–11:30: Flogging.
11:30–12:30: Lunch.
1–3:30: Bondage and Genital Torture.
3:30–5: Free time.

slave rudy and I enjoyed each other greatly and had a rollicking time. At one point the flight attendant asked us to try to be more quiet and, since he had other passengers to take care of, could we please write down some of that stuff about pumping for him.

I still hear from slave rudy. Recently he sent me photos of him with his new master, taken during the Folsom Street Fair in San Francisco. He's on his knees in a body thong with his arm around his master's thigh. His master, a sweet-looking man in deliciously scary leather, has his hand on rudy's gleaming, shaved head, and they both couldn't look happier.

On your next holiday, do your traveling with an open mind and you just might meet someone interesting. Maybe someone like the woman I had beside me one year who, during turbulence, prayed fervently, saying she'd stop screwing her husband's boss if God would keep her from vomiting on her new Donna Karan. Or perhaps you'll meet someone like slave rudy and end up with a new friend and vocabulary (Apadrava, down; Ampellang, across). Either way you get a fun story guaranteed to horrify your relatives. This year I'm actually looking forward to the flight to visit my parents.

Now if only someone could help me deal with the part that happens once I get there.

Bath Time

The English town of Bath is a privilege just to walk through, filled with the kind of charming sights and quaint shops Disney minions search out to co-opt and wreck. A father-and-son team built most of it, so there's a consistency to the architecture that makes it look like it was ordered in sections from Harrods. Also, Bath has a marker in a public park in honor of James "Beau" Nash, an internationally known dandy of the 1700s. Any place that can raise a memorial to a man because he knew how to dress is my kind of town. Fred and I had been rushed through Bath on our first trip to England, but this time we were spending several days in a bed-and-breakfast I'd found in a gay B&B guide. Unfortunately, by the time we arrived it had changed hands and there was nothing gay about it in any sense of the word.

The bed was a nightmare of angry and bent springs, and the breakfast consisted of stale cornflakes and milk well on its journey to become whey. Our smelly, cramped garret had to have the only hideous view of Bath to be found. The one tiny window overlooked a car park behind the building and an expanse of roof littered with used condoms and hypodermic needles. That night we also discovered it was directly over a noisy disco. Surprise! The one good point about the place was that it was ample inducement to get the hell out and soak up some local color.

Which we found our first morning in town. As we passed a small truck parked on the side of the narrow, picturesque street, a squat but beefy driver leaned out of the window and bellowed at us, "Oi!" We looked around, but here was no one else on the street. "Yes?" Fred answered. The man held out a nasty-looking meat pie called a pasty with one very large bite taken out of it. "D'you want this? 'Ere, tike it." Fred and I looked at each other with wrinkled noses. "G'wan!" the man yelled. "Oi just 'ad one boit of it and it's fuckin' diabolical!" As tempting as he made it sound, we declined politely and moved on, filled with joy at God's wisdom in making that man a lorry driver and not an advertising writer. Our destination was the Royal Crescent.

In the late 1700s this was the place to live in Bath. It's a stately, curved row of town houses built to house the rich shits of 18th-century England. Number 1 Royal Crescent is a museum. My favorite item was the boot rack in the hall for gentlemen to remove their boots so they wouldn't track mud inside, but also to keep the men from "appearing too masculine among the ladies." I wondered what appearing too masculine among the ladies would cause the women to do. Ovulate? Besides, given the string of callow Hugh Grant-ish actors we've been getting from England of late, all the boots in the world couldn't butch these guys up enough to elicit more than a yawn. Maybe it was different back then when Heathcliff and Mr. Rochester types were running around half nuts. But I still wondered what footwear the men of Bath wore, once the boots were off, that were sufficiently nonmasculine for the ladies. Our guess was fuzzy bunny slippers.

Bath has three natural hot springs, all with iffy-looking water that stinks like hell and makes one poop to beat the band. The English, being English, naturally flocked here to guzzle it down by the imperial gallon. Back in Jane Austen's day the elite "took the waters" and paraded their diarrheic derrieres around to see and be seen in the Pump Room of the baths. Today it's filled with tacky tourists like us, taking high tea at high prices and having a high time listening to the live string quartet, sticking our pinkies out, and pretending we're posh. I always liked Jane Austen because her leading ladies were forever poor but were kept by sympathetic rich relatives and friends in the best of places, like Bath. When I read her novels in high school, that was my life's ambition, to be a permanent guest in some house that made Balmoral look like a beach hut. When *Dynasty* came on TV in the '80s and poor Krystle was stressing because she was new to Blake's millions and didn't know how to treat all the servants, I kept thinking, *Get with it, blondie! Order 'em around! That's what they're there for!* I could have been very happy in old Bath calling for my sedan chair to take me to the spa. We learned all the landings in the Royal Crescent houses had been built absurdly wide to accommodate the sedan chair that took you from the spa, wrapped in more towels than Martha has languishing at Kmart, through the town, in your front door, up the flights of stairs, all the way to your nicely warmed and cozy bedside where you hopped out and under the covers. As a Jane Austen–style guest, I wouldn't have to pay for all that. Am I the only person who doesn't have a problem with this? And could you have cook send up some sandwiches?

For a change of pace, one day we took the train to Cardiff, the capital of Wales, where we visited Cardiff Castle. *This* was where I wanted to live! It was owned by the third Marquess of Bute, who at the time was the richest man in the world. During the Victorian era he lavished the very best on it, some rooms taking 30 years to restore. Can you imagine? We just had our bathroom replumbed and I thought *that* took forever. But the Cardiff Castle results were amazing. You have to love a man who uses precious jewelry as an architectural element. And that gold tile? It's gold. Not colored, not plated, gold. It sorta took the sparkle off our brand new copper bathroom plumbing at home. Each room was decorated beyond excess with inlaid wood, marble carvings, stained glass, ivory, gold leaf, and amazing painted designs. The man had far more money than anyone with such garish taste should be allowed to have. The man was out of control, something even the tour guides seemed to acknowledge, because they wouldn't allow any photography indoors, as if to say, "Please don't tell people what this straight man perpetrated in the name of decor." I imagine his servants lived in fear of being sent to certain rooms. Still, after the opulence of Cardiff Castle, coming back to our baleful bed-and-breakfast in Bath really bit the big one.

Why couldn't we have servants to abuse, or at least a wait staff at our bed-and-breakfast? Or even a breakfast that was better than freakin' cornflakes? Well, we combined all those miseries by going to the Bath Pizza Hut for lunch. After a third night in that god-awful B&B bed, I was so cranky that when our sausage pizza finally arrived with nasty two-inch-long wienie-style gray sausages in hard, opaque casings and purely accidental cheese on taste-free crust, I blew up at our server. Fred wisely decided to wait for me outside. Meanwhile, the manager was called. I listed the pizza's imperfections to him in a frazzled American accent and demanded our money back.

The manager sneered, "You people complain about everything. It's perfectly good pizza. Besides, you've eaten half of it, you bloody yank."

I was both angry and desperate to communicate my displeasure in a way he would understand. And Bath had given me the perfect words. "Listen, you," I said, "Oi just 'ad one boit of it and it's fuckin' diabolical!"

Out on the street, Dr. Fred correctly diagnosed me as constipated. Actually, what he said was I was full of shit. But with the restless nights and unfamiliar food, of course I was constipated. I told him I was uncomfortable, though, about taking any over-the-counter cure Britain had to offer.

"Maybe you need some Bath water," he said.

So we went back to the Pump Room and like the privileged Victorians, Georgians, and Romans before them, I took the waters.

I was indisposed for the entire rest of the afternoon, but by that evening it had passed, along with everything I'd eaten that week. Thus relieved, I ended my stay with nothing but love for the town and its inhabitants. Bath and environs had worked its lovely magic on me. Both inside and out.

Road Rules—Are You Ready to Travel With Your Sweetie?

Ah, the open road. Nothing brings out people's true natures like traveling together long distances in the car. Which prompts the question: Should you? After a few hours, the normal filters are removed and you find yourself saying, and hearing, all kinds of things. Are you really prepared to have your weekend date shatter a pleasant hour's peaceful silence by saying, "Did I ever tell you I once blew a sheepdog?" just as you pull into the only motel for 100 miles? And what about him? Do you really think he wants you to prove you can sing the entire Björk library while crossing Kansas? It's that kind of thing that leads me to believe there are many more shallow graves along roadsides than the authorities are telling us.

These thoughts may occur, but they don't stop us from blithely jumping in the car with those we think we know and heading out on Interstate 10 in L.A. bound for Jacksonville, Fla. My point is, perhaps they *ought* to stop us, hence the following test. To find out if the concept of a road trip with that special someone is a good idea for you, answer these questions.

Road Rules

When driving long distances with your sweetie pie, you like him to put on:

(a) dance tunes.

(b) corrective makeup.

(c) a large ball gag.

He wants to stop at every cheesy roadside attraction. You:

(a) indulge his whims because he's adorable and besides, that's the fun part of traveling.

(b) tell him, "No, that's for pinheads and geeks" and endure his resulting icy, sullen mood the rest of your vacation.

(c) stop. And then leave his tacky ass there.

You're making good time driving when poopsie says he needs to take a pit stop. You:

(a) pull over at the first McDonald's.

(b) beg him to hold it because you'll be there in a quick couple of hours.

(c) give him an empty bottle and a stern warning about dribbling on the floor mat.

Eating on the road is:

(a) why you packed a dozen sandwiches, fruit medley, frisee salad, a saucy pinot noir, and homemade lemon squares.

(b) not what you intended, so you get back at lover boy by ordering the double bean burrito and eggs.

(c) a great way to ditch your partner and his damn *Les Mis* karaoke tape at a truck stop.

You wouldn't even consider going on a road trip with someone without taking:

(a) your Clinique.

(b) your Valium.

(c) your .22.

You're driving when you realize your rocket scientist boyfriend can't read a map. You:

(a) assure him it's OK, pull over, and study it yourself.

(b) verbally abuse him for having missed the turnoff until he is sobbing. Then make fun of that.

(c) slow down to 40 mph, reach over him, open his door, swivel your legs around and kick his stupid geography-challenged butt O-U-T out.

After 10 hours in the car together, you arrive:

(a) happy, like Damon and Pythias.

(b) bitchy, like Madonna and Sandra.

(c) tragic, like *Sid and Nancy.*

Upon arrival, you want to go hiking but he wants to go swimming. As a compromise you go:

(a) dancing. Together.

(b) tricking. Alone.

(c) home. Separately.

OK, what did you pick? The more A's you have, the better. You're open to the romance of the road and the lure of travel with your loved one. Not only that, but you'll probably both return alive. If you're still speaking, especially after what he did with the bratwurst at your family reunion, you may even start making plans for another. Good for you!

The more B's you chose, the worse your prospects are for traveling together. You might want to rethink inviting anyone on any trip longer than from here to Sizzler. On the other hand, if you're too craven to end that bad relationship, get out the map and start looking up national parks. By the time you get back, you'll have achieved your goal as well as open animosity, and be fighting bitterly over how to divide your Janet collection. Try to remember, with your next boyfriend, take the plane.

Any C's at all and it's bad news. You couldn't take your pet across town without it trying to run away—into traffic. Do not, under any circumstances, take anybody anywhere with you in the car. If a friend asks you for a ride, give 'em bus fare. And when it comes to vacation you should just camp in the backyard by yourself, perhaps spending the time wisely by considering why you can't maintain a relationship.

But don't be too hard on yourself. Traveling together is a test of any relationship, and you can't know if you're truly compatible unless you try it. Start with small trips and leave the Broadway CDs and sharp objects at home. After all, if it doesn't go well, you don't need *Sweeney Todd* giving anybody ideas.

Part Four: Hollywood, Or Ready for the Dragon Cage

Twinkle, Twinkle, L.A. Stars

For Los Angelenos, celebrity sighting is the sport that connects us all. We're too blasé to get really excited, but it's always fun to have a bit of dish on someone famous. "Guess what star of *Pretty Woman* I just saw in Kate Mantalini's pulling her pants out of her crack?" I'm not very good at it, but I'm proud of my celebrity encounters. Just the other day I saw Pat Boone in the elevator of my building. OK, I admit I didn't know it was him until a friend told me when we got to our floor. I just remember looking at the man thinking, *Spot the guy who didn't get the memo on wearing white boots.* I rarely recognize celebrities unless Fred, who is Mr. Publicity, points them out to me. Since he works in PR, I figure it's his duty to identify the famous so that I, the writer, can be petty about them in print.

In Tower Records, Fred recently pointed out Lars Ulrich of Metallica buying classic Broadway musicals. If you ever hear a hard metal version of "I Feel Pretty," you'll know why. Another time Fred pointed out Heather Locklear in Jerry's Famous Deli, putting away the freebie pickles like she was carrying triplets. At the table next to us at Intermezzo, Jodie Foster was being interviewed by an appalling, sniggering journalist right after *The Accused* had opened. "So didja have bruises, you know, down there?" Check, please.

Fred's always pointing people out to me in the French Market Place on Santa Monica Boulevard in West Hollywood. Zelda Rubinstein, Charlene Tilton, and—a big one for Fred—Billie Hayes, the woman who was Witchiepoo on *H.R. Pufnstuf* and Weenie the Genie on *Lidsville.* Oh, and handsome John Wesley Shipp, who played Dawson's dad Mitch Leery on *Dawson's Creek,* eats there. Regularly, I might add. I'm not implying anything by that; I'm just saying he's there. A lot. The place is also crawling with gay porn stars, which is every bit as cool as so-called "legit" stars elsewhere. At L'Orangerie we ate next to Hugh Grant and Elizabeth Hurley and they both smoked at the table. I paid $80 for duck something, and thanks to them it tasted like an ashtray. Plus the bitch had just crossed picket lines to shoot a commercial for Estée Lauder. I'll take porno people over Eurotrash any day.

I love it when stars throw their weight around long after they have any weight to throw. At a U2 concert, Billy Idol sat right in front of us with his hulking bodyguard, whom he had harass passersby for no reason other than to draw attention to the fact that this was Billy Idol. Apparently Billy had left it to us to explain to the just-hassled and confused 20-somethings who the hell he was. "Remember that stupid song about a white wedding your parents used to play?"

Seating also reveals status. At the Cirque du Soleil, Arnold and Maria, along with their kids and entourage, were shown up to the stage, where they met some of the performers. Everyone around us was craning their necks to get a glimpse. Then the Schwarzenegger-Shrivers were taken to their seats—several rows *behind* us. Our entire section was palpably smug about that.

At a Tina Turner concert we felt smug ourselves about having better seats than Farrah Fawcett because we were directly in front of her. The joke was on us, though, because for the entire evening, she would not shut up, yakking nonstop at the unimpressed man with her. We tried to be big about it, though, putting it down to that head-bashing-against-the-driveway thing with her former boyfriend and all. And I don't mean to seem insensitive, but I'd love to have witnessed that, just to see how it compared to her work in *Extremities.*

At my job we sometimes get important visitors, which I hear about because my office is right next to reception. One day I heard the receptionist announce that Dick Morris was in the lobby. The name was familiar, but I couldn't place it. Then I realized this was the White House boob who had just been fired by President Clinton for telling national secrets to his mistress. Still, I thought it couldn't really be him—could it? I stuck my head in the lobby and called over to the receptionist, "Is this *the* Dick Morris?" She made a face to try to warn me and pointed toward the corner. Too late. A man leaped up from his seat on the other side of the lobby and bustled toward me remarkably quickly for someone so shaped like a giant ham. He looked like someone who would need to hire a mistress, and he grabbed my hand for an aggressive self-introduction and handshake. Trapped and embarrassed, I fumbled for something positive to say: "I can't wait to tell everyone I met you." He was there for a guest appearance on the Michael Reagan radio show, which my company produced. I had just shaken hands with a man who not only hires women for sex but was an intimate adviser of Bill Clinton's. I shuddered to think where his hands had been, so I excused myself to the rest room. Inside I saw Michael Reagan himself, standing a foot and a half back from the urinal, hands on his hips, pissing for all the world to see. I quickly washed my hands and left, thinking that in the space of five minutes I had just been exposed to a current president's ex-Dick and an ex-president's son's current dick.

Come to think of it, I had another bathroom encounter at a restaurant called Tommy Tang's on Melrose. I was headed for their tiny one-seater rest room when Harvey Keitel snagged it just before I got there. So I waited. And waited. And hoped Harvey had the fan on. A drunk guy waiting behind me was in no mood to hold it anymore. He lurched past me and, to my horror, beat on the door with his fist, shouting, "Hurry up in there, asshole!" Then he mumbled something and staggered away in the direction of the alley. A moment later the bathroom door was thrown open and a seething Harvey Keitel was glaring at me. I started to explain but realized it was hopeless. Mercifully I noticed he had forgotten to zip his fly in his rage, allowing me to go on the offensive. "You wanna put that away?" I said pushing past him, "I think we all got enough in *The Piano.*" I shut the door and stayed inside a long, long time, until I was certain he had gone.

I tend to meet my celebrities in bathrooms. After a celebrity screening of the well-intended yet execrable Bill Murray remake of *The Razor's Edge* in New York, I found myself taking an urgent leak next to Charles Haid from the popular and then-current TV show *Hill Street Blues.* Not only is he talented, but I've always had a thing for him and here he was right next to me. "I love your work, Mr. Haid," I gushed as I gushed, "I think you're fantastic!" He glared at me and said, "I'm takin' a piss." I was so excited he talked to me, I said, "Wow, so am I!" Only then did what he said register. Fortunately, just then Bill Murray walked in and sucked all the air right out of the room. If you don't believe he could do that, rent *The Razor's Edge.* It'll feel so good when you turn it off.

I had a cluster encounter in another bathroom eons ago, at the Burt Reynolds Dinner Theater in Jupiter, Fla. The interior was a shameless celebration of what passes for elegance down there, padded red and black everything. Jim Stafford, who had recently had a novelty hit with an insidious country tune called "Spiders and Snakes," was to have the lead in an atonal musical called *The Robber Bridegroom,* which I had just done in Jacksonville. I had gone down to Jupiter trying to get a role in the only theater my parents had ever heard of as well as something approaching a living wage. When the stage manager let the auditioning actors inside, there was a celebrity press conference breaking up. Martin Sheen, Dom DeLuise, and Will Sampson (Chief Broom in *One Flew Over the Cuckoo's Nest*) were focusing their combined, if oddly eclectic, star power on some cause I couldn't be bothered with because I was full of acid coffee that desperately wanted out. I ran to the rest room and, through ecstatic piss shivers, realized I had been joined by Martin Sheen to my right. His role in the press conference had been intensely serious. His acting was always intensely serious. And when he peed, he was also intensely serious. Dom DeLuise, who was enormous, nevertheless flitted in and out like a gazelle. Will Sampson was so tall he had to duck to come in the doorway. His sheer size completely filled the toilet stall he entered, towering over the partition until he sat down. As I was leaving, Jim Stafford came in. He was good-looking but so small I wondered if it was physically possible for Will Sampson to wipe his ass with him. It would serve him right for that damn "Spiders and Snakes" song that still gets stuck in my head for days.

My most memorable star meeting wasn't in a rest room, but in line for *Ruthless People* at the Chinese Theater in Hollywood. I noticed people looking past me and pointing, so naturally I turned to see what it was. I didn't know it at the time, but I was staring at football star Lyle Alzado. What I did know was that this was the biggest, butchest, most bulging and beautiful man I had ever seen. Actually I was staring a little above his navel—he was that large, and brimming with muscles. We now know that was steroids, but at the time it was an overwhelming rush. He was with a tiny slip of a woman, and I wanted to shout at her, "Run away, honey! He will break you like a pencil!" Instead I turned away with a calculating, randy excitement. *I must touch this man!* I thought. *But how?* He was obviously an athlete but I knew nothing about pro anything, having no idea even what game he played. A detail like that wasn't going to stop me, though, because I was dying to ask if I could just rip his clothes off right here and use him like a jungle gym. I refrained, knowing it might lessen my chances and provoke comment. Then I got a delicious idea.

I would make *him* touch *me*.

I turned back to face this towering man. "I would just like to thank you," I said, "for some of the most exciting moments in professional sports." Then smiled big and dopey. His large, macho face melted into a generous grin. “Why, thank you,” he said. And his mighty hand stretched forth for mine. He took it, took it in blatant social intercourse. It was massive, engulfing mine, swallowing me to the wrist with vigorous, pumping thrusts. I was swept away by this sensual pressing together of hearty male flesh. I had won this huge man, and I now held him in a warm, moist, callused, manly, firm, assertive, masculine, powerful yet gentle, lingering…handshake.

To this day, I can’t tell you what the movie was about, but I get a chubby every time I pass Mann’s Chinese.

The Debbie Allen Dance Number

I am dressed completely in black. Not because it's West Hollywood, or I'm into goth, or because I have no imagination and I'm incapable of color coordinating like all the other people who do it, but because I am in mourning. The powers that be have announced that for the 72nd Academy Awards presentation there is to be no dance number. How could they do this to us? Every Oscar telecast for the past decade has allowed millions of homosexuals to howl with hilarity at the Debbie Allen Dance Number, that cobbled-together orgy of poorly thought-out dance moves designed to illustrate the connecting theme of the nominated pictures. That theme, at least as far as we were concerned, was always "*What* were they *thinking*?" As bad as you knew it would be, there would always come at least one jaw-dropping moment of truly transcendently stupid choreography. Entire gay ghettos would erupt with screams to spouses in the kitchen, "Get in here! You gotta see this!" Couples and friends would watch with hands over their mouths, not daring to move until it was over, and then shriek in gleeful horror. It was the hoot heard round the world.

The Debbie Allen Dance Number has won a cherished place in

the pantheon of dependably bad ideas. It was as if every idea Cher rejected as being too embarrassing, even for her show, flowed downstream to collect in the cloaca maxima that was the Debbie Allen Dance Number. It was staged annually in bare skin, glitter, G-strings and top hats. It was a train wreck with lasers and flying by Foy. It was heterosexual high camp.

The Academy said the dance number was "inappropriate." Well, duh! They just figured this out? Of course it was inappropriate! That's what Hollywood is about. Maybe in another 72 years they'll figure out giving Adam Sandler $20 million a picture is inappropriate. The Academy also said the Debbie Allen Dance Number was "undignified." They were wrong. It was fucking god-awful, and that was its genius. It made us feel superior to an entire auditorium full of beautiful, rich, and glamorous movie stars who, every other day of the year, we wished we could be. But during that 15-minute dancing debacle we saw the Hollywood hotshots for the high-rent trailer trash they are. If the Debbie Allen Dance Number was Hollywood's idea of sophistication, doing "YMCA" at your cousin's wedding reception at the Ramada didn't look so bad. If this was the best choreography Tinseltown could come up with, line dancing at the rodeo suddenly seemed downright elegant. And if the whole thing became truly unforgivable, which is to say dull, we could always go to the kitchen for a microwave burrito. Not even Streisand can do that.

Speaking of Babs, I'm getting a little tired of that silver outfit, you know, the one she wore for her zillion-dollar-a-seat concert? It looked like the same thing she had on at the Golden Globes. Does the woman have another dress? She can't snap her fingers and have James run out for something pink but intimidating? And have we all learned that giving someone like Barbra a Golden Globe tribute award means an hour and a half none of us will ever have back again?

I know I'm straying from my subject of the Debbie Allen Dance Number, but I'm bitter. First they move the awards to Sunday so you don't even get to ditch work, and now this. What's next? No preshow bitchiness with Joan and her forgettable daughter, all because that's undignified and inappropriate? I've got news for the Academy, Oscar night is about the industry bending around to kiss its own ass. They don't save lives, they make movies. Movies that are undignified, inappropriate, trashy, gaudy, amazing, and wonderful—but useless. What could possibly exemplify, nay, glorify that better than the Debbie Allen Dance Number?

If you need to save time, get rid of that Parade of This Year's Dead reel. Not only does it bring down the room, but it reminds us of who we should have picked in the online Death Pool. Lose the Irving Thal-butt Time-to-Go-to-the-Bathroom Award. Stop hiring presenters who can't dress or read. But don't take away our Debbie Allen Dance Number. It was the very essence of all the soaring, glittering crap Hollywood squeezes out and we can't get enough of. We need it! Screw presidential politics, I'm starting a petition for next year's Oscars. If you believe choreography should be overbudgeted, overblown, underrehearsed, and televised globally, sign and mail the form below and change the world for the worse.

Dear Academy of Motion Picture Farts and Sciences,
Puhl-e-e-eze give us back our Debbie Allen Dance Number!
(Signed) ______________________________

The dance disaster you save could be your own.

Queer as HGTV Folk

People complain and moan about how there are no real gays represented on nonpremium TV channels. Oh, sure, there's *Will & Grace* and whatnot, but let's face it, that show, while funny, is written by gays for straight people. The characters are no more realistic representations of gays than *Friends* is accurate about heteros. So other than behind an anchor desk on E! where do you go to find nice, normal, dull faggots and dykes?

HGTV. This channel shows gays without comment or fanfare, and it's like looking at how life would be if the country's IQ went up about five points. The homes and gardens are owned by all kinds of people and it is utterly refreshing how often they are gay couples. Actually, given the amount of design involved, it's amazing how many straight people they show.

On shows like *Restore America* there's nothing blatant about it at first. Tom and Ralph have made over a house that has four bedrooms. This one is Tom's office, this one is Ralph's studio, and this one is the guest room. Do the math. Then, in case Middle America's gay panic and/or denial causes any lingering doubt, the host takes us into what is plainly stated as Tom and Ralph's master bedroom. There's no art by Kake or rainbow tchotchkes cluttering up the room, but you know that nightstand drawer contains a big bottle of Wet.

The show *This Small Space* recently featured an obvious lesbian couple redoing their tiny bathroom. I know I'm going to get grief for sounding so stereotypical, but they really did roll up their flannel sleeves and go to a salvage yard stacked with old bathtubs to choose one. After getting it home to their garage, they went to work on it in a manner so organized, effective, and cheery that it was like seeing lesbians in their natural habitat. They used something called Naval Jelly, which is this scary goop that eats right through rust. I understand it's a common item, but I'm so nonhandy I thought Naval Jelly was something entirely different. Something that involved seamen. Lesbians, though, apparently just know this kind of stuff. In no time they had a beautifully restored iron tub and were calling over their male neighbors to help them drag it upstairs. The neighbors' names were Evan and Thom. Need I say more?

Gardener's Diary frequently drops in on gardens designed by gay couples. One was owned and maintained by an Anglo man and his lover, a Vietnamese man. Using large-leafed plants and different colors of crushed glass, they had turned their small yard into a stunning fantasy of Southeast Asia to help ease the Vietnamese man's homesickness. It was so touching I wanted to cry. Especially after I priced crushed glass.

On *Designing for the Sexes,* the couples are always heterosexual, but designer and host Michael Payne, who for the record is straight, still fulfills the traditional gay role of interpreter between that which is seen as masculine and that which is called feminine. On every show the woman wants one style in the home while her husband wants another. It's amusing every so often when the husband is clearly uncomfortable around Payne, but otherwise all sexuality is totally ignored—as it should be. The only thing that bothers me about Payne is that in every bathroom makeover, he installs a big shower at one end with no door or curtain. Yes, it looks fabulous, but if that's the only bathroom, there will come a time both people need to use it. When someone's in the shower I don't want to have to grab an umbrella to take a crap. I can't help thinking Payne learned shower design from a disgruntled designer out for revenge against straight people who have too much money to spend on a bathroom.

A recent *Country at Home* presented a holiday show where they took us into a rural home owned by Dave and Tré. Dave looked like some backwater bohunk who beats up truckers while, Tré, natch, was a thin little nelly redneck country queen. I'm not being judgmental; there are many ways to be gay. And being Tré's kind of gay in this country's heartland takes more balls than frankly most of us, including myself, have. Every square inch of their home, inside and out, was loaded with antiques, some valuable, some crap, but all of it rustically, absurdly, gloriously overdecorated for the season. "Ah buy th' stuff," Dave drawls as stoic as American Gothic. "Tré here makes it work cuz he's ver' organic." Well, Dave had recently bought an enormous box of children's shoes from the '30s and '40s. Tré had worked the whole box of them—I kid you not—into a fireplace garland. "Ah've allus b'lieved Christmas is fer children," Tré gushes, hands flitting around the display, "and ah like to think of all these children grown with happy children and grandchildren round 'em now." He was adorable, and I loved what he did with the shoes. I just hope that box didn't come from Germany.

I'd like to point out that there's another level at work here too, in that we are seeing not single homos but long-term same-sex couples. I can state this with surety, because if you and a partner have ever tried to put together so much as a wall unit from pictographic schematics and did it without throwing claw hammers at each other, you know you've achieved a deep level of commitment. These people are ripping out entire walls. Sure it's for the better, but it's hell while it's going on. With the cost, inconvenience, and duration of the work, few things will test a relationship like remodeling. Snoring comes close, infidelity maybe, but damn little else. By showing these people, HGTV has ended the invisibility of real-life committed same-sex partners and I say hooray. The only institution doing more to support gay couples is the state of Vermont.

You never know when these shows will feature the gay couples. Unlike on network television, there's no hyping these episodes with sniggering sensationalism like "Tonight on *By Design,* wait'll you see what two gay men spray on their bedroom walls!" You don't hear crap like "When Bob Vila comes to look at flooring, he finds a lesbian couple in love—see Bob get down on his knees to inspect their joists in a very special *This Old House.*" It's just presented as it is. It may not be Must-See TV, but it is...normal.

Golly, gay people shown as intelligent, contributing, successful, resourceful, caring, creative, but otherwise unremarkable people. What a concept.

That's Why They're in Cages, People!

The story of Sharon Stone's ex-husband, Phil Bronstein, in the Komodo dragon cage at the L.A. Zoo demonstrates an idea whose time has come. In case you've forgotten, it happened something like this. Actress Sharon Stone gave the L.A. Zoo a check so big they forgot their animals were wild and potentially dangerous. I mean, come on, that's why they're in cages, people. Hello? In exchange, the zoo allowed Sharon to give Phil an up close and personal tour of the animals for his birthday. After all, what could make one feel better about getting older than seeing how rotten your life could be in a cage where the highlight of your day is throwing your own feces and masturbating for tourists. Which describes Tom Green's career, but I digress. All went well until Sharon and Phil came to the Komodo dragon cage.

The mouth of a Komodo dragon is a truly vile place. It is so nasty, and harbors such bacteria, germs, and general ick that even a light nip, if left untreated, will fester and kill. I've had men with mouths like that. "Want me to go down on you?" Uh, no thanks, but I'll give you 20 bucks if you'll blow my ex-boss. Anyway, that's how the Komodo dragon works. All it needs is one decent chomp, and then it waits around a few days until you drop.

This is basic information the zoo attendant had to know. My theory is that this attendant was an evil queen. I'm sure he was thinking, *Oh, my God, Mr. Sharon Stone wants to pet the dragon! This is too good to resist.* He bit the inside of his cheeks to keep from smiling, and said to his guests, "Sure, right this way." Then true inspiration struck. "Wait!" he giggled, desperately trying to keep a straight face. "Why don't you take off your shoes first?"

Now, Phil is no dummy. He's the executive editor of the *San Francisco Chronicle,* for crying out loud, so that suggestion seemed a bit suspicious. "Why on earth," he surely asked the attendant, "would I take my shoes off before approaching a carnivorous 10-foot lizard?"

Inspiration, being a fleeting thing, was now gone. The attendant was forced to come up with the lamest possible story. "Because, uh, because we, uh, feed it white rats and your shoes are white so the dragon might think it's a white rat?"

"Oh," Phil said. "Why, that makes perfectly logical sense." And he took off his shoes. I guess it never occurred to him that his pasty feet were at least as luminously chalky white as his shoes. Well, we all know what happened next. Phil ended up in the hospital with serious damage to ligaments and a gruesomely chewed big toe.

I wish Phil and Sharon no ill will. Sharon is a gay activist, after all, and we need all the friends we can get, so I hope she'll forgive me for seizing on their specific misfortune to point out what I believe to be an excellent idea in the abstract. I love the concept of exposing people of privilege to peril.

For instance, not long ago David Schwimmer was in line for a movie at the Beverly Center. That week he had made news, along with his other *Friends* costars, for negotiating $750,000 *per episode.* When he got to the window, he said, "You know who I am? So I don't have to pay?" The minimum wage–earning ticket seller made a withering face and said, "Yes. And yes." Once inside, Schwimmer whined to his date du jour that now he barely had enough for popcorn. This is a man ready for the dragon cage.

Speaking of *Friends,* Jennifer Aniston and Brad Pitt bought matching rings from a jeweler who must have been pissing in his pants to have this stroke of fortune walk into his store. They made the jeweler promise not to sell any more rings of that design so these two privileged people could feel even more smugly privileged. As soon as they left, the jeweler naturally ran to the back and started cranking out duplicates, dreaming of how many rings he could sell by cooing, "They're just like Brad and Jennifer's." Well, the couple found out about this and sued—not for the price of the rings, but for $50 million. $50 *million*? I guess those millions are to make up for the emotional distress of having their love sullied, and we all know stars suffer more than ordinary mortals. Especially when they discover something about themselves they thought was special has been made ordinary. So they feel betrayed, big fucking deal. You and I suffer lies, petty betrayals, and generic unpleasantness daily. When was the last time you sued for $50 million over it? I say throw these two in the dragon cage. Hell, rub them with meat first.

While we're in the lawsuit territory, Tom Cruise recently sued two men for $100 million each for alleging they had gay sex with him. For the sake of this piece I'm not even going into what could cause such a massive overreaction on Miss Cruise's part. But I do think it's totally uncalled for because I never believed one of the guys in the first place. He claimed to have a videotape of the sex. I'm so sure. If that were true, this tape would have been on the Internet faster than you can say *A Few Good Men.* If a videotape had existed and the guy had tried blackmail, a person of Tom's ferocity and financial resources simply would have had the guy killed and we never would have heard of him at all. Why not? Even if Tom had been arrested for putting a hit on the man, this is Hollywood, and he would have been out doing preproduction on *M:I 3* in a month, if not guest shots on *Ally McBeal.*

The other person, Chad Slater (née Kyle Bradford), immediately denied ever saying he had sex with Tom, yet Tom still slapped him with a $100 million lawsuit. Can you imagine waking up to that kind of shitstorm? Whether they had sex or not, believe me, Tom fucked him royally.

Tom justifies this high-rolling hissy fit by claiming if the public believed he was gay, it would affect his earning power as an international heterosexual. Maybe, but I have to ask, how many hundreds of millions more do you really need, Tom? After half a billion or so, doesn't it just start getting in the way? Are we not just pursuing money here for its own sake? This is why I think Tom's ready for the cage: to be reminded of what's important (here's a hint, it ain't another bazillion dollars) and what's real. People say all sorts of untrue things about me, Tom, it doesn't change who or what I really am. And I certainly don't go around suing people hysterically for it. Life is too short. Think about that while you're running from the Komodo dragon.

Another candidate for the cage is Jennifer Lopez. For a recent interview at KIIS radio in L.A., she sent her minions in ahead of her to bully all station personnel not to even look at her. It would have made sense if they had warned everyone not to ask her about the box office for *Angel Eyes*, but looking at her? We all have bad hair days, J. Lo, wear a hat and get over yourself.

These are only a few of the people who deserve Phil Bronstein's fate, and I would gladly put any one of them in his place. I don't know much about Phil, but I don't believe he deserved to get mangled. To their credit, neither he nor Sharon Stone was angry at the lizard. I would imagine, however, that there's an out-of-work zoo attendant out there somewhere. No doubt by now he's moved on to where he can do real damage, like NASA or television. Or the clergy.

If our society had such a Peril Policy for anyone who got too big for their britches, we'd have a much healthier world. Not to mention entertainment news that was actually entertaining. "Honey, did you see where they fed Dr. Laura to the dingoes?"

I say call the zoo and let them know half of Hollywood and all of Congress are on the way over. If they ask what they're supposed to do about that, tell them for starters they can stop feeding the dingoes.

NOTE: Given Mr. Cruise's propensity to prosecute for alleging in print that he's gay, let me clearly state: **TOM CRUISE IS NOT GAY.** So, Tom, when you read this during a rest break at Slammer, please don't sue me.

Kisses,
Joel

Fraud!

Nooch, my friend downstairs at work, called me up at my desk and said, "I just got back from auditioning for *To Tell the Truth.* You gotta go on it!" I wasn't sure I wanted to. "What are you, stupid?" she yelled into the phone. I love her for her shy, demure qualities. "It's a guaranteed $300 even if you suck." Well, $300 would almost cover my Visa bill for that month (I had recently discovered online purchasing). Still, I didn't think I wanted to commit a precious Sunday to hanging out at NBC. "Oh, please," she scoffed, "what do you do on Sunday anyway besides go to church and masturbate?" Nooch was right, although I did point out that those activities were separate and not simultaneous. "Yeah, yeah, yeah, just do it," she ordered and hung up. I decided what the hell.

For those who don't know, *To Tell the Truth* is a game show from the '50s and '60s, brought back to life for the new millennium because there's just not enough crap on the air. There are three contestants per game. One of them has an oddball profession or some other marginally sad claim to fame, and the other two are impostors pretending to be that person. There's a host and a panel of C-list celebrities who ask the contestants questions. The point is for them to be able to spot the impostors and thereby not look any more foolish than they already do for appearing on a game show panel in the first place. The more celebrities who are fooled, the more prize money the contestants get to split among themselves to assuage their shame for appearing on a game show. It's the American Dream.

The audition staff had us fill out a brief bio and answer whether we knew other languages, if we had traveled to other countries, what exciting hobbies we had, and other questions designed to make me realize how little I'd done with my life. Then they asked for a list of our major achievements. All I could think of was the time I ate a whole ham in two days. I thought about putting down, "Can take it up to the elbow," but my luck would be they'd choose me for the segment and I'd be forced to demonstrate. I left "Major Achievements" blank, which felt depressingly telling.

Next we each met for a quick one-on-one with a staff member. Mine was Mike, who looked like he'd been Lancômed and Cliniqued since the age of 5 and was dressed in that industry manner of $200 casual shirts and Cole Haan shoes with no socks. He helped me come up with something for "Major Achievements": above-goal lifetime Weight Watchers member. In retrospect it seems a bit snide, but at least I'd achieved something.

Six weeks later Mike called asking if I was available for taping the next Sunday. Sure, I could put my usual Sunday, um, activities on hold. I was to be an impostor for a man who made his living as a comical nonmotivational speaker. "Think you can you do that?" Hell, I've tried to motivate people all my life only to be laughed at. That $300 was mine!

I had to go in on Saturday to meet the guy and the other imposter and go over our stories so we'd be believable, or in the case of the real guy, unbelievable. That's when the surreal nature of this whole thing hit me. I was to pretend to be an impostor for a person who pretends to be a motivational speaker but who is an impostor even though that's his real job. I was already getting a headache. The other fake guy was a stand-up comedian named

Terry, and the real fake guy was named Paul and had started out in stand-up before getting into this bogus motivational speaker gig. It turned out that Terry and Paul knew each other from the comedy circuit, a detail I was going to pretend I didn't know. As an impostor I already felt like a fraud.

We were assigned to two production assistants, Gavin and Lisa. Their job was to make sure we had plausible answers ready for the celebrities and that we didn't wander off to steal things from the *Friends* set. They grilled us with rapid-fire questions: "How much do you make? Are you married? Where do you go? How do you make a living at that?" It was a lot like visiting my parents. Terry and Paul had their answers down pat, but I kept faltering. Since any prize money would be split between us, we'd have to work as a team, but I felt utterly out of place. We were two stand-up good ol' boys and a fag. Two regular joes and a fat guy with a beard, shaved head, and tit rings. At one point I caught Lisa staring at us and singing: "One of these things is not like the other..." The more I tried to be plausible, the worse answers I gave. I was told to go home and relax.

On Sunday, Gavin and Lisa got us presentable and led us to the soundstage for our segment, which was called "I Am a Bad Motivational Speaker." Each show has two segments. The other segment was about a woman who, instead of being a clown for hire at children's parties, puts on wings and glitter so as to avoid all the emotional baggage of clowns. Hers was called "I Am a Professional Fairy," and I kept wondering if I'd been called in for the wrong segment.

While we waited for our taping, I asked Gavin and Lisa if they were used to dealing with stupid people like me. Without batting an eye they said, "Yes." They told me they'd been production assistants on the failed *Donny and Marie* talk show. Their job had been to stand off to the side and wait for the inevitable moment when a guest would make a statement and the hosts would just sit there in dead air, smiling inanely. At that point, Gavin and Lisa would hold up one-word cue cards prompting the empty-headed hosts to ask, "Why?" or "How?" They assured me I was in good hands, but I didn't feel better for it.

At last the three of us were led into the studio. There was a quick rehearsal on the set to make sure we could hit our marks on the floor and move to our seats. Then we taped it. The host was John O'Hurley, and the panelists were Meshach Taylor, Paula Poundstone, Alan Rachins, and some model no one had ever heard of. Once the game started, it went by in a glittery flash. The panelists were less concerned with asking questions than getting airtime for themselves by chattering and attempting jokes, so it actually turned out to be pretty easy on me. The only glitch came with Paula Poundstone—who actually was funny and, worse, smart—questioned my bogus story about having started out as a door-to-door aquarium salesman. "I'd just like to know," she said, certain she had me, "what your sales pitch was when you rang a person's doorbell to sell them aquariums?" We hadn't thought of that. Thank God the buzzer went off and her question period was over.

When it came time for the panel to choose who they thought was the real guy, we fooled everyone except Paula. Alan Rachins even voted for me, which tells you that the dim bulb he played on *Dharma & Greg* was no stretch. Gavin and Lisa were pleased, but Terry and Paul were thrilled. Forget the lousy $300 minimum, we got $4,000 to split between us, $1,333.33 each! I could go back to online shopping. Not only that, but since all of my friends tell me they absolutely *never* watch game shows, no one would ever know I'd stooped so low.

My friends lied. This stupid episode of *To Tell the Truth* has been shown five times already, and everyone I know gives me shit about it. As far as they're concerned, I could come up with the cure for cancer and all I'll be remembered for is that damn show. Yes, I was a contestant on a game show. I will have to live with that shame. But I also have my cash winnings. And honey, $1,333.33 buys a *lot* of margaritas.

Hooked on Hollywood

Why are so many gays addicted to screen icons like Judy Garland and Marilyn Monroe? Poor Judy was phenomenally talented but the studio fed her pills like they were Tic Tacs until it eventually killed her. Do I want to look up to that? I realize that we gays identify with a similar sense of being born with a sparkle and beauty that was viciously mauled by a society that seeks to destroy what it doesn't understand. But is clinging to that healthy? I mean, I've worn out my copy of *The Essential Judy* too, but let's face it, the system killed her and it wasn't pretty.

Same for Marilyn. She oozed sex, innocence, vulnerability, and victimhood. She did the nasty with sports icons, playwrights, and presidents and, some would say, was among the first to suffer from death by Kennedy. She was used and abused and dead by 36. I'm thinking there might be someone else a bit more beneficial to emulate. I love Marilyn's movies, but give me Katharine Hepburn. She survived Hollywood, made a couple of decent flicks, and did it on her own terms. And even though she's gone, I'm taking this opportunity to tell her now, "Thanks, you grand old hard-assed battle-ax, you. Thanks from all of us."

A better addiction is Barbra Streisand. She managed to seize the Hollywood machine and make it do her bidding, even if that meant foisting *The Mirror Has Two Faces* on us. The point is, she knows she's a woman battling a misogynistic town, yet she doesn't let that stop her because she also knows she's fabulous. We too are hated and fabulous, so let's be like Babs and not give a damn what anyone thinks either. This is a woman who has the balls to go out and hire Lauren Bacall to play her *mother.* Never mind that Lauren must not have read the script or her Fancy Feast ads had stopped running. She was there on the set with everyone because Barbra was strong enough to say, "Damn it, I need some class, get me Lauren Bacall!" and backed a truck full of money down Lauren's driveway. We need to latch on to that kind of strength. Sure it gave us that *A Star Is Born* remake and *Yentl,* but there's also the occasional *Prince of Tides.* Besides, when was the last time *you* produced a Hollywood musical, hmm? Especially one with a romping, naked Mandy Patinkin and his pee-pee? (Love that DVD pause feature!) Barbra's an addiction that's at least halfway healthy. As long as we too can learn to say screw everyone else and make fabulous things—if not movies, our lives—Barbra offers us a terrific archetype to emulate. I'm going for it because she's richer than God, neurotic as hell, and a bitch to work with. Of those, I figure I've already got two out of three down pat.

We need to identify with those who overcame their awful stuff and went on to be amazing anyway, or at least Movies of the Week. Like Ann Jillian. She's no *Funny Girl,* but she's a helluva trouper. She lost both breasts to cancer and still continued her career. All right, that assumes you consider *Sammy the Way-Out Seal* a career, but she overcame. Instead of succumbing to depression, she went out and used her tragedy (not *Sammy,* the other one) to help in the fight against breast cancer.

Greg Louganis was deeply closeted, not only by being gay in the sports world but also by his HIV-positive status, and addicted to his abusive manager-boyfriend. On top of that, in the finals of the 1988 Olympics he cracked his head open on the diving platform and still won the gold medal. Hell, If I get a hangnail I call in sick. Greg gets stitched up poolside—*without* anesthetics, thank you—and goes on to Olympic gold. He later dumps his boyfriend, comes out, writes a best-seller about his life, and is played in the TV movie by dreamy Mario Lopez. Now, that's success. In fact, when my life is made into a movie, I'm having all my Speedo scenes done by Mario. Greg also has taken his HIV-positive status and used it to create awareness of HIV and AIDS. He took the shit he went through and turned it inside out to help others. OK, so his second book was a piffle about his dogs, but hey, who wouldn't want to hump Greg's leg? All that and he goes home to hunky Steve Kmetko. You go, girl.

Anyone who's been sucked into watching hours of those VH1 *Behind the Music* shows (talk about an addiction!) knows of Elton John's descent into drugs, booze, and bulimia. The man was addiction central, and yet he finally checked his abusive ass into detox, put his career on hold for a year, and healed. He now talks openly about his former addictions so that others can draw strength from his experience and seek help. Oh, and he's known to contribute a dollar or two to AIDS foundations too. If you can overlook that "Written in the Stars" abortion with LeAnn Rimes, Elton is a living lesson in healing. Look at any gathering of gays and tell me how many people you see that could use some of that. "Didn't I see you tweaking at that sex club?" "Yeah, but then what were *you* doing there?" Gulp. Hey, I never said I was better than anybody else.

Elton John, Greg Louganis, Ann Jillian, and, yes, even Babs are people who were wounded or maligned in some way. So were all of us. When it comes to being messed up, I know I have more issues than *Newsweek*. But it's time we put down the icons of victimization and started identifying with people of power, those who show us the way through our own hurt and into healing. So can we please lose our addiction to doomed icons? (Are you opera queens listening to this too?) Honor the Marilyns and Judys because they were wonderful for what they were, but it's time to let them go. It's time to move on to the next stage: total empowerment—not just being a survivor, but being fa-a-abulous!

Lights, camera, now let's see some action.

Seen Any Good Movies Lately?

Every year we honor gay-themed movies at festivals like L.A.'s Outfest, and every year I get more depressed. It's not that there aren't good films. I always hear people raving about the movie I couldn't get in to see, that will not be shown again, and that will never be seen within 100 miles of wherever I happen to be. My depression stems from the fact that out of 150+ films, *maybe* four will be collected into a nearly impossible-to-find compilation video, and one *might* be shown next June on HBO7's Gay Film Festival at 2 A.M. between the one millionth running of *Priscilla* and *To Wong Foo.* Each festival has one full-length feature with, if we're lucky, two people you've ever heard of, and they're both gay for pay. But we mustn't complain about any of this because that would be attacking our own.

Wrong! I applaud every bit of the talent, work, passion, and personal sacrifices of these filmmakers. I know what it's like to be underfunded on an important project, to languish in development, to have your lead not show up because he had "an important party to go to." What ticks me off is that so many talented filmmakers are killing themselves to make movies no one but us will see, and damned few of us. Gay festivals are ghettos. Fabulously catered and attended by beautiful people, but still ghettos. They're the WeHo of Hollywood.

The people I feel the worst for are the documentarians. They have the most passion about their subjects and the least likelihood of finding an audience where they're not preaching to the choir. How many straights go to Blockbuster thinking, *I'm really in the mood for an unflinching yet humanistic look at the lives of one-legged gay bowlers*? And if they do, God help them with finding it. Some documentaries do break out, like *The Brandon Teena Story,* but that was the rare exception. Even then, it was made into *Boys Don't Cry,* and you can bet rent-boy money that you won't see it on network TV during sweeps month.

And let's face it, these festivals are also loaded with dross. What-were-they-thinking entries that could only have been scheduled because the filmmakers had incriminating photos of judges having sex with goats or, worse, human partners of the opposite sex. These are the screenings you come out of angry, because you'll never have that hour and a half back again. The ones you come out of thanking a merciful God that Absolut is a sponsor.

Then there are the feature-length movies everyone goes nuts over because they're just as slick, banal, and empty as mainstream movies. I'm sorry, but in a *Dude, Where's My Car?* kind of world, that's hardly a compliment. I have a difficult time lauding something like *The Broken Hearts Club,* no matter how sincerely made. Box office will bear me out on this when I say it's like praising baby's first boom-boom in the potty seat—only family is going to care. And I want much, much more than that for our family's filmmakers.

We are among the most imaginative, brilliant, resourceful people on the planet. When folks want catering, style, wit, color, drama, design, musical theater, or need tips on anything from throwing a party to giving a decent hummer, the world comes to us. Why, then, do we not have the definitive all-out homo-lesbo-tranny queertastic fagalicious movie so amazing that everyone on the planet is dying to see it?

I'm talking about a movie so incredible that redneck Okies take their dates to it because (a) they dig it; and (b) their girlfriends are so touched they put out. One so good that Jesse Helms sneaks in to see it and gets his first hard-on in 50 years. One with so much humanity that it gives Fred Phelps such a spasm of contrition that he dismantles his Godhatesfags.com Web site and builds one called Jesuschristwhathaveidone.org.

Am I asking too much of a movie? Yes, but I can dream. That's what movies are about. I dream of a queer movie so amazing that people are lined up around the block for the next two shows in freaking Lubbock.

I want *Independence Gay,* with Will Smith and Jeff Goldblum fighting alien invaders between sucking each other's cigars.

I want a *Braveheart,* only without the homophobe. You get that many men in blue makeup and dresses, there's bound to be some kink going on and I want to know about it! Call it *Fabulousheart.*

I want a hugely successful series like *Lethal Weapon,* again without the homophobe. Give me Danny Glover, Joe Pesci, and Sean Hayes solving crimes in wacky ways while maintaining the delicate balance of their three-way home life.

I want *Home Alone 2: Lesbian in New York.* It's a day in the life of Sandra Bernhard kicking ass in the Big Apple and taking no prisoners. Or, as Sandra would call it, Tuesday.

I want oversexed same-gender superheroes getting it on off-camera. Oh, wait. They did that. *Batman & Robin.*

I want a freaking gay *Titanic.* Hell, there were 2,000 people on that ship. Taking just half of Kinsey's one-in-10 ratio gives us 100 people I wanted to know about a hell of a lot more than Leo and Kate. God knows it's not like there wasn't enough time to include some of us. How long does it take to shout "I'm queen of the world!"?

But until we get that, I'll just have to make do with what we have. Outfest claims to be the largest film festival of any kind in Southern California. And even though that smacks of saying, "Yeah, he's a Republican, but he's got the largest dick of any kind in Southern California," I know I'll attend. Why? Because I keep hoping for a *Crouching Lesbian, Hidden Homo,* an *E.T., the Extra-Transsexual,* or even a *Dances With Bears.* At the very least, I'd like an *Apollo 13 Inches.*

However, I could be at the wrong sort of festival for that last one.

Shrink-Wrapped

I amuse myself by rating my friends according to the amount of potential real damage they can do. For a period of several months, the winner was Jeff, who for a standard tour of 16 months was commanding officer of an antisubmarine warfare helicopter squadron with nuclear capability. During that time—but only for that while—he narrowly beat out my friend Greg, who teaches tender, impressionable third-graders. I had just gotten used to Greg being back on top when I learned this morning that two of my high school friends have become licensed psychiatrists. I may have to completely revise my list.

Next to a parent, no one has the potential to wreak lifelong head-screwing havoc like a therapist. And I do love stories about therapy nightmares. Perhaps that's because going through therapy can itself be a nightmare, even when it's doing the most good. But few things make me cackle with horrified glee like the deep-down damage only a shrink can do.

A bachelor friend I'll call Teddy is a minister who had started taking medication for mild depression. A few weeks later, the psychiatrist asked Teddy if he'd noticed any side effects. Teddy said he was sleeping better, but it took him a very long time to come when he masturbated. The shrink made a face of hideously ugly judgmental disdain, hissing, "I am shocked to hear such language from a man of God!" Teddy ended the session and left, even though he was at the end of his meds. Months afterward, he still couldn't jerk off because every time he started, he'd think of that shrink's scowling face. "It's kind of spoiled it for me," Teddy told me. "Now when I need to feel better I just go a couple of towns over and have a hooker blow me. I get the same results, and with the money I'm saving, I'm funding our Meals for Shut-ins program." See, God does work in mysterious ways.

When it comes to therapy, Los Angeles is like no other place on earth. Over dinner the other night, my talented but unsuccessful actor friend Ed was telling me about his therapist, Dr. Fielding. The good doctor had been making the rounds about town pitching his idea for a television show. His concept was to show music videos and then psychoanalyze the visual content—as if we didn't know the motivation behind Madonna's latest calculated affront isn't about a bad childhood but about $$$. Anyway, some studio had given Dr. Fielding the go-ahead to shoot one of these shows and he was thrilled. So thrilled he felt compelled to tell his client Ed, who was very excited for him—until he got home and thought about it. Then Ed realized Los Angeles has to be the only city in the world where your therapist can get a pilot but you can't.

I'd had a similar situation happen when my own therapist asked if I was OK with him pitching an idea to a magazine for which I regularly write. He wanted to do a column dealing with gay issues from a therapeutic point of view. I was a supportive client and told him I thought it was great. I didn't tell him I felt I had already been doing that, only trying to use humor instead of Zoloft. It turned out the magazine wasn't interested, which I found disappointing. I was looking forward to letters like, "Dear Doc: Is it wrong for a 50-year-old gay man to be watching TV and pop a chubbie over Vivian Vance?"

I got my very favorite therapist story from a woman named Sue with whom I did an industry workshop. Sue's husband had left her for a cigarette girl at a casino in Bell Gardens, so Sue had great roiling internalized rage at her ex-spouse. Her big issue now was trust, especially as it related to being abandoned and to allowing herself to be vulnerable. These were the things she felt were keeping her from meeting men, a problem that depressed her profoundly. It took her a year and a half of therapy before she finally felt comfortable enough to bare her innermost thoughts to her therapist, Richard, a man whom she felt was free of anger toward women and clearly centered. Just as Sue began to make progress, she opened the *Los Angeles Times* to see a photo of Richard over the headline, "Prominent L.A. Psychiatrist Found Dead." Richard had hanged himself from the suspended pot rack in his ex-wife's extensive kitchen. From other clients she learned he'd left an erratic note mentioning "you unfaithful whoring cunt," "sucking me dry," and "all this goddamned fucking Calphelon." Not surprisingly, the suicide sent Sue into a clinical depression for which, again, not surprisingly, she refused to seek professional help. She only came out of it through the aid of a friend who gave her some of his ex-boyfriend's medication he'd left in the medicine cabinet. As a footnote, I should tell you the boyfriend had left it there because he had convinced his shrink he didn't need to take his meds. A week later he was arrested in Marina del Rey for shooting holes in boats with a semiautomatic rifle. But back to Sue.

A year or so later, Sue decided she was finally ready to trust another therapist. She decided on Kat, a female therapist because she felt another woman would empathize with her difficulty in meeting men. It turned out Kat more than empathized.

One day Sue was home from work. She had been stood up by her date the night before and, too depressed to go to work, had spent the morning crying. After somehow managing to fix herself a can of soup for lunch, she turned on the TV. There on the screen was Kat, the therapist Sue was seeing because she was desperate to learn how to meet men who weren't pathetic, on *Blind Date*, a game show about desperate women trying to meet pathetic men (and vice versa). Sue turned off the TV, called her therapist's machine, and fired her. Being able to express her rage and do the abandoning felt so empowering, Sue decided to hell with therapy. She was going to go back to work and embrace being an erratic, flaming bitch on wheels. Within a year she'd been promoted to an executive position. The lesson from Sue's story is that therapy isn't necessarily for everyone. Sometimes you just have to go with your neuroses and find yourself a niche where it pays to be manic-depressive, abusive, and dysfunctional.

Of course, it helped that she worked in a talent agency.

Part Five:
Adventures in
Publishing

Sex Advice

Strange and wonderful things come my way. For instance, I am allowed to rant and rave in a humor column in *Frontiers* magazine and get paid for it. Not much, but it keeps our VCR in fresh porno. I frequently wonder how much Sarah Jessica Parker's character gets paid for her column on HBO's *Sex and the City.* While I'm scanning the Sport Chalet ads for $30 Reeboks because my last pair fell apart when I was pushing my car, she breezes into Henri Bendel and buys $800 Pradas to make herself feel better for getting a zit. And all while wearing Vera Wang. Writing a sex column clearly pays a lot better than cranking out alleged humor. But something wonderful and strange came my way that might change all that for me.

Instinct magazine offered me a sex advice column. And, oh, did I enjoy scribbling that letter to my parents. "Dear Mom and Dad, you'd be so proud..." The first time I stopped by the office to pick up the letters I would answer, I had to get all my squealing done in the car. After all, I didn't want to sound like a 12-year-old girl in the well-appointed offices of a glossy national gay men's magazine. The well-appointed offices turned out to be a cramped storefront in Studio City next to Cliff Cadaver Piercing.

"OK," I told myself," they're saving all their money to spend it on what really counts, the writers. I'll be sashaying into the Key Club draped in Gaultier in no time." Yeah. Right. Note to would-be writers: Get used to wearing Hunt Club.

The money was a bit of a letdown. If *Frontiers* affords me discount cross-trainers, this magazine could supply the gum I'd step in. Still, I would be getting the juicy questions. I took the stack of E-mail they handed me, came home, poured myself a lascivious glass of merlot and sat at my computer, ready to cure the world's sexual dysfunction. I took up the topmost letter. It read:

> Long story short: Boy falls madly in love with married man, they part sadly. Two years later, boy is almost over married man when he calls announcing he's divorced. Boy is happy again, but ex-married man is still far away. What should we do?

That was easy. "Long answer short: Find someplace in between, move in, and fuck. Next question."

Hey, what could be simpler? Maybe I could actually pull this off. I read the next letter and frowned. This one required some actual thought, which immediately gave me a headache. But I am a professional, so I tackled it.

"My boyfriend wants me to swallow. Should I?"

"Yes, but only after chewing thoroughly. Oh, you mean *that*. Yeah, I know some guys think you're being rude if you don't swallow. On the other hand, you could go ahead and swallow, get you-know-what and wind up a couple of years down the road vomiting blood and pooping yourself. Now, *that* is rude. And what the hell are you doing letting him come in your mouth anyway? You both know he should be using a condom for these shenanigans. Oh, and don't whine to me about condoms tasting like rubber. Do us all a favor—get a degree in chemistry and invent a dick-flavored condom."

All right! I liked this job. I felt powerful and sex-positive, like I was giving back to my community. And getting paid for it. Not

Sarah-Jessica-in-Roberto-Cavalli "paid for it," but enough to afford Calvin underwear someplace other than Ross Dress for Less. I turned to the next letter.

"How hard should I fuck?"

I was impressed. "God, that's beautiful," I wrote, "It's like the first line of a haiku:

How hard should I fuck?
As hard as your love can stand it.
Fuck strong, like the sea!

"And now in prose: As long as the bottom is only yelling because it's 'good' pain, I say ride 'im, cowboy. If you are concerned this may not be the case, establish a memorable word between the two of you that can be called out when things get too rough. Make it a word you wouldn't ordinarily use in this situation, like 'blueberry!' or 'Zanzibar!' because words like 'Ow!' 'Stop!' and 'Rape!' may be part of the fantasy and role-playing. If they are, though, just be mindful of what the neighbors might think."

I began to feel worldly, experienced, cocky. I was changing lives and opening people up to fantasies they needed to explore. OK, so it was really fantasies *I* needed to explore, but I sounded knowledgeable. They don't need to know I'm a leatherboy wanna-be and besides, anything in print has instant credibility. Next question!

"How do I get a bubble butt?"

Oh, for crying out loud. "Lather, rinse, repeat. Oh, and don't read those hundreds of fitness magazines already out there or anything. Honestly, people."

That one ticked me off. It wasn't even about sex. Damn it, I'm a sex columnist, give me queer love! I looked at the next letter.

"I have a friend I am secretly in love with, but I don't think he's gay. I'm going to visit him in France this summer. Should I tell him the way I feel?"

That's better. "I say *oui*, tell him. Europeans are much less hung up on this macho crap than Americans, so if he's not gay, he's not nearly as likely to freak. If he is gay, you're home free. And if he does spit in your face for whatever reason, well, what did you expect? He's French. They're rude. And they eat stinky cheese."

Top that, Sarah Jessica Parker! I've just gone *internationale.* Plus it felt good insulting the entire nation as retribution for that pissy waiter at the French Market in West Hollywood. Well, it is French.

By now I was getting tired of pretending to care about other people. I counted the words I'd written to discover I was 20 words short of what I'd agreed to write. Damn. I needed one more question. It had to be the right question, though. One that had pressing timeliness and an urgent relevance for my readers. A question to which I could bring my years of worldly experience and answer with genteel candor. And above all, one that could be asked and answered in 20 words because *Buffy* was coming on. I found it.

"I would like to know how to suck a thick 12-inch cock."

"So would I, honey. So would I."

I Am Revealed

Alyson Books came up with a nifty idea for the cover of my first book, *Funny That Way.* The concept was a gay version of those children's books where the top third of the page is animals' heads, the middle third their bodies, and the bottom third feet and you could mix and match for funny animals. Our cover was to be my head and shoulders on top of someone else's torso on top of still another person's legs. One glance and it would scream gay and funny, yet oddly disturbing. I loved it. But they needed a photo of my head and shoulders for this, so they arranged a shoot with a professional photographer. Scott, my editor at the time, called to tell me about scheduling all this. I had contractually agreed to provide Alyson an 8-by-10 black-and-white head shot for publicity purposes, which I had not yet done, so I asked if the photographer would include that in the shoot. Scott said he'd tell the photographer but I'd have to negotiate this with him once I got to the studio. Fine with me.

With other projects going on I needed to schedule the shoot for Saturday morning at the ungodly hour of 9. I picked up a dozen doughnuts to try to assuage the pain for the photographer. His name was Phil and he lived in a nicely middle-class area of L.A. called Larchmont. He had pale skin with dark hair and was so thin that despite being gay he could afford to eat two of the doughnuts. As he nurtured me with just-ground espresso and lovely bone china for my half-doughnut in his spare but chic gray kitchen, I looked at the fresh-cut flowers in a charming vase on the table and thought, *Oh, do I love gay people.*

After some chitchat, Phil gave me the newspaper and left to go set up the living room, which had better morning light than his studio. It gave me time to relax by doing the crossword and eating a couple of more doughnuts unseen, which I planned to blame on his dog.

He called me into the living room that he had rigged to diffuse the bright sunlight streaming in the bay window. Because the previously photographed torso was naked, Phil asked me to take off my shirt so it would match. I did, although I didn't see how my tufted shoulders would blend with a hairless, if flawless, torso. I posed and let the man work. The picture of me Alyson ended used was one where I was giving my sexiest "come fuck me" look. On the finished book cover, it translates as "non-threatening dimwit." Don't blame Phil. An artist is only as good as the material he's given.

When we were done with that round of photos, Phil said, "I'll take your head shot if you'll agree to give me the rights to the other photos I'd like to do of you." By this time I felt we were working very well together, and since I liked the photos he had framed on the wall, I signed it all away. We did several head shots until he felt satisfied I had something I could use. Then he looked at me and said, "OK, my turn. Take everything else off."

I hesitated. Was this leading to some sort of cheap and disgusting sex play? I figured that highly improbable because (a) I'm not that lucky; and (b) the man was a professional. In that case, was I being taken advantage of just to get filthy sex pictures he could peddle to the porno trade? Unlikely, unless there was something on newsstands titled *Hairy Spare Tire* magazine. Oh, wait, there is, it's called *Bear*. Then I wondered if this was how lurid career-ending photos appeared on the Web? Ooh! Possible scandal! And me with a book to sell. "Why not," I said, "what the hell." If he wanted to take photos of this doughy furball, why not? I dropped trou and kicked my tightey whiteys away. "Now what?" I asked.

It was freeing and wonderfully affirming having a man take such an obvious, if merely professional, interest in my body. True, I had to strain to remain immobile, but it felt great being naked. That is, until all that straining to keep from moving started the sweat machine.

Worrying that your ass is sweating through your host's living room upholstery becomes decidedly unsexy and begins a panic reaction. You still sweat, but now it becomes tinged with a mortifying fear the dog could smell. As I remained motionless while Phil snapped the back of my shaved head, his dog was sniffing at my balls. Good grief, do Colt models have this kind of problem? Phil went into the back for some more film, so I shooed the dog away and I grabbed my T-shirt to wipe my pits and other sweaty areas. Phil called out from his office, "Try to stay in that exact position." I froze in my pretzel-like pose with my T-shirt in my crack. *You've got to be kidding,* I thought, then realized he meant the earlier pose. I tossed the T-shirt and resumed the original position as best I could.

On his return, Phil became avidly interested in how the light was playing on one of my fingers, making it seem translucent. He contorted himself in various ways to catch it at its best as I watched the dog snuffling at my now-fragrant T-shirt on the chair across the room. While Phil captured the sublime artistic essence of the eternal life-giving sun passing through the mortal flesh of my hand, I watched his dog pick up my stinky shirt and drag into the back of the house. What could I say? "Your dog took my ass-sweat soaked shirt?" Screw it. I'd brought a couple of other shirts for the shoot; I'd just wear one of those when we were through.

All in all it went very well. When Phil was done, he seemed

pleased with the finger shots and I was allowed to dress and go home. I remain glad for the experience, but feel I owe a debt to society, which is the reason for writing this piece. So let me take care of that with the following: He may have concentrated on my finger, but he took plenty of other buck-naked photos earlier, so if you wander into a gallery and see my ass on the wall, you have been warned!

I Was a Whore for *Instinct* Magazine

There I was at my day job of writing nationally syndicated radio comedy, trying to decide if I could get away with the phrase *rim job* in Sandusky or Ocala, or if I should just go with *butt licking,* which had been rendered acceptable, if tired, by Beavis and Butthead, when the phone rang. It was JR, the publisher of *Instinct,* a magazine for which I write. It seems Channel 7, the ABC affiliate in Los Angeles, wanted to do a review of fashions worn by stars attending one of the zillions of awards shows Hollywood foists on the world. They had already asked mainstream *Los Angeles* magazine, a well-known, tasteful, and respected publication, to do this. The producer of the show, being "family" and a loyal reader, made the inspired choice to call *Instinct.* He asked if *Instinct*'s fashion editor would care to join this highly legitimate fashion maven. Of course JR said yes; it was the ABC flagship station, darling, so you do not say no. One problem though: *Instinct* didn't have a fashion editor. So JR was calling me to ask if I would be willing to prostitute myself in an attempt to pull off this charade on live early-morning Los Angeles television.

"Oh, I get it," I said. "It's like a morning-after postmortem bitchfest?"

I could practically hear JR wincing on the other end. "No, no, no!" He was hot to develop a professional relationship with the producer. That's so L.A. You don't just know somebody in this town; you have a relationship with them, as in, "I have a relationship with someone very high up at Paramount." (Translation: I know a lighting gaffer.) But JR knows how important it is that his magazine smooch butt, er, I mean create a relationship with a producer at KABC. I was to behave myself.

"What time do I have to be there?" I asked.

"Six A.M., and we air at 6:45."

Ugh. That meant setting the alarm for 4. Oh well, at least I wouldn't be competing with Joan Rivers, who would have done her thing the night before, and since I shave my head I wouldn't be plagued by that mashed bed-hair look. I said, "What the hell," I told him. "I'll do it."

I wondered if *Instinct* knew what they were getting into. The last time I appeared on TV was roughly 15 years before on another early-morning show in Jacksonville, Fla. I was part of the cast of some tired musical we were desperate to get people to attend. The chatty hosts, though, were going on and on about the recent marathon called the Jacksonville River Run and the likelihood of the city getting a football team, possibly named after the highly successful marathon. Annoyed that we hadn't been allowed to tout our show, I piped up with "What? You call 'em the River *Runs*?" Shock, silence, instant cut to commercial. I decided not to tell JR about that.

To appear somewhat knowledgeable, I actually watched the wretched award show on Sunday night. It was full of people whose names I'd never heard of in productions I never saw. I was distressed at how many of the new celebrities have three names apiece. I am impossible when it comes to names and these people were mostly underfed and interchangeable. Many were newbies from movies with "scream" in the title and breasts on the screen, neither of which interest me. I did look at the clothes, and I tried to remember JR wanted me to be nice. That wasn't going to be so easy because there were far too many outfits that made me want to crawl through the TV, shake the bony little twit and scream, "What were you thinking?" Ages later, the thing was over and I went to bed, utterly unable to sleep. All I could think was, *I'm an impostor! And tomorrow all of the greater metropolitan Los Angeles demographic will know.* Thank God I had only told a couple of hundred people I'd be doing this.

At 4 A.M. I dragged myself into the shower, shaving from the neck up. My pasty hairless head gleamed like a gardener's gazing ball. Should I wear a hat? All I had was leather, which seemed a tad much for so early in the morning, or two cloth caps, one that advertised a brand of condoms; the other I'd bought because it had a cheer for the University of South Carolina emblazoned on it: "Go Cocks!" I decided to forgo a hat, hoping the show's makeup people would be able to knock the shine down.

I dressed in black Calvin jeans and a black dress shirt with no collar. All fashion people wear black. It must be because there's nothing you can say about black, and that's good if you're going to be trashing people for wearing tacky gowns that cost more than you'll ever have in your 401(k). Besides that, black is slimming and I can use all the help I can get in that department.

JR had arranged with me to link up near the studio at 5:45. He wanted to confab, go over strategy, establish passwords, synchronize watches, and drive to the studio together. I sat at the meeting place until 6, popping Tums and listening to Mexican radio stations to try to wake up. At the stroke of the hour I was outta there without him, flooring it to KABC and the first bathroom I could find. Thank you, Starbucks.

The production assistant (PA, in Hollywood-speak) deposited me in the tiny green room and left. I called JR to let him know where I was. He had only then arrived at the rendezvous point. Gay Standard Time lives. He was on his way over.

The green room had makeup all over the place, but it became apparent that talent would have to apply their own paints. I started to panic. I don't know from makeup, and I was shiny like the sun. "Don't worry, I'm here," JR said, sweeping in the door. Damn it, I didn't need a publisher; I needed a femme lesbian. I remembered that back in my theater days we used to kill the glare on any mirrors on the set by coating them with hair spray, so I grabbed the industrial-size can of Aqua Net and sprayed my head. It did nothing, and now I was sticky. I hastily dusted it with powder, praying it wouldn't be hot in the studio. If I started to sweat I'd have mud.

The woman from *Los Angeles* magazine arrived—in black. Hey, maybe I could blend in and pull this off after all. She was wearing black pants and a black jacket with a red top under it. And oh, my God, was she serious about fashion. She knew the celebrities' names (all three of them for each), their shows, and their designers. She was talking fabrics and color, and I just nodded and smiled and felt like I had FRAUD! tattooed across my sticky-powdered forehead. JR was beginning to look nervous at my silence so I waded into the conversation blathering words picked up from years of watching *Ab Fab.* Line! Ornamentation! Details! Actually, the line I was thinking of was the one I was going to give JR when the producer saw through this charade and threw us off the lot. The only ornamentation I know anything about hangs on my Christmas tree. And *Details* is a magazine I don't read because they won't just come out and say they're gay. But she bought my shtick and even agreed with me on the importance of buttons, of all things.

The PA came in and rattled off the celebrities we'd be dishing. I jotted down their names on a paper towel, which greedily absorbed the ink. I prayed I wouldn't forget and dab my head with it. She herded us into the studio where we were wired for sound. That's where we met the producer, Edd.

It turned out Edd had been at my house three years prior at a Christmas party, the one where we accidentally set a woman suffering from multiple personality disorder on fire. Back then I didn't know him nor did I know he was there, but such were the parties we used to throw. There was no time to reestablish the connection we didn't have, though, because the real style lady and the faux fashion fag were shoved over to a set with seats. There was no getting out of it now. My throat tightened. With a gurgle from the lower intestine, a full-fledged panic attack started to surface. I knew the next five minutes were going to be stupid, unpleasant, embarrassing, and empty, like *The Blair Witch Project,* only with better sound.

Then over on the other side of the studio I saw the weatherman pick his nose. Suddenly everything fell into perspective. My part in this wasn't an evil deception or cruel hoax, it was a joke. Hell, everything is just entertainment, anyway. I relaxed. I even crossed my legs as artsy-casual as anything Mr. Blackwell could pull off. The anchorwoman joined us and seconds later we were live.

I said Susan Lucci's daughter looked like the Good Witch Glinda's younger sister. I said Camryn Manheim's outfit, a Brunhilde number right out of *What's Opera, Doc?* was a big f-you to anyone who said she was too fat. The fashion lady strongly felt otherwise, but I said we should give Camryn a spear and horns and stand back. I said it looked like the producers yanked Gwyneth Paltrow out of the Westside Pavilion Mall. Said that Leelee Sobieski's dress looked great, but why was she wearing Madonna's hair from last year? I said Courtney Love looked like she'd been run over—seven or eight times—crossing Wilshire. Oh, and on a personal note, I told her over the air that she needed to get therapy. I made lots of friends in Hollywood that morning.

When it was over, Edd said it went well and he might even make us the regular fashion police. I liked that idea. It's just the beginning of awards season, and lots of famous people with more money than taste will be traipsing up and down red carpets all over this tacky town. JR had established his relationship and was beaming, so I figured I didn't suck too badly. I even got him to spring for a post-taping coffee at Starbucks. A *venti.* He must have been very pleased.

Viewing the videotape was eye-opening. Nothing bestows credibility like being on television. I always used to wonder where these shows came up with all the highly knowledgeable and qualified experts who told us what we should be thinking.

Now I know.

Getting Yelled At

Every so often I write something that upsets someone so much they have to let me know about it. I suppose if enough people see any given opinion, it'll eventually provoke an extreme reaction from someone. If I were to put it out there that Julia Roberts was a very pleasing and attractive actress, somebody would be incensed enough to scrawl back, "That scabby, stretched-out, pockmarked *whore*? How could *anyone* think that, you brain-dead filth!" Or the like.

Case in point: In an Oscar awards piece I went off on a self-admitted petulant tear on Barbra Streisand for, I don't know, being Barbra. It lasted a paragraph. A man in Glendale sent back a most angry and detailed letter—which got printed—that took up an entire column. He ripped into my piffle on Ms. Streisand like Medea preparing dinner. I had spat upon his sanctum sanctorum and it would not stand. I was really annoyed by his response. Not because he was coming at me hammer and tongs, but because his letter was unwittingly twice as funny as my article. Bastard.

I've also heard from a number of people that I shouldn't be writing about God and church and all that noise. There are some in our community who are angry at me because they want nothing to do with religion, and the ones who are religious are upset with me because they think I'm too disrespectful. Such a *tzimmis.* And that's just the homos. If a Pat Robertson were to see me in my leather pants and shirt serving communion to same-sex couples, he'd have such a fit of fury he'd swallow his tongue. Which would be doing the world big favor. Listen, if you're one of the gays who hate religion, who can blame you? You've had the shit beat out of you with it. Been there, done that, told I wasn't worthy of the T-shirt. But that's religion, not God (Goddess, Creator, Great Spirit, Adonai, Allah, the Universe, whatever—it's all good). Don't let that religio-crap keep you from finding and celebrating the divine within you. I'm not telling anyone what he or she should believe. I hope I'm telling people it's possible to come through to the other side of the spiritual wounding and find some happiness and peace. And if you're one of those others, I'm not disrespectful, just joyous, ya big boob.

Speaking of church, some time ago I did an interview by E-mail for the monthly publication of St. Jude's Metropolitan Community Church in Wilmington, N.C. (Yes, I'm that big and famous.) I had hit it off with the interviewer over the phone in a conversation that was jolly and delightfully profane, so I approached it casually and free-associated like crazy. Being an awful blowhard, I wrote answers that went on for days to simple questions like, "Where are you from?" When I finally finished, I hit "Send," vaguely hoping there were a couple of lines he could pull out of it that wouldn't make me look like a total idiot. Well, he printed the whole damn thing. Four pages of ramblings in a flier that only had 12 pages to begin with. Plus, I assumed he would clean it up. This has to be the only church publication Wilmington ever saw containing the phrases "pain in the ass," "full of shit," "eat me," the word "dick" as a very improper noun three times, and various forms of the word "fuck." It caused a stir. And the publication now has a new editor. Oh, well. Oops. I try to be more careful what I tell interviewers these days.

Not that I don't give my opinion. Another person wrote that he hated my politics. I'm not surprised. He should hear what my father thinks of my politics. What did surprise me was he called me a "flaming Democrat." What, just because I tweak Republicans he thought I liked Democrats? Let me settle this once and for all, and piss off plenty *more* people. It has been my experience that Republicans are generally motivated by three things: personal greed, personal greed, and more personal fucking greed. As a whole, they would be very happy to see gay people, and anyone else who doesn't look and act just like they do, dead. Democrats are every bit as vile, only they have a twinge of guilt about it. The poor things haven't figured out what to do with that darned vestigial conscience. The way that plays out for gays is that the Democrats want us to come out and vote for them, then crawl back under our rocks like good little abominations until next election. And if people feel I'm a tad harsh, let me quote Lily Tomlin and Jane Wagner, "No matter how much contempt I have for society, it's nothing compared to the contempt society has for me." I love Lily and Jane. I wish they would run for office. I don't know, maybe that's not a good idea. Searching for signs of intelligent life in the universe is one thing. Searching for it in Washington is something else.

I hope I'm not going down the sniping-back-at-the-reviewer road, but I must mention one who got quite angry with me for "perpetuating demeaning stereotypes." I can see how he might think that, but I believe he misunderstood my intention. It wasn't to perpetuate stereotypes but to fuck with them. On the other hand, there do exist such things as bitter queens, nelly fags, vanilla boys, leather freaks, flaming homos, macho clones, disco divas, and mincing fairies. I know because some days I've been all of them and a few more.

But playing with stereotypes can induce one to go too far and I am woefully guilty of doing just that. I wrote a piece on Home & Garden Television wherein I heavily implied that the host of *Designing for the Sexes,* Michael Payne, was gay. Actually I said he's "a prissy fruit." At least I followed it with, "I just love him...." I meant it as a compliment, but it was not received as such. Two indignant letters came back, one from a Mr. Hauser, who is a former segment producer of the show, and one from a Ms. Garson. She is apparently his agent or lawyer, a confounding choice to be sure, but she wrote, "Mr. Perry's facts in the article regarding Michael Payne's sexual identity are misinformed. For future reference and in the pursuit of journalistic professionalism and accurate reporting, please be aware that Michael Payne's sexuality has been inaccurately reported...." I can understand her irritation at me. After all, I get annoyed when people assume I'm straight. Ms. Garson is entirely in the right.

Mr. Hauser was more succinct, writing, "Do your research, buddy!" He's right too. I blew it. He also wrote, "I find Joel's assumption and stereotypical attitude that men who have the capacity to design with a flair are prissy fruits [offensive]." He's right. I totally screwed up. I try to be the one telling everybody there are infinite ways to be gay, just as there are infinite ways to be straight, bi, transgendered, and androgynous, all of them perfectly valid. Witness Mr. Payne. The fact that he is able to balance the male and female sensibilities of his clients is a testament to his talents and abilities. If more straight men could do that, there would be a lot less patriarchal abuse and damage thrown around, plus gays wouldn't wince so often when walking into our straight friends' homes.

I have to admit that I fell into my own trap of stereotyping, and that it is indeed possible for straight men to be sensitive and artistic. The works of Van Gogh make me weep, but he sliced up an ear over a prostitute, not a rent boy. He gave us some of the most beautiful paintings in the world and he was a full-on bat-shit crazy fucked-up heterosexual. Before I get grief for that, let me state I know plenty of those who are gay. I dated them. But in this case I was being homosexist in the extreme.

Mr. Hauser also said my "myopic views that gay men can't have masculine qualities drive home one of the reasons why executives avoid having same-sex couples on *Designing for the Sexes.*" Do they, now? That's an interesting decision for the executives to make in light of the fact so many other shows on HGTV see no need for similar distancing. When their host has the balls to break the tyranny of society's gender constructs and be himself, something I'm willing to bet those executives view as less than dick-swinging macho, I can't help but wonder whose baggage is getting in the way here. I'd love to meet those uncomfortable executives and ask them point-blank. I'd be sure to choose something frilly to wear for the occasion. In his letter, Mr. Hauser points out that the show is produced by Pie Town Productions, which is owned by gay partners Tara Sandler and Jennifer Davidson. Are they aware this foolishness is going on?

Then again, perhaps it just has to do with the show's title. After all, if the executives were to allow the talented Mr. Payne to drop in on a same-sex couple, the program would necessarily be called *Designing for the Sex.* That's an altogether different kind of show, one that sounds more suited to late-night Showtime or HBO, but I'd tune in just as avidly. Perhaps I should pitch it to Pie Town.

Since I have no interest in hurting innocent people's feelings, especially those I admire, I wrote an apology to Mr. Payne, which I assume he will share with Ms. Garson and Mr. Hauser. There is enough ill will in the world already and I refuse to add to it, even if it is unintentional. I am happy to report that Mr. Payne was most gracious in his reply. I remain a respectful fan and hope to have enough money some day to have him design a bathroom for me with several well-placed yet tasteful nozzles.

And finally, in another area, I learned that according to more than one source, I was "the self-appointed expert on all things gay." If that is so, I cannot tell you how profoundly I apologize. If I felt someone was presenting himself to me like that, I'd have to reach for the extra-strength Maalox too. I can think of few things more obnoxious. Possibly a Republican-controlled Congress. But little else. So I'm sorry if I came across as some sort of poofter pundit. As therapy has proved time and again, I'm not even the expert on me. I'm not an expert on anything outside of snack foods. I just write how things affect me, and I'm fortunate that some people seem to enjoy that. If you don't like it, write your own book. Seriously. Take that as an invitation. We need your ideas too, especially if they're different from mine. My opinion is no better than yours. But you did just drop $14.95 to find out my opinion, though, didn't you, now?

Blow Me

I never set out to be any kind of expert on sex. I took the sex advice column because I thought it was a great hoot. From there a most undeserved reputation grew. One month, the editor wanted me to visit all the sex clubs in L.A. and write a feature article comparing and contrasting them. I declined, reminding him I had a spouse and that this was not the sort of thing that was going to be healthy at this point in the relationship. It was also not a task I felt up to, preferring to be in my nice warm bed by 10; still, it's always nice to be asked to dance.

When it comes to outright sex, I'd rather play a bit more demure role, at least on the outside. In fact, when my first book came out, the publishers wanted me to subtitle it *Queer as They Come* or *Queer Ol' Me* or *Faggoty Bent Queer and a Half* or something like that. I begged them not to do that, because I still had the naive idea that once I was in print, my father might actually put the book out on the coffee table for visitors to notice, and he certainly wouldn't do that if it had anything that could be construed as "My Cocksucking Son" on the cover. The publisher acquiesced and it was subtitled *Adventures in Fabulousness,* whatever that means.

Then for the cover, they put my head on a beefcake torso, naked except for a feather boa and a scant yet enviably filled leather thong. So much for the coffee table.

Still, sexually charged things just seem to come my way. Alyson Books asked *Instinct* magazine if they would do a how-to book for them in the cheeky yet informative and sex-positive *Instinct* style. *Instinct* asked me if I would write it with their editor, Ben. I happen to respect Ben a lot, mainly because he doesn't screw around with the material I send him. I said yes, and found myself the coauthor of (we hope) the definitive book on how to give a blow job, titled *Going Down: The Instinct Guide to Oral Sex.* Coffee table? I'll be lucky to get this one in the door.

A couple of chapters in, it became apparent that I was going to need to talk to some experts about this subject. A friend put me in touch with a man who was quite proud of his expertise in the field. After missing each other a few times, he left a message that he was on his way to his Hollywood job but to call him on his cell. I had been out to dinner, so when I got up with him, he was in Numbers, a bar known as the premiere hustler bar in L.A. I didn't think anything of it, though, because I've been there myself a few times with friends and we were just drinking. Thinking he must have finished his Hollywood job earlier in the evening and was also drinking with friends, I jokingly told him, "Pick up someone for me," to show off my casual worldliness and knowledge of this bar. He said he was actually hoping someone would be picking him up. Well, what single man doesn't hope that on a Friday night? I asked where he worked in Hollywood. He said, "At Numbers." "Ah," I thought, "he must be a part-time waiter or bartender still on duty." I then asked when he got off, a term that caused some confusion at the other end. The light dawned. He wasn't working *at* Numbers, he was *working* Numbers! My reaction? "Cool!" So I made my first date with a hustler. Hey, I have no problem with sex workers. I figure if they're good enough for Jesus to hang out with, they're good enough for me.

We met for dinner on the Boulevard early enough for him to get to work on time. Even for West Hollywood, our table chitchat was a bit outré. Snatches of conversation, like "If a guy with a long dick comes while you're deep-throating him, do you gag?" or "When I was 16 I was meeting cops on the Internet and blowing them in their squad cars" and my favorite, "Bulimics give the best deep throat," were wafting through the air like sin in a whorehouse. His point-by-point description of a date who had paid him extra for snowballing caused an entire table behind us to relocate. This man was in such demand that he got between $350 and $450 a night, and that was just doing one date per evening. I got much expert advice. And he was so generous with his knowledge, he said he was considering leading a workshop on the subject at the upcoming California Men's Gathering. I made a mental note to attend.

I made more notes at the Beverly Hills library, where I plunged into male anatomy. There's nothing like asking a Beverly Hills matron, "Where are your books on fellatio and the penis?" But from that I learned words for things I never knew had names. That little ridge-like line running from the bottom of your cock down your scrotum and back to your anus? It's called the raphe (pronounced *ray-fee*). And when you shoot, your sperm comes out between 25 and 28 mph. A city bus only goes about 25 mph, so it's possible your sperm could beat you to work. Another figure I learned is that a normal male will ejaculate approximately 14 gallons of splooge in his lifetime. That really impressed me. The gas tank on my new Corolla only holds 11.4 gallons.

Does any of this information make for a better blow job? Only indirectly. It depends on how well you work it into your sparkling party repartee and who picks up on it. People, you should pardon the expression, eat that stuff up.

We interviewed many folks and learned that while the techniques could be reduced to a relatively few basic moves, there were paradoxically infinite variations based on the individuality of the people involved. And believe me, we heard all about it. You'd be surprised how fast people are willing to tell you their intimate sexual techniques, well, once they dispense with the obligatory pretense of finding such talk scandalous. You might also be surprised to learn how quickly this talk grows tiresome, especially after they open up to you and drift into other areas like dating a man with a third nipple or how their episiotomy affected their sex life. That was why I usually conducted my interviews near sources of alcohol. Bartender, another double, please.

So despite most of the advance going toward booze, we managed to collect enough information (as well as titillation) to put together an entertaining little manual. And if it's not entertaining, there are always the illustrations to get off on. Hey, if we can improve the quality of cock sucking in this country even a little, it will have been worth it. The way Ben and I look at it, the next time somebody slobs your knob and it's really great, you're welcome.

Some people have asked me how I could demean myself by agreeing to do a how-to book on sucking dick. Are they kidding? For the rest of my life I'll be able to say, "Don't tell me what to do, buster—I wrote the book on blow jobs!"

Part Six: Getting Through It

When Work Doesn't Work for You

What is the biggest sin? Infidelity? Murder? Stripes with plaid? That's kid stuff. The worst sin is *boredom.* If you work 40 hours a week, 50 weeks a year, minus holidays, you spend close to 1,900 boring hours a year at your job. That's a heaping helping of dull. That's like sitting through *Blair Witch 2* over a thousand times and almost as stupid. How do you survive the ordeal?

By stirring up trouble, of course.

"But why would I want to do this?" you ask. "Why would I want to distress my coworkers, summon up the demons of evil mischief, and add to an already dark world's misery?" Simple: Because you can.

"But I should be concentrating on my work," you whine. Yeah, and your employer should be paying you what you're worth, but that isn't happening either, is it? And just how secure are you in that homophobically run job you should be concentrating on, you big ol' dick-sucking butt pirate, you? And how much domestic-partner coverage are you offered? And who chose that awful art-work out in the lobby? Get over it. You're a fucked-up homo from a dysfunctional family in a gay-hating society. If anyone ever had a reason to act out their resentment and neuroses, it's you.

And if by some freakish chance you actually are healthy and well-adjusted and get fabulous benefits, then the rest of us could use the entertainment. It behooves you to make life interesting for the poor saps who have had their souls sucked dry by the tedium of toil and day-to-day drudgery. It is vitally important that you valiantly lead the way into amusement for all the peons in your workplace. These people desperately need variety in their lives, at their workstations, and, if you can work it, inside the desks, drawers, computers, and lockers they think are "secure." Straight people are looking to us to provide this kind of stimulus and excitement; it's one of our roles in society. Well, that and discovering new trends for Madonna to rip off next.

But the main motivation, the inspiring incentive, the prompting provocation is that it's plain old *fun*! And isn't that the only real reason to do anything? Where better to foment fun than a place that (a) needs it; (b) isn't expecting it so probably is not going to be able to handle it; (c) has devious little you in it; and (d) pays you while you're doing it? You have no choice. The universe has forced your hand in this. You *must* create workplace fun. And because I'm a giving, loving person who loves his fellow humanity, I'm gonna tell ya how.

All you have to do is cause any kind of disturbance. The fun comes in watching the reactions to it. Workplace fun breaks down to five main areas: Pranks, Stunts, Moving Stuff, Misinformation, and Random Shit. Let me start with the most direct.

PRANKS

These are stupid, petty, small-minded things to do that annoy the shit out of people. That's what makes them fun and life worth living.

1. Put labels on everything. And I mean everything: "Door," "Spatula," "Disposable Hat," "Fan," "Copier," "Carpet," "Ketchup Stain," "Nose Goblin," "Bad Toupee," "Bi-Curious," "Closet Case." Make sure they're really difficult to remove.

2. Pick a phrase and say it after everything. About the 173rd time you say "Would you like fries with that?" someone is bound to snap. Especially if you don't work in fast food. "Serving you is a pleasure!" is guaranteed to get on any boss's nerves after a couple of days of hearing it every fucking single time you speak. The beauty of that one is, you don't even have to go for the sarcasm, they'll get it.

3. Have any sex toys you're tired of? Bring 'em to work and, after hours, discreetly drop them in someone's desk, leaving the drawer open enough for the goodies to be seen by all who pass. Enjoy the gossip.

4. This prank is so well-known and stupid that it's frequently overlooked. Make a chain out of all the paper clips you can get your hands on and drop it in someone's paper clip holder. It's a classic because it's asinine, puerile, infantile, easy, and mindless to assemble while you chat on the phone (preferably company-paid long distance), plus it's guaranteed to piss off whoever goes for that one paper clip and comes up with yards of them hopelessly tangled. There is cosmic beauty in the fact that each clip must be carefully unhooked by the victim one by one by one by one... That or they just throw it all away in disgust, costing the company money. That works too.

5. It shouldn't be too difficult to get your hands on the résumés of some of your superiors. Xerox them and leave them around fax machines. Management will think they're using company time and equipment to look for another job. Is there anything more sublime than watching your boss get shit from his boss?

STUNTS

What do you do when boredom becomes unbearable and there's nothing at hand? You use your fabulous self, that's what. It doesn't matter where you work for these stunts to be effective.

1. Make up an accent and use the wrong words deliberately and enthusiastically. "Dees outfit on chew is bitchy! Chew are one bitchy lady! Chew in dees outfit suck my world!"

2. You know, you're not the only person bored at work. Share some of the fun by staging an ugly fight with a coworker. "You

wouldn't be behind this perfume counter if you weren't blowing the company rep!" "Oh, yeah, well, we're through! I'm throwing your butt plugs and vacuum pump out on the lawn!" Bystanders love this. Unfortunately, many managers do not.

3. If you're with an obnoxious customer, start twitching and calling them horrible things. It works best if you pick one thing and repeat it obsessively. "Cunt! Cunt cunt cunt cunt! CUNT! Cuntcuntcuntcunt—*CUNT*!" Afterward, apologize and say you suffer from Tourette's syndrome. Cunt cunt cunt. If you already suffer from Tourette's, you know this is a horrible and inaccurate stereotype. But other people don't, so go ahead and get all your anger out in this fashion, and if anybody even tries to give you shit about it, you sue their asses off! You deserve it.

MOVING STUFF

This category may seem overly simple, but with the right victim, it is an insidious delight. This category is an area that deals with two hot-button issues for any victim: vulnerability and control. Not having control over things in life is a reminder they also have no control over death. They are as vulnerable as an unattended Hershey Bar in a bottom left-hand drawer. You're actually helping these folks on their spiritual path because they need to know they have this issue so they can work on it. And demonstrating to them that they do have it can be such fun!

1. Go to the staff refrigerator and rearrange the food. People go ballistic over this because it looks like someone has rifled through their vulnerable, unattended lunch and/or swiped some of their food. They feel outraged. Powerless. Violated. Is that fun, or what?

2. Change all their shit. Alter the presets on their radio, put their clocks back an hour, and, when they're out to lunch, change the color field on their computers.

3. Choose your most anal-retentive coworker and move everything in their work space, from pictures on the wall to drawers in their desk. Watch them have conniptions. Suggest they switch to decaf.

4. Another approach is to choose just one thing and move it

incrementally over a period of days. By the end of the week, the chosen item should be on the other side of their office, if not out in the hallway. Enjoy their apoplexy.

MISINFORMATION

The workplace functions on facts. Because workers operate in this environment, they assume the information they receive is going to be accurate. What does this mean? It means you have a workplace full of sitting ducks.

1. If your office is just getting online, take the opportunity to "teach" your boss (and anyone else) how to use E-mail. If you're clever you can have them sending extremely sensitive and private messages to everyone in the company. That'll keep the water cooler buzzing.

2. If you're already online, go to person A's desk and use their computer to IM (Instant Message) person B. Type something like, "Did you hear I quit?" When the reply comes from person B, type, "I can't talk now, I really need to take a walk." When person A returns, enjoy the conversation.

3. A variation on this is to IM person B, "I have two tickets to [movie/show/whatever], want to go?" This works especially well if you happen to overhear that person A actually does have the goods but is planning on taking their spouse or sister or trick. Even better, though, is to do this IM dance whenever you've overheard a juicy dark personal secret. It's a great way to spread embarrassment, discord, and entertainment.

4. Fake a note from the boss that says, "See me." Underline it several times and attach it to someone's time card or just leave it on their desk. Do it when you know the boss will be away for a good while. That allows for maximum buildup of your victim's anxiety. If they mention it to you, commiserate deeply, then ask what they think it could be. Naturally you will focus on all the recent possible mistakes your victim has made.

5. Paging systems are fun. "Mr. Farnswerger, please meet your parole officer in the front lobby." "Anyone knowing the whereabouts

of Mr. Blodgett and young Miss Chapman, please come to reception and tell Mrs. Blodgett." "Whoever left a vibrator in the men's room may claim it at the front desk." Use the paging system to tell everyone there is free food in the third-floor conference room and watch the stampede. Then go back on and apologize for the error, saying the free food is actually in the fifth-floor kitchen. They're already away from their desks, so they may as well run upstairs. The fools.

6. Posting fake stuff on the bulletin board is always entertaining. "For sale, leather sling with hardware, minimal bloodstains." Then leave the phone number of whomever you wish to upset. Or perhaps you merely wish to upset those who read the postings. "For sale, pig with three legs and one fresh ham." That's especially good if the bulletin board is in the lunchroom.

RANDOM SHIT

This is stuff you do just for the pure joy of pulling utterly unnecessary crap on people. Sure, doing it is what makes people go to hell, but the joy of doing it is also what makes us want to get out of bed in the morning.

1. Call a truly nasty 976 porno service, put them on hold, and buzz your victim. "Tina, pick up on line 3." (You might want to disguise your voice.) You can also call up the service, then transfer them to another person. If you plan on doing this a lot, use somebody else's phone. Phone bills detail where all calls originate, and you don't want them coming back to you. Much better to have it traced back to some homophobic asshole. Generic assholes work well too.

2. Taint the coffee. Put something unpleasant-tasting in the pot when you make coffee. A couple of dashes of hot sauce will suffice. An old trick, yes, but the novice does it just for one pot. You are a pro, so keep doing it. Lead the complaints about the coffee. See how long it takes for the machine or even the coffee service to be changed. See how many services you can go through. Stop when you find one that sends a cute representative to restock the supplies.

3. If you work in a doctor's office, call a false name for the next patient. "Mr. Williams? Is Mr. Williams here?" When no one

responds, feign annoyance and go flouncing into the reception area. Get in someone's face and accuse them of being that person and of having something embarrassing. "Look, are you Mr. Williams?" "No." "Are you *sure*?" "Yes!" "So you're *not* here to get your anal warts burned off again?" That sort of thing makes patients very nervous. When you do call their names, you'll be amazed at how quickly they respond rather than risk having you come out after them.

4. When the boss (or someone equally vile) goes into the walk-in freezer, close the door. Wait two minutes. Two minutes is a very long time at minus 2 degrees, especially when they don't know it's going to be only two minutes. But it is long enough for deep panic to set in, and that's the point, isn't it? After the two minutes, open the door like you needed to get something and be surprised to find them there. **NOTE:** Don't forget that last part about opening the door. If you leave them locked in the freezer, they will die. Fun, maybe, but the authorities will have to be called.

CONCLUSION

"Shame on you for even considering these things," your better self is probably saying, "These are terrible tricks to play on people!" On the contrary, they are excellent tricks. Don't think of them as mean-spirited. Remember, you are doing it as an act of love. The coworker who is going mental from the monotony truly needs to be shaken from his torpor. If infuriating him until blood vessels burst in his cortex is the cost, it is a small price to pay. The boss grown petulant with power needs to be reminded who is in charge. That would be you. And the person with control issues needs to be gently awakened to the fact that they are shit out of luck on a hostile planet that doesn't give a rat's ass whether they live or die, let alone whether someone swiped their Pepsi out of the fridge for the 15th time.

You are merely the jolly gnome whose job it is to remind them of this with humor, joy, and mind-fucking.

Now get to work.

Stars of Stage and Screen

Mr. Cutler, a boss I once had who was straight, asked me why there were so many homosexuals in the theater. I didn't know where to begin. To me it was like asking why there was air. There are so many gay men in the arts *because* there are so many gay men in the arts. I mean, think about it. If you're a homo, you want to meet other homos, right? Where are they? In the arts. If I were a lesbian, this would be a piece about softball and I'd have a great right arm. Actually, I do have a great right arm, but it ain't from softball.

Growing up, the theater was the one place I could pretend to be something else and literally get applause for it. Most gays have pretended to be something else for so long, it should surprise no one that we're already pretty damn good at it. So there we are, all over the stage and screen. And each other. But it goes beyond that. At least, to me it did.

For me, theater was where magic was not only allowed but demanded, every day. When I woke up at home, I was fat and shy and painfully ordinary, in some vague way a disappointment. But when I walked onto the stage that evening, I was sure, I was right, I was needed, I was special, and I got applause. I wanted to sleep there. I wanted my mail delivered there. I wanted my life to be lived there forever. I've more or less managed to do just that. I can't help but think those umpteen-million-dollar-a-picture movie stars started out feeling the same way and having similar experiences.

During my teenage years in Wilmington, N.C., I was involved in a summer stock company that each June through August was like falling into heaven. It was seven weeks of a new show every week. That meant that in the midst of the season we were blocking one show in the morning to get the basic movements down, having lunch, rehearsing a second show in the afternoon, breaking for dinner and then performing a third show that night. I was in high school, so I wasn't getting paid, but I was working with people who were making $75 a week—professionals!

Every week, my greasepaint family changed roles with the shows we were doing. I wished my birth family could have done that just once. Even if they had turned into *The Little Foxes,* at least I would have understood what they were about. As it was, my poor parents were struggling to understand me. I thought it was perfectly normal to be in the shower belting out the most over-the-top song a 14-year-old could sing from *Man of La Mancha,* "Aldonza, the Whore." My mom would tap on the bathroom door, "Dear, could you choose some...other song?" Not a problem. *Fiddler on the Roof* was coming up. I launched into "Tevye's Dream." The Frumah Sarah part, naturally.

In that production of *Fiddler* I was, sadly, not Frumah Sarah, but Reb Nochum, the beggar, who has only one lousy line in the opening number and is scenery for the rest of the show. He's the village blind man, but he somehow manages to keep up with a boisterous dancing crowd in "To Life." During the wedding scene that ends act 1, the Cossacks have to rudely knock over tables and chairs. Our Cossacks were way too nelly to pull it off, so they were recast as wedding guests and a stagehand the size of Poland was given the part of destroying the wedding. It looked like the Russians had gone out and hired Mongo from *Blazing Saddles.*

Tevye could have saved all of Anatevka if he'd just come up with that Candy-Gram gimmick.

In *Cabaret,* I was also scenery. I was cast as a sailor, engagement party guest, and Nazi, among other things. It was as Kit Kat Club patrons, though, that we chorus members made our mark. The director wanted us to smoke real cigars to create the authentic smoky, smelly club atmosphere. None of us had ever actually smoked a cigar before, and we didn't get them till opening night. Three of us threw up during "Don't Tell Mama."

When I was 16, I was inexplicably cast in *Brigadoon* as the father of the female lead. I was thrilled to be given the part, and I diligently practiced my Scottish brogue until it was truly heinous. Saying lines like "Auch, aye, laddie," it's hard not to sound like a pirate. It was the last show of the summer stock season, and everyone was exhausted so this production got very short shrift. We weren't even taught one of the big numbers until the day before opening. It was a dramatic piece called "Run and Get Him," where all of Brigadoon would vanish forever if we didn't run and get young Harry Beaton and drag his tartaned *tuchis* back to town. We were blocked to be running all over the enormous, perilous rocks on the set while belting out the song with appropriate drama and alarm. Due to the concentration it took not to kill ourselves on the damn rocks combined with the lateness of learning the tune, we ended up shout-singing in dire, manly tones, "Run and get him! Run and get him! Run or blumf flumph la de da da hermfin lermun berman! *Run and get him!*" We may have been inarticulate, but we were most urgent about it.

Later, at the ripe age of 19, I was cast as a muleteer in my second production of *Man of La Mancha* in a summer stock company in Burnsville, N.C. The stage was severely raked, which means on a slant so steep just walking downstage in boots was a feat. The day we blocked the fight scene was a festival of first aid. Nevertheless, we were actors, and by damn, we would pull it off. The director, imported from New York, gave all the other muleteers their instructions for the scene, involving punches, falls, kicks, and various pratfalls. Recalling years of choosing sides for games in P.E., I was the very last to be put into the scene. I could see the director thinking, "What can I do with the sweaty fat kid?" I think he wanted me out of the scene, because he told me that for this bit I was to get hit in the groin by Don Quixote, then kicked in the butt by Sancho, sending me into a double somersault ending with a fall down the well onto an inadequate mattress below stage where I was to quickly roll away so Aldonza could immediately hurl a small wooden barrel after me, all of this happening on a 20-degree tilt. "Can you do that, kid?" I had no idea, but I loved being in the theater so much that if he had asked me to set myself on fire and fly, I'd by damn give it my best. And you know what? I did it on the first try. The director was so impressed, he thereafter called me "Bobo," which I later learned had been his nickname years earlier when he was a muleteer in the original Broadway production. Every so often I think of that incident. If he was impressed with that, he should see what I'm able to do now when I get out of bed and step on the cat.

During those shows I did character parts and crowds, helped change costumes, ran props, pushed sets, and flew scenery, sometimes all in the same production. Every now and then there were a couple of shows in which I had acting roles large enough to preclude me from doing anything else. Those occasions were the ultimate gifts of affirmation, like being welcomed into Valhalla, only with rented costumes. And always there were terrific parties after the shows.

At these parties I literally sat at the feet of the professional actors while they told wondrous stories of performing shows in real cities like New York, Boston, Raleigh. These were outrageous, fun, flamboyant people who were thrilling to be around, completely different from the homunculi I lived among. These people's behavior was exotic, strange, mercurial, and exciting, their very existence a romance. If you haven't figured it out yet, they were screaming, alcoholic, maladjusted theater queens. Even the women. Hell, especially the women. They were horny as hell and pissed off the men wouldn't fuck 'em. It was gloriously dysfunctional. And every Wednesday, Thursday, Friday, and Saturday night we made magic together out of sweat, paint, canvas, limelight, and love.

How could I choose any other life over this? What other life could be as noble? Where else could I feel half so alive?

I still work in the field of entertainment, albeit in a niche most people don't even know exists. I write and produce radio comedy bits for a nationally syndicated service. I have over 200 affiliates coast to coast, so there's a very good chance you've heard my work and never known it. I am proud to say I make people laugh. I do it because I know the oppressive dullness of the ordinary. I do it because I believe in my heart it is desperately needed. When asked what he did for a living, one of my coworkers used to say, facetiously, "I write comedy and save lives." I've stolen that as a slogan, but I'm not facetious about it.

In my 20s and 30s I tried my damnedest to be cynical but failed. I somehow managed to remain hopeful despite rampant hate, terrorists, plagues, gay Republicans, and Oscar winners doing haircare infomercials. It's because I know there is a place where magic abides. In my teen years, when I loathed myself in a way that makes Fred Phelps's hatred look like amateur night, it was the combined power of laughter and theater that saved me. Now, every time I go to the theater or movies, or watch the Academy Awards or even TV dramas or sitcoms, I know there are people up there who started out like me, desperate for love, acceptance, and, let's face it, attention. That's why there are so many homosexuals in the theater, Mr. Cutler. No, they're not all gay, but a helluva lot of 'em ain't straight either. It's sad that so many feel they still have to hide to get the acceptance they crave. I don't envy them. It's a long road to win a Best Actor award for being someone else, but for many of us, it was a longer one learning how to be ourselves.

And that beats the hell out of any Oscar.

Bed, Bathhouse, and Beyond

OK, I've done the bathhouse thing, so it's not like I'm above it. In fact, I've done it and done it and done it, had a Pepsi, and went back and did it some more. But it got increasingly difficult for me not to notice what was happening beyond all the sex. Can we talk about some of these people?

Take Mr. Fantastic Body. And you can believe I took him as often as he would let me. The question that eventually surfaced, though, was, "Why does *he* need to come to a place like this for sex?" The man is drop-dead gorgeous, so why does he need to prove to himself he's attractive? Or maybe it's about being worthy of love? If so, a lotta good that's gonna do him in a fuck palace. Suddenly he's looking less like Steve the Stud and more like Nancy Needy. And not nearly as hot.

There was also Mr. Look But Don't Touch. If that's his attitude, why the hell is he paying money to come to a sex place to *not* have sex? Besides, it's just plain rude. If you're going to bring a body like that to the party, be prepared to share. What kind of power trip is he acting out in that steam room?

There were the obvious cases, like Mr. Amazing Slut who just finished #175 for the evening and is now serving #176. Hey, I like a good fuck, but there's being into sex and then there's having a hole in your soul Dirk Diggler couldn't fill. In all these cases and many more, it felt like something unhealthy was going on.

I realized that all too often, what was going on was not sex. Sure, it looked like sex, felt like sex, required a shower and breath mint like sex, but it was really about something else that was just playing out as sex.

For me, the big factor in my own sexual behavior was internalized homophobia. Being gay I still struggle with feelings of not being masculine enough, that I am not worthy of manhood, blah blah blah. Back then I compensated for it by dominating butch-looking men in sexual arenas like bathhouses and sex clubs, but I never got anything out of it that lasted longer than a rash. Since in my messed-up mind gays weren't real men and my conquests were only among gay men, I couldn't win. Still I kept returning in a cycle sicker than Tina Turner going back to Ike. Eventually even Tina got a clue, gained some self-respect, and went elsewhere for strokes, fulfillment, and whatever else pop divas need. If I had respected myself enough, I wouldn't have needed that sex club masculinity "fix." Unfortunately, this crippling baggage is too often the thing I see roaming the hallways in towels and hanging from slings. If issues of masculinity, attractiveness, power, child abuse, insecurity, lack of love, and other forms of low self-esteem are what's pushing people to this kind of sex, did I really want to get in bed with that?

I also had to figure that if I'm having sex with men who are going to these places to act out their own behaviors born of low self-esteem, that means I am taking advantage of their weakness, which makes me a sexual predator. Yuck. And if I allow someone to do to me what they need because they're at the mercy of their old unresolved issues, I'm allowing them to prey on me. This is just all-around icky. Just thinking about it has me looking around desperately for a moist towelette.

Another thing I see all the time is drugs and barebacking. Personal expression, or yet another choice made out of either simplistic defiance or just garden-variety sucky self-esteem? Any shrink or 12-step program will tell you that people who feel good about themselves do not engage in potentially self-destructive behavior. Wake up and smell the poppers, people.

Now, I'm not saying bathhouses or sex clubs are evil or infested with sin or some other such nonsense—although, when they are, it's usually a much better evening. And I'm not telling you to stop going. God knows there are times when a body just needs some good old-fashioned tension-releasing man sex. And who doesn't love that? I do, however, think we should be aware of all that's going on behind that security door we're getting buzzed through.

And just in case I haven't pissed everybody off yet, I want to say a word to those out cruising tearooms and public parks. At least in a designated space like a bathhouse, sex club, or private party, you're not likely to get arrested. Having a cop slap handcuffs on you is a great fantasy, but when it happens outside the men's room it's a real wood kill. There are a lot of nice, attractive, respectable homos out there who literally got caught with their pants down. Every one of them thought, "It won't happen to me." Two words: George Michael.

OK, fine, let's say you don't get caught by the pigs in the park, does the term *fag basher* mean anything to you? 'Cuz they're out there. If you want to fuck up your life, go invest your 401(k) in a pyramid scheme, date Tommy Lee, marry British royalty, but don't do this. And if you already are doing it, take the trouble to find out why so you can get some control over your life. Chances are, whatever is causing you to loiter in the loo is screwing up other areas of your life as well.

On top of that, masturbating in the men's room or balling in the bushes doesn't reflect too well on the rest of us either, so take some responsibility. Plus it gives those religious right assholes more ammunition. Remember, self-destructive behavior is a result of having had all their hate and homophobia heaped on us, which we are still internalizing. Don't help them. And fuck how it reflects on us, just get some help for yourself. Down deep, probably not even all that deep, you're a terrific person. Really. Hey, you bought this book, you've already got my stamp of approval.

About now a lot of men are ready to scream, "Who the hell does this asshole think he is to tell me what I can and can't do with my dick?" Trust me, I want you and your dick to have lots of sex. I want your dick to have more sex than the guys in the Colt Video catalog. I want your dick spurting like Old Faithful and at least as often. The only thing I'm asking you to do with your dick is have sex with it that's healthy. That way you'll enjoy your dick more, plus you'll get to stick around to keep enjoying it longer. I want you alive because (a) if you're dead, that kills any chance I'd have of fucking you; (b) most gay rights are won by the living; and (c) dead people don't order nearly enough gift copies of my books for their families and friends. Call me wacky, but I think nothing's as attractive as a man who's got his shit together.

So I'm not telling you, "Don't have sex." I'm saying maybe it's time to try some sex that's not tangled up in negative crap. Wouldn't you like to have a guy go down on you simply because it was hot and not because you needed to prove to yourself you were manly, attractive, or worthy? Wouldn't you like to get ass fucked because it felt great—period—and not because you were acting out some dark abuse issue or other? That's all I'm saying. I want you to have sex out the wazoo. Or in the wazoo, if that's what you like.

That bears repeating. I want you to have sex. But I want you to have sex that gets you off free and clear of anything but a good time. I want you to have sex that won't get you arrested, fer cryin' out loud. And finally, I want you to have sex that won't get you dead. These books don't sell themselves, you know. I need all the readers I can get.

Qu'est-ce Que C'est Gay?

A while back I was assigned to write a magazine article on gay holiday gifts. My first reaction was, *Gay holiday? What's a gay holiday? Halloween? The Oscars? Sean Hayes's birthday?* I was told they meant holiday gifts *for* gays. Then my question became, *What makes a gift gay?* Other than wrapping it in rustic hand-made paper topped with dried statice and cinnamon sticks woven together with antique gingham and Belgian lace, I had no idea. It was like being told to go to the grocery and pick out the gay canned goods. This same general question, more or less, has come up in several conversations I've had lately. What exactly is "gay"? Is it changing? And am I going to need a new outfit for it?

I concluded "gay" is whatever the hell I decide it is. Why should it be limited to what I do in bed? Hell, thanks to late-night HBO shows like *Sex Bytes* and *Real Sex*, what we do in bed is becoming more and more unremarkable. Indeed, a gay couple I know has confirmed to me that their sex is totally unremarkable. I suggested they needed better toys and more attention to detail. But my point is that "gay" is evolving into something that has little to do with sexuality. It is about sensitivity and awareness, having an open mind and an outsider's perspective. It helps if you have beads and Disney figurines, but they're not essential. What you do need is joy and a healthy disrespect for convention.

It's important to note that being homosexual does not necessarily make you gay. The man in leather chaps, tit clamps, and harness who ridicules the drag queen is not gay, merely confused about what constitutes drag. The gym bunny who sneers at my friend Patty because she's a lesbian is not gay either. He's stupid. Not just because we are all brothers and sisters, but because Patty could beat the crap out of him any day of the week. The fact that she doesn't do that is very gay, because gay is about not only allowing yourself to be free but creating that space for others.

I don't care how many same-sex genitals you've bumped, if you hear an antigay "joke" and say nothing, that's not being gay. That's just being a victim, which, in case you didn't hear, went out with puff-paint T-shirts. Incidentally, if you're heterosexual and said nothing about that fag joke, it didn't make you straight. It only made you a coward and we're all embarrassed for you.

So what is and isn't gay? The AT&T booth at the pride festival is not gay. They're not there for us, just our money. They're like blowing a straight man; do not expect reciprocation. The movie *101 Dalmatians* is not particularly gay. I mean, it's a straight couple and their dogs, for God's sake. But Cruella De Vil is emphatically gay. She lives out loud, can't be "cured," doesn't give a damn what other people think, and truly knows where to shop. (And yes, I have the figurine.) Doing crystal meth is not gay. It's cliché. The fundamentalists who come to our parades to harangue us are now such an institution of those parades that the fundies themselves have become this new definition of gay. Feel free to tell them that. Watch them just shit.

Can a place be gay? The gay ghettos certainly are. After a certain saturation point, even the remaining straight people start quoting Martha and dressing better. It's hard to argue with the gayness of a Home Depot on Saturday mornings or Bloomingdale's any day with a vowel in it, but what about someplace neutral, such as the post office? I say if you're gay and you're there, that's enough to make wherever you are gay. All it takes is one gay man or lesbian to change everything. After all, drop one nugget into a bucket of sand and you've changed that sand into gold ore. And we're not even trying. It's like shuddering when we see stirrup pants or jelly shoes; it just happens. We can't help it.

Gay is like MasterCard: It's everywhere you want to be. You have that power. So go forth and make the world gay. Walk into Kmart and spread your fairy dust. God knows they need it. And please start with the Jaclyn Smith collection.

To sum up, gay is not just connected to how we have sex. It's how we react, how we offer a fresh viewpoint, and how we give others permission to be different. And that's why I tell you gay is whatever you say it is. It's surviving and thriving. It is making a thing of beauty—a flower arrangement, a barn, a life—in the teeth of oppression. It is flying in the face of conformity to live your truth, regardless of whether you have sex with men, women, army boots, or, like me, Häagen-Dazs. It's also way fun watching the looks on other people's faces when we do this. And when the moralistic prudes sniff and say, "Yes, but what *do* you have sex with?" answer, "Wild abandon." That pisses them off. Check out their spouses and you'll understand why.

Gay is playful and youthful in its refusal to become dull, stodgy, and boring. It is the sparkle you carry and the magical kingdom you bring with you. Golly, it actually *is* beads and Disney figurines. Who knew?

And for those of you wondering if any of this makes me gay, you already know I own the figurine. As for the beads, well, I have both natural pearl and anal. You take it from there.

Part Seven:
Bitch, Bitch,
Bitch

Starting Out With That Fresh Feeling

When times of new beginnings come around—whether a new year, a new birthday, another new look from Madonna—it's important to start fresh, which means you gotta take out the garbage. You know, all that old stuff still rattling around in your tiny brain. My brain being especially puny, it's vital I make room by cleaning house. So with this being the start of a new chapter, here goes.

The first thing I need to get off my chest is that there's too much news. Not too much happening, but too much being reported all at the same time. On CNN there's an anchorperson scrunched into a corner telling me one news story, a graphic on the side with additional info, a stock market ticker at the bottom, another "crawl" of a completely different story under that, weather around the country on the next line below that to the right, airport delays on the left, and an animated logo just to keep your eyes twitching. I'm overloaded with information and have no idea what's happening anywhere. I come away with nothing but frustration and a tic worthy of Herbert Lom.

That's not true. I do retain some information, but it's always the least meaningful story. I was watching something about, oh, a war somewhere with terrorists, I think, and I notice the crawl at the bottom of the screen telling me, "Penélope Cruz says her acting depends on her shoes." Her *shoes*? We all knew it wasn't talent, but does this qualify as news? And later, erroneously assuming I care, the crawl announces that Penélope has moved in with Tom Cruise. Is it possible to block this kind of information? When did headlines turn into spam?

I also think we need to stop whining about straight people coming to "our" events. I am so sick of hearing, "The heteros are taking over Halloween in West Hollywood." In case you haven't been paying attention, we've spent the last few decades trying to get straight people to accept us in our unapologetic diversity. The fact that they now feel comfortable enough with us not only to show up themselves but to bring their kids down to the Boulevard—in strollers, no less—is huge progress! And can you imagine the influence that kind of intensely focused outrageous imagination is having on those kids? If I had seen Halloween or, even better, pride from a stroller, I would have come out while still in diapers. Our displays give early and massive permission for infinite possibility to these toddlers and they are going to be light-years ahead of us at their age. In 15 years you can ask one who his first crush was and he'll say, "Joey Hopkins at Gymboree. He was so hot in his Scooby-Doo pull-ups." So be glad straight people are coming to the WeHo Halloween frolic and frenzy. They're the smarter ones anyway. They're not taking over, they're taking notes. Which is as it should be.

I've had it with the people who abuse the rest of us with their cell phones. I know I'm beginning to sound like a queer Andy Rooney (and I truly apologize if that gave you a visual), but I can't go to a movie or play or any other function without having it interrupted by some moron's phone playing the first 7½ notes of some tune they want you to know they saw on Broadway. And it's played over and over and over because the idiot can't fish it out of his Esprit backpack due to a lack of both functioning cortex and opposable thumbs.

Starting Out With That Fresh Feeling

At the beginning of all plays and most movies, there's a request that people turn off their phones, pagers, and all other things that go beep in the night. It's a waste of breath since it's ignored, probably because they were yakking to someone while the presentation was starting. If you're that grossly inconsiderate, ushers should be allowed to take your phone and crush it with a 20-pound mallet—preferably against your head. You should then have a spotlight trained on you so the rest of us will know at whom to direct our contempt, popcorn, and airborne sodas. For people like this it's time to bring back Hawthorne's scarlet letter, only the A doesn't stand for a kind of sin but a kind of hole.

This Sunday I was in church when a cell phone went off during the sermon. The guy took the call! I'm sorry, but if you are in a house of worship and it is more important that you talk to someone other than God, you need to reexamine why you bothered to put on a clean shirt Sunday morning.

And if you are dining with me and your cell phone goes off, I am going to continue talking. You're gonna have to choose to whom you wish to speak. If it's somebody else, why the hell should I stick around? My favorites are those people who apologize profusely for getting a call but take it anyway. "Oops, I'm really, *really* sorry, just let me get this call." Ram it up your redial. They are about as repentant as Barbra Streisand is for bitching at Jon Peters for her hair in *A Star Is Born*—and that was just last week. In classic abuse fashion, these phone phucks are just setting you up for the next time. Cell phones are the most passive-aggressive thing since E-mail. Don't put up with it. If you went out to dinner with a guy who spent half the time talking to the guy at the next table, he'd be history. So why tolerate it when he's talking to a guy across town? Check, please.

Going back to kids in strollers, I'd like someone to tell me if I'm going to hell over my fetish for young fathers. There is no hotter accessory a man can have than a little kid, as long as it's quiet or adorably unconscious. It's a total sex thing, I know. With other men you assume they have sex, but when a guy has a child with him, well, there's drooling proof he got hard and shot his potent wad. And my behavior is only getting worse. I used to be trusted to lust from afar. Now if I see a man alone with his kid, I go over to him and compliment his little DNA sample. I squat down to say hi to the little tyke but, more important, to get eye level with Daddy's dick, mere inches away. If I'm lucky, I can get the proud papa to bend over to shake a rattle or something and I can look down his shirt at his chest.

Hmm. Another thing I need to work on is giving out just too much information. Oh, well, at least the brain is now rid of that other stuff and ready to take in all new disturbing things. I feel so…so fresh! And if you really want to keep straight men from bringing their kids down to Halloween on the Boulevard in strollers, just let 'em read the previous paragraph!

Why He Never Called Back

I was sitting with my friend Casey at an extended brunch where he, on his fifth mimosa, was beginning to get a little weepy. "Why?" he cried aloud. "Why is it that every time I give my number to a man, he never calls?" It's only April and this is the sixth meal this year I've endured with him boo-hooing over his Cook's sparkling wine and frozen from concentrate orange juice. Ever the optimist, once his number is given out he refuses to turn off his cell phone, even at the ballet, once even during his performance review, another time even during his stepmother's funeral. After days of obsessing, he would call me to sift through the pathetic rubble of the relationship that never was, trying to understand why, why, dear God, why?

As much as I love Casey, I've had it with the whining, the gloomy brunches, and especially the nasty cheap-ass Cook's. So for Casey and all of you out there like him, I'm going to tell you in classic easy-to-grasp outline form all the reasons why your man never called you back. Maybe then I'll finally get to enjoy a decent brunch. The reasons fall basically into two main categories.

CATEGORY 1: IT'S HIM

A. He's a commitmentphobe. He liked you, but he panicked. He does this every time he goes out, but this is a guy who couldn't commit to a magazine subscription. Little wonder he wasn't going to call you.

B. He sobered up. I mean, who wouldn't look good when the other person's on Jose Cuervo and crystal? And after a while, the highest high wears off—a fact you should have taken into account before E-mailing him your photo the next day. Oh, well, at least you have his E-mail address. Now you can sign his judgmental ass up for all kinds of porn spam at work.

C. He has validation needs. He just got you to drool over him because he pathetically needed that in order to feel good about himself for that moment. Lucky you know real validation comes from within, huh? Right. Hold on to that thought while you have another bowl or three of Breyers.

D. He has a fear of dating. He's so terrified of meeting new people that it took four sour-apple martinis for him to get up the balls to ask you for your number. Now that he's sober he can't remember what he did with it. But did you really want to go out with someone who needs bottled courage to hang with you? That's not dating, that's enabling. And if you simply must be around drunk people, well, that's what holidays and weddings are for.

E. Bad timing. It was too soon after the breakup with his ex. Ending his eight-year relationship earlier in the day made his frightened decision to cruise you that evening a poor choice. By the time he got home from the bar and saw his ex's photo in the "I ♥ You" frame from Sea World, he broke down and called his shuggie-woogums at the Motel 6 in floods of tears. All was forgiven and you were forgotten.

F. He's already got a boyfriend. If so, you don't need to get mixed up in that. If he's pulling this crap with his current boyfriend, why wouldn't he do the same thing to you once you became his new boy toy? OK, fine, you're so desperate you don't care. Then maybe he was just using you to make his lover, who was at the other end of the bar, jealous. God, being used is so depressing. There's gotta be a better explanation. All right, then, maybe he was just toying with you in order to feel powerful himself and you haven't heard from him because he never intended to call you in the first place. Ugh, that's even worse. Ooh, ooh, I know! Maybe his boyfriend caught him with your phone number and, in a fit of rabid jealous rage, murdered him in an operatically gruesome way! Yeah! Really consider going with this excuse; it's nice and empowering in a delusional sort of way.

CATEGORY 2: IT'S YOU

A. You moved too fast. If it's the first date, you might want to rethink mentioning all the romantic B&Bs in Vermont near tuxedo rental shops until *after* you've had dessert. Also, showing up with a suitcase for your second date may not have been the best idea. I mean, what are you, a lesbian? And having your mail forwarded to his place after that elaborate 36-hour anniversary party also could have been a little misstep.

B. You were too pushy. Telling him he should dump his crummy friends could be considered rude, especially if they are present at the time. Telling him he needs better shoes and this year's pants could be misconstrued as demeaning. And telling him there was nothing wrong with him a little collagen and Botox couldn't fix might have given him pause.

C. You were too needy. Hinting for lavish sprays of red roses in your "I love you" notes the next morning is pushing it. Calling every 15 minutes on the quarter hour gets rather old around 2:45 A.M. And pumping his mother, father, siblings, boss, and priest for information before the second date wears awfully thin.

D. You're too high-maintenance. "But how could he tell that?" you wail in your Hermès sweater, putting a manicured hand (with polish) to your cunningly plucked brow. Well, when you excuse yourself more than twice during a meal because you're "feeling shiny," darling, you're tipping your hand. You love to hear him talk, but only if it's about you. In fact everything has to be about you.

Well, get over it! The sun does *not* shine out of your ass. Although God knows your ass is big enough it could.

E. You gave him the wrong number. Like rattling off the one that started with 555 out of habit. Honestly, one little case of stalking and you put up walls all over the place.

F. Too much information. Did he really need to know about what your stepfather did with you after lights out when you were 10? Did you have to tell him you could take eight billiard balls? And did he have to know about the webbed toes? All on that first meeting in the elevator?

G. You're not his type. It was bear night at Big Al's and you had just shaved your swimmer's chest to show up in chinos and powder-blue puffy shirt from International Male. Get a clue. Or maybe it was the leather harness and jockstrap you wore to that bar where S/M stands for "sweaters and mascara." Do your grief work and move on. Preferably to a more appropriate hunting ground.

These are the kinds of things that keep men from calling. Given the damage walking around in our community, the miracle is that anybody gets called back at all. I hope this puts to rest a great portion of the whining and self-pity we have to listen to and allows the rest of us to get on with conversations worth having, like if Britney is the new Madonna, does that mean we're going to have to suffer another puerile 20-pound metal-bound coffee-table book?

But I know Casey's fragile ego, so when I can't stand his blubbering any more, the reason I always give him as to why they never called back is this: The poor guy recognized the reality that you were just too damn good for him. Yeah. That's it. Really. What else could it possibly be? You are, after all, you. Golly, doesn't that make it so much easier to let go? Good. What a silly thing to have worried about. Now let's go home and see what's on *Judge Judy.*

The Young and the Restless

When it comes to today's youth, I'm reaching the point where it's just too hard trying to keep up. I'm sorry, but my mind is full. For instance, I have decided I will make no further attempt to learn any actor born after the bicentennial with more than two names. I don't go to movies starring these people, so what's the point? When I meet them at Hollywood parties, my spouse, Fred, will come over and tell me I was just talking with Tiffany Amber Pinkett Smith or something. I say, "Oh," and ask if he knows her from his office. He tells me no, she was just in that smash-hit comedy where they screw pastry and run from killers in hockey masks. I say, "That's nice. Stay away from the rumaki."

One of my editors, Ben, is 22 years old. If I'd had a son when I was 21, he'd be that age now. Ben is gay, and being that young, he pisses me off like you wouldn't believe. He's against marriage, same-sex or otherwise; doesn't know from Harvey Milk; and, most unforgivably, doesn't laugh at my gay references. It's hard for me to realize that when *Dynasty* was filling the airwaves, he was filling diapers. It's even harder making a David Hodo joke to a brat whose only exposure to the Village People is at straight weddings. How can I communicate with that?

Fortunately, my other gig, in radio production, keeps me up on the latest pop and rock music. It's my job to know that "Voodoo" is a song by Godsmack and not the other way around. I get paid to know the (purported) differences between Backstreet Boys and 'N Sync, which in reality is like a taste test between Evian and Arrowhead water, only not as substantial. Nevertheless, it gives me a means of conversing with anyone born since the *last* time pukka shells were worn in public. Ben seems forever impressed someone my age would still have his hearing, let alone use it to listen to Sevendust. He assumes I eat bran and go to bed at 9:30. OK, I do, but it infuriates me that he assumes it.

I have to remember that he's the future and pissing me off is in his genes. But that's good. If kids aren't upsetting their elders, they're not doing their job. It's not only normal to piss old farts like me off, it's vitally important. You young people developed your worldview at a different time, so your ideas are going to be different. If they weren't, who'd need you? I just ask you to be kind to your tribal elders as you come into your own. And that you at least fake laughter at my *Mommie Dearest* quotes.

Don't expect us to give over to you easily, though. After all, we fought damn hard to get into power. Once there, we found out our ideas didn't work any better than our parents' ideas. Well, maybe a few of 'em turned out better. Like that one about replacing Connie Francis with the Rolling Stones. That turned out OK. We also traded the Carpenters for Pansy Division, which was definitely a step in the right direction. Then again, that whole "Let's Go Metric" thing during the Carter years didn't catch on at all. Unless, of course, you deal drugs. Oh, well, we tried. Good luck with the wacky stuff you come up with.

This coming-on-the-scene-with-new-ideas thing is only natural and has been going on forever. I'm certain the Cro-Magnons bitched at their hairy offspring. "What the hell is your problem, Urgh? A simple cave was good enough for your mother and me but not for you, oh no! You and your friends Grogh and Umph have to paint *bison* on the wall. What the hell is *that* about?" See? You were the first interior decorators. (What, you think straight people came up with wall art? Wallpaper, yes, but wall art, no.) I'm sure the argument carried over into other duties as well. Can't you just hear young Urgh going, "A mastodon hunt? Dad, that is like *so* Neanderthal. Tell you what, me, Grogh and Umph are gonna stay here and mash berries for the cave. When you get back you're gonna love it."

The kicker is that you know Urgh's exasperated parents caught hell from their parents too. "What's with this standing upright? Why can't you walk on your knuckles like everyone else?" Today, we know that clever walking-erect idea was a great leap forward in evolution. Mainly because it allowed for much easier cruising.

So I guess there's no escaping the fact that you younger folks are here to stay. You're out for the most part, and as much as it chafes my leather chaps to admit, you're fabulous. You haven't had to put up with as much of the abusive crap we did, so you're not screwed up like we were. Instead, you've found your own totally new ways of being screwed up. And you're doing a terrific job of it. Really. You are. In fact, I want to offer you three tips:

1. Never accept being told, "We tried that; it didn't work." Maybe it wasn't the right time when it was tried before. I have a friend who tried to launch a service in the mid '70s that would send paper copies via phone wires. Every time he pitched it, he was laughed out of the room. It didn't help that he called it Telephonic Universal Reconstructive Display, or TURD. Ten years later, though, someone younger pitched it as FAX and retired at 29. Bastard.

2. Do not listen when people say, "That's a stupid idea" (unless your idea has the acronym TURD). It may turn out to be stupid, but the world will never know unless you have the guts to try it. Clothing ads showing only naked people sounds like a stupid idea, but go tell that to Calvin Klein.

3. Take it with a grain of salt when you hear, "You'll understand when you're my age." Translated, that often means, "You threaten me, and I'm going to shut you up by saying this." Sometimes though, we say it because it's true. Some things can't be explained,

only experienced. Like 10 years into a relationship discovering infidelity and still staying together. Like gaining wisdom and perspective along with inches and pounds. And, a personal favorite, like looking a decade from now at embarrassing photos of yourself in today's trendiest clothes. "Cargo pants! What were we thinking? Who decided knees needed pockets?"

I'd also advise you to be kind to us older people. If you are lucky, you'll get to be one—and sooner than you think. It'll happen when people in stores start calling you sir or ma'am. You'll have the most wonderful look of shock on your face. And we will laugh and laugh and laugh at you. Just like our parents laughed at us.

Now get the hell off my lawn, you damn punks!

Hot and Bothered

Maybe it's the heat that's been making me irritable lately. Fred would probably say it was age. I'd thwack him on the head for that, but it's just too hot. So I sit in my torpor and underwear beneath the ceiling fan. I'm annoyed that it has only "low," "medium," and "high" speeds when what I want is "B-29 propeller." I'm so irritable that I've started a list of things that annoy me.

I read that aspartame can affect your memory. Of course I can't remember where I read that. But they finally come out with an artificial sweetener that actually tastes sweet, they put it in every diet soda in the world to the cheers of the world's overweight masses, and the damn thing can make you forget? I wouldn't be so irritated about this if it would make me forget I was fat. Or, even better, make other people forget the fact. And what was I talking about?

Oh, yeah, things that aggravate me. This moron in my office went to a psychic during lunch. "She was amazing;" he enthused. "She told me my past, present, and future for only $50!" Big deal. I wanted to tell him I could read his past, present, and future for free. "In the past you desperately needed to go to a dermatologist but didn't, you've never so much as looked at a fashion magazine in your life, and whatever you paid for that tie was too much. As for the present, you don't separate your whites from your colors, Head & Shoulders shampoo is not in your shower, and your best friend would be a breath mint. In the very near future you're going to be spending a lot of money at the dentist, at the rate you're going you'll be buying a bigger belt inside of a month, and you will never get a girlfriend with those shoes." But I didn't say that because the poor man has a brain the size of a goat pellet. And he's my boss.

Psychics exist to give stupid people a place to go other than Tom Green movies. If psychics really had the power to pick winning lottery numbers, they'd be living in mansions, people, not in the back of some hole-in-the-wall with sputtering neon. Besides, anyone who really knew the future would have bought IBM at $10 in 1978.

The other day at the grocery, I got annoyed at scented deodorants. How the hell am I supposed to know what "cool active" or "power zone" smells like? A gym? I saw two side-by-side announcing their scents as "arctic peak" and "glacier." Sounds to me they would smell in the neighborhood of "polar bear." There are a lot of scents with "fresh" in them, like "powder fresh" and "active fresh." I saw one deodorant advertising a "fresh blast" scent. Remembering that "fresh" merely means "recent" or "new," I decided I could conjure up one hell of a fresh blast myself—just give me a bean burrito and Circus Peanuts. One deodorant claimed an "aqua sport" scent, which I can only imagine as sweat with chlorine. There were two others touting "sport scent" and "musk," both of which sound like the very stink I'm trying to hide. Fuck 'em. I purchased "unscented."

I love the fact that makers of rice cakes have finally admitted their product tastes like foam core. You know they have because now they offer rice cakes in flavors like caramel, barbecue, sour cream and onion, cheddar (both traditional and white), banana nut, and apple cinnamon. All it took was coating them in massive doses of salt, sugar, and spooky chemicals that combine only in zero gravity. Then, through the power of suggestion, we can believe they really are sorta kinda banana nutty-ish-oid-esque. The irritating thing is, they managed to turn the fact that plain rice cakes taste like puffed cardboard into a marketing opportunity and get even richer. And that I bought so many.

The number 1 thing on my list of petty, irritating things, though, is Word for freaking Windows. For instance, if the "normal setting" under View is indeed the norm, why does it give me other unbidden presentations of my document? And doesn't that by definition make them *ab*normal?

It pisses me off that I can use "select all" to set all my margins and tabs, but when I start typing it gives me whatever the hell it feels like. Damn it, I used "select all." What part of "all" does Bill Gates not get?

And I really, really hate that goofy-assed animated paper clip that comes down whenever I'm trying to type a note to someone. "It looks like you're writing a letter. Would you like help?" Gee, yes, because somehow I got this far in life *without ever writing a letter!* And I'm so happy that my epistolary savior has appeared to me, lo, in the form of a fucking paper clip. You wanna help? Type this: Dear Mr. Gates: Crawl up my hairy ass and fight for air!

Bitch, bitch, bitch. Now I see I've managed to become as petulant and irritating as the things I'm whining about. Clearly God put my mouth at one end and my dick at the other so I could literally piss and moan at the same time. Ugh, it's still hot and I can't even stand myself. I need a drink to help me forget.

Bartender, get me a Diet Coke.

We-a Culpa

Goodness gracious me, Cardinal Mahony made an apology! The pope made an apology! Even Dr. Laura apologized! OK, so that one lasted five minutes, but she still did it. (Bet that'll be the last time her people let her get into the Manischewitz.) Clearly, though, this is the season for saying "oops" to those on whom they've been shitting for millennia. Since I can't resist a trend, it is in this warm and loving spirit of his Holiness, his Eminence, and Mrs. Schlessinger that I offer our own mea culpa to the straight world on behalf of gays everywhere.

We are sorry for recruiting your children. It didn't work. For some reason a life of being reviled, fourth-class citizenship, the threat of physical violence and death, the possible abandonment by our birth family, and the likelihood of losing employment, housing, our own children, and our seat at the Wednesday night bingo games was a hard sell. Go figure. Maybe we should have mentioned the free condoms at pride events or talked up the tea dances, but it's too late now. Besides, it turned out we didn't need to do anything at all. *They* came to *us*. Funny, huh? So we're all really sorry for upsetting you needlessly and for time wasted. You may now stop shrieking that gays recruit kids, because we've all moved on to something less controversial. Adopting them.

We are sorry for the two or three gay serial killers who steal the media glory from the hundreds and hundreds of straight serial killers. When 99.9% of the serial murders in this country get upstaged by a few rabid homos, it must really bring up resentment issues among your "normal straight" killer populations. We apologize for that. And we're really sorry our couple of loonies upset people so. We recognize that your worst nightmare is a faggot with a gun—as it should be—so perhaps that's why we got all that coverage. But we can't help it. They may have been homicidal maniacs, but they were gay homicidal maniacs, so they naturally had more flair. You need to tell your multiple murderers to use a bit more imagination. Numbers are newsworthy, but only on a local level. For global headlines you need to blow away internationally known fashion designers, dress like a clown, or actually eat your victims. Watch the news and learn.

We apologize to all straight single women who lament that "All the good ones are either married or gay." I should point out, though, that there are plenty of us who are kept satisfied by those who are married *and* gay.

We are sorry for not letting disco die. That, however, is not entirely our fault. All we ask of the recording industry is a few good dance tunes, and when the only alternative they offer is fucking Kid Rock, there's nothing else to do but keep the Donna Summer handy. I mean, even Madonna has gone off into this electronica thing. Or worse. Somebody should apologize to *us* for that cover of "American Pie." So we try to compensate by laying dance rhythms over diva ballads but it doesn't fool anybody. Nothing clears a dance floor like a Barbra/Celine circle jerk with a backbeat. All we can do is get a Marc Anthony or Pet Shop Boy up on stage and hope for the best. If it weren't for Ricky Martin, we'd be doing the fox trot by now. And for you straight folks who like Ricky Martin, on behalf of the homosexual community, you're welcome.

We apologize for keeping Martha Stewart afloat. By and large we don't have children, so we have the time and resources to actually do some of her projects. If you have 2.6 kids like you're supposed to, you're too busy trying to keep them alive till bedtime to give a rat's ass about antique brocade. We not only care deeply about antique brocade, we are the only people in the whole damn world you can buy it from. When Martha whips up a delicious *perdrix aux épinards,* we take notes. You missed a key ingredient while you were force-feeding your .6 child her Ritalin, so if you want this dish at your next soiree, you have to have us cater it and it's gonna cost you. Martha tells you what's possible and makes it look incredibly easy, never mind that it's collecting glacier water from Base Camp 2 on Everest for the perfect hollandaise. You see the fabulous stuff she does and you can't live without it. Neither can you re-create it. So you get on the horn to us. It's how we get back for all those years growing up when you wouldn't let us play Mystery Date. Now our date is Martha. And it's a good thing.

We apologize for making the mainstream religions so uncomfortable. We had no idea that all-inclusive love didn't include us. We feel so silly. Tell us, what part of "all" are we not getting? It's gotta be tough, though, belonging to an organization that says you have to love someone you don't understand. That or kill them. And when you do that, there's all that "thou shalt not kill" stuff to deal with. Ouch! Better to teach hate on Sundays in the name of love and let others do the dirty work. That makes it easier to deny responsibility for what happens when you preach that it's OK to treat us like less than humans. What terrible, terrible stress we must put on you. Words fail at expressing the amount of sympathy we have for you on this.

We're sorry for constantly saying that everyone is gay. Ya see, my generation wasn't allowed to know about any gays whatsoever while growing up, so now we have a tendency to overcompensate. That's why you'll hear us outrageously proclaiming that everyone from Stephen Hawking to Hillary Rodham Somethingorother is gay. We need famous people to claim as our own so we can feel a part of society. Along the same lines, we also apologize for playing head games like this: Backstreet Boys has five guys and 'N Sync has five for a total of 10, so if one in 10 is gay, who's the fag? (And two of the Backstreet Boys have fiancées, so it's probably not them, although when we heard Brian and Kevin were engaged we assumed it was to each other.) We don't mean for our minds to go off into this same-sex fog, but when you start telling us about the funny thing Bobby Junior did yesterday at Pop Warner football, it's either that or open a frickin' vein. And it isn't going to be one of ours.

We apologize for the return of bell-bottoms a couple of years ago, and we're sorry for those new "digger" pants DKNY was pushing that looked like capri pants for men. Some queen must have been very angry that day. We're sorry for that terrible NBC show a while back with Nathan Lane. They made our dear Nathan a straight opera queen, what were they thinking? We apologize for all those Rupert Everett movies. He's good, but even we are getting tired of him. He's turning into the gay Janeane Garofalo. Somebody should tell him he's allowed to say no to a project. And finally, we apologize for making everything pastels one year and earth tones the next. We get bored.

For all of this we are sorry, sorry, sorry. I hope it is understood that this spasm of contrition is meant with all the sincerity of the more famous apologies that recently made the news. May this wipe the slate clean so we can begin anew, all cuddly, happy, warm, and fuzzy.

If not, get the fuck over it.

Part Eight:
Telling
Tales

Let Me Call You, Sweetheart

I recently attended a memorable same-sex wedding, not in gaily liberal Vermont, but in conservative Wilmington, N.C. Still, I'll bet Vermont never saw a show like this.

The two men getting married were Pat Cobb, the best caterer in town, and Colin Cumbee, whose father had gone to glory when Colin was just a baby. His mother, though, was still very much alive in Johnson City, Tenn., where she terrorized the assisted-living home she was in. Mercifully, she was confined to her bed. She had suffered a stroke when she walked in on Colin and the strapping son of her maid at a point when neither was able to stop what they were doing. In the hospital, Colin convinced her that the two of them had just been turning the mattress. He didn't bother to tell her that they had been "turning the mattress" since they were both 16. But never underestimate the power of denial, because that cock-and-bull story—no pun intended—reassured her mightily. Colin is, after all, the only one to carry on the Cumbee name. I was sure he'd told her by this time, though, what with the wedding and all. Still, thank God for being far away and bedfast.

Pat's rise to catering stardom began four years ago when his company was hired for a reception at the Country Club. Colin not only managed the Country Club, he also managed to find himself alone in a catering truck with Patrick, who proved to have skills far beyond those found at an ordinary cash bar. They bought a sprawling love nest together, and it quickly became known that if you wanted Colin to give you preferential treatment at the Country Club, you hired Pat to cater your party. It was purest queer pro quo.

The day before the wedding, I came by to drop off my gift, an antique crystal decanter I had liberated from the back of my parents' closet on my last visit. I was met at the door by a handsome young man with deliberate black roots under yellow hair the color of Easter Peeps. "Well, hey, Andrew," I said. "Are Colin or Pat home?"

"Hey," Andrew said back in the Southern manner. "Pat's out, but Colin's here. If that's a wedding gift, I flat hate you. Come on in." Andrew was Colin and Pat's best friend, who worked in a salon out at the beach, and they affectionately referred to him as a hair burner. Unhappily, Andrew never had any money because, well, he burned clients' hair. He led me into the living room which was filled impressively with still-wrapped wedding gifts. "Throw yours on the heap, " he said sadly. "All I can afford is to do Colin's hair." I hoped it wasn't a perm.

Fortunately, Colin's gift was merely a trim. I found him seated regally in a chair in the middle of the kitchen, sipping bourbon from under a pink stylist's cape waiting for Andrew to return. To cheer him up, Colin coaxed him into telling me about his new boyfriend. His name was Beau and he worked for the phone company, which in Wilmington is called—what else?—Southern Bell. "I never thought I'd be into uniforms," Andrew enthused, "until he showed up one day in his hunky phone man outfit and, well, honey, my rates weren't the only thing that went down."

Conversation turned to the wedding. Colin bragged that he had invited the elite for (a) the gifts they knew they better give unless they wanted to sit next to the kitchen the rest of their Country Club careers; and (b) to rub their noses in the fact that Wilmington's service economy was run by homos claiming marriage, so get used to it.

In the South, vengeance is as good a reason as any to get married. At least their family and gay friends had been invited for the joy of the occasion.

"Will any of your family be there?" I asked.

"No. Sadly, Mother can't travel," said Colin refreshing his drink. "Pat's family is coming up from Georgia, though. They all went in together to give us a cruise."

"I wish I could do something great like that for y'all," murmured Andrew, shaving Colin's neck, "something memorable, something really special."

"You already are special, Andrew," said Colin. "It's people like Joel who have to buy their way into other folks' affections. How much did you spend on our gift anyway, Joel?"

I arched my eyebrows. "A gentleman never tells."

"My, my. That little?"

"It's time I left." I said to Andrew. "I do believe the bride is getting her period."

I hugged Colin goodbye, and an excited Andrew saw me to the door. "It just now came to me!" he whispered. "I know the absolute perfect gift. I'm gonna give Beau a call and, oh, just wait'll you see!" I wondered what he had in mind, but as it didn't involve setting gel and heat, I was sure it'd be just fine."

The wedding was the next day at sunset in the Magnolia Room at the riverfront Hilton. The room was filled with old money holding their noses at having to mingle with queers who, during the rest of the year, served at their parties but today, they had to treat as equals who had outdressed them. Andrew and his new beau, Beau, were in the back running the electronics, which included a tape of "Up Where We Belong," "The Wedding Song," and "Having My Baby." I hoped that last one was just to see who was paying attention.

The tape was changed to a stately Elgar march, and Pat and Colin came down the aisle together as equals. The pastor of the Wilmington Metropolitan Community Church took her place in front of them.

"On behalf of Colin and Pat," she said to the assembled crowd of blue-hairs and party boys, "I want to thank you for being here to witness their love in this ceremony. I know Pat's family traveled hundreds of miles to be here. Other family members are unfortunately unable to attend in person. However, I understand the couple's best friend, Andrew, through the telephone expertise of his lover, Beau, has arranged a special speakerphone hookup with Colin's mother in Johnson City, Tenn." Colin gave a start that made people in the front jump. The pastor continued, "Through the gift of technology, Colin's mother, although bedridden, may share in her son's joy." Colin grabbed Pat's arm in an iron grip of panic as the pastor called out, "Are you there, Mrs. Cumbee?"

Crackling from loudspeakers in the room came the gravelly voice of Colin's mother. "Jesus, Mary, and Joseph, the preacher's a woman."

The pastor didn't even flinch. "Can you hear me, Mrs. Cumbee?"

"Go ahead, Miz Cumbee, answer," came a distant nurse's voice.

"You leave me the hell alone," Mrs. Cumbee ordered.

"Let's go ahead and get started," the pastor said. "Colin Ray Cumbee, before God and this community you have pledged your love and your troth to your spouse, who stands before you. Do you promise to honor, attend, support, and above all, love Pat? If so, answer 'I do'. "

Still rigid, Colin managed to make a high-pitched noise, which the pastor took as an affirmative. She turned to Pat. "And you, Patrick Stephen Cobb—

"What?" screeched the loudspeaker.

The pastor repeated it louder for microphone, the better for the happy mother to hear. "And you, Patrick Stephen—"

"Not Patricia? *Patrick*? Oh, my gawd!"

Pat looked at Colin. "You didn't tell her?"

"My gawd! My gawd! My son's marrying some faggot fruitcake!" Everyone's openmouthed gaze was riveted on Colin.

"You're upsetting yourself, Miz Cumbee," came the nurse's voice over the speakers. "Calm down!"

"My son's a homo!"

"Calm down, Miz Cumbee."

"Fuck you, bitch!" Breakable objects in Johnson City were being hurled. The nurse was heard shouting urgently for a doctor.

A red-faced Colin whipped around, glaring down the aisle. "Andrew!" he seethed. As one, the entire congregation turned in their seats to see poor Andrew frozen in horror at the sound controls.

"I don't know how it works," he squeaked helplessly, "and Beau went to the bathroom." Then Andrew started to cry.

"Damnation!" roared Pat. The congregation turned back to the front. "Who goes to the bathroom in the middle of a wedding?"

Meanwhile, a doctor had entered Mrs. Cumbee's room and, with the nurse, was apparently wrestling her to the ground. All eyes were on the loudspeakers as shouts, curses, and crashes combined for riveting radio drama.

"Mother, get back in bed!" yelled Colin over the din. "You know you're an invalid!"

More oaths were heard over the phone. "Oh, I'm coming to get you, boy! I'll beat that shit outta you with a belt!"

"Nurse, get a sedative STAT!"

A distraught woman with too much hair spray and not enough Prozac stood up and shouted frantically, "For God's sake, turn it off!"

"Shhh!" went every gay male guest in the room.

The nurse could be heard running back in. "Where is she, doctor?"

"Call security," he answered, "before she hits the lobby or gets to the—" Abruptly it stopped. Beau had returned from the men's room and cut the connection. The guests made an audible sound of disappointment. Andrew could be heard weeping.

"If you don't mind," said the pastor at last, "I think we should start over from the top."

The reception featured pancetta-wrapped scallops with lemon, hunter's style chicken, Jerusalem artichoke gratin, and nobody gave a rat's ass. The entire meal was nothing but an opportunity for an animated play-by-play rehash of the earlier telephone train wreck. The pastor felt Mrs. Cumbee's ambulatory recovery was a wondrous thing—provided she had indeed been stopped by security at the lobby. Andrew and Beau had been forgiven, and the newly joined couple were already on their way to a Caribbean vacation where they had called ahead to request a room with no phone. Some of the wealthier people were miffed that society had changed to the point that their daughters' lavish weddings had been upstaged by a pair of drama queens. Their sons, meanwhile, were being plied with lavish champagne by the gay guests who most conveniently had rooms in the hotel. Some things don't change.

Azalea Festival

Each spring the gardeners of Wilmington, N.C., are justifiably proud of their many camellias, dogwoods, and magnolias, but they go bug-ass, frog shit, fruitcake bonkers for azaleas. Wilmington, known as the Azalea City, celebrates this bush in a weeklong spring arts frenzy called the Azalea Festival, the highlight, indeed the very pinnacle of the Wilmington social season.

For decades, Jenny Jonathan's family had treated her with disdain for marrying a common dirt farmer. Now that her husband Jim had turned the farmland into a highly profitable real estate development, she had money but, living in rural Burgaw, zero social position. The dreams she and her husband shared of mingling with established Southern elite, to say nothing of having the ultimate last laugh on her family, made them ravenous for a place in society. So they left lowly Burgaw, moving 15 miles south to the great sophisticated metropolis of Wilmington, where Jim Jonathan donated an extravagant sum to the Azalea Festival Committee. He made it quite plain that his daughter, Jackie, should be strongly considered for Azalea Queen. As queen she would give the Jonathans entrée to Wilmington society. Parties, dinners, the

Coronation Pageant at Trask Coliseum, and, of course, the ultimate moment: reigning supreme atop the Azalea Queen's float in the televised parade that bumped its way down Third Street on the final day.

Sadly, another girl's father had made an even more generous donation to the Azalea Festival Committee. Jackie was, however, named First Princess in the Azalea Queen's Court, so at least she would be at all the events, just not in the spotlight. Though somewhat disappointed, as far as society and Jenny's snooty family were concerned, it was a major coup. Besides, there was always the chance that something tragic and disfiguring would happen to that damned Azalea Queen.

Jerry adored his twin sister, Jackie, and was thrilled for her. Jerry was thin, unmanly, and effeminate, causing his father to be disgusted and ashamed of him outright. His mother had long ago shifted her constant attention and stifling projections onto her daughter while considering her son yet another disgrace for her to rise above. Jerry escaped to Myrtle Beach, S.C., and the Carolina Opry, where he had risen to the position of wardrobe and makeup manager. He was quite happy there, dreaming of the day he could raise the astronomical sum of $115,000 to buy his own beauty parlor.

The week of the festival, Jackie begged Jerry to come to Wilmington to help her. Jackie hugged and kissed her brother as soon as he arrived, swearing she loved him forever. Then, late that night, she climbed out her window and ran up the drive, where Lud, the youngest Hedgepeth boy, was waiting for her in his battered pickup to drive her far, far away from her parents. Tuesday morning Jerry found the note she had left. There was nothing he could do but show it to his parents.

"Oh, land sakes, Lord have mercy!" keened his mother. "How could she do this? Run off with some tobacco trash from Leland, oh, Lord, Lord!"

Jerry's father was brimming with fury. "So help me, I will hunt down that sumbitch and shoot his hairless little balls off!"

"Damn it, Jim. Will you forget about him? What are we going

to do? I have family coming from Spartanburg and Fayetteville! This weekend! How could she do this to me?"

"You'll have to call 'em up and tell 'em."

"Tell 'em that our Azalea Princess eloped with some no-account swamp rat? Are you out of your cotton pickin' mind!"

"Well, it's the truth."

"The truth is irrelevant!" she screamed at him, then she put a hand to her mouth. "Oh, my Lord, what are we gonna tell the Azalea Committee? The Welcoming Gala is tonight, Jim, what are we gonna say?"

"Mama, let's just tell them she's sick," said Jerry at the side of the room. "Maybe by tomorrow Jackie will come back."

His mother pounced on the idea, as well as a bottle of whiskey. Later in the day, after much medication from Dr. Johnnie Walker, Jenny put on the lightest demeanor she felt she could get away with to describe how her daughter had a violent yet non–life-threatening case of food poisoning and would be emetically unable to attend tonight's gala. Thus the first disaster was averted. But come the next day, there was no Jackie.

"Where is she?" fretted Jenny Jonathan. "Why is she punishing me like this"

"I don't think it's about you, Mama," Jerry offered.

"Well, it's fixing to be about all of us because there's a TV appearance, the Garden Tour, and a benefit dinner scheduled for today, all going to be one First Princess short in a glaring fashion. Your grandmother and Aunt Tilly are coming for the Coronation Pageant tomorrow night, and cousin Earle and Jane and their brood of little monsters are descending on us for the parade on Sunday. Dear Lord, I will never hear the end of this."

Jerry intervened. "Why don't I go down to the committee and explain in person that Jackie's still recuperating? I think they'll buy it if I go. I know most everybody on the committee."

"I'm not surprised," Jim snorted from his bourbon and Coke, "the whole thing's run by you faggots. Rich bored housewives and faggots."

"Jim, settle," Jenny told him. She turned to her son. "Would you do that?"

"Any excuse to get out of this house," he said snatching up his car keys. Already out the door he yelled, "Call everybody and tell them not to come." The back screen door slammed behind him.

Jenny knew that was what should be done. Instead, though, she took what remained of the bourbon upstairs to lie down and pray to a Baptist God for one hell of a miracle.

The next day around 4 in the afternoon Jerry's grandmother and Aunt Tilly arrived.

"Yoo-hoo! Where's our little Azalea Princess?" called Aunt Tilly as she prodded Grandma in the front door. "

Jerry pulled his mother into the dining room. "You didn't tell them?"

"I couldn't, I just couldn't!"

"This is insane! Mama, I can't keep this up."

She grabbed him by the shoulders. "You listen to me. We have lied through our teeth to some of the best people in town all week. Lying to my stuck-up sister and that old bat out there will be a snap. I know because I've done it for decades."

Aunt Tilly stuck her nosy nose in the room. "Are you two telling secrets?" She imperiously took Jerry and his mom by the hand, yanking them into the living room. "Come tell mother why our Azalea Girl hasn't come down to greet her."

Jenny smiled too broadly and hugged her mother with as little touching as possible. "Jackie's not here, she had to…go back up to Duke."

"Today?" barked her mother.

"She had an exam," Jenny said. "An emergency exam. That she forgot. And she has to keep her grades up. You know. To be a Princess."

"Isn't that her car outside?"

"It doesn't work. It has…tubing problems. In the hood area. She went back with a sorority person."

Her mother narrowed her eyes. "Does this person have a name?"

"Of course. Oprah...Springer. Her friend Oprah Springer." Jenny's smile was by now a clenched grimace. "Mama, the point is she's gone, OK?"

"That's all right," Aunt Tilly said, patting her mother. "We'll see her tonight at the coronation, and afterward." She looked at Jenny. "Right?"

Jenny looked to Jerry to say something, anything. After a beat, he said, "Sure. Why not."

While Jerry helped his aunt and grandmother get settled into their room, his mother was arguing with his father. "I'm not asking you to kill anyone, just veer off the driveway."

"Use your mind, woman. We'd just end up taking another car, and there are currently five in the driveway. After the second or third accident it's gonna look a little suspicious. I mean, they're gonna think we're trying to kill them."

"We can live with that. We can't live with them finding out about Jackie; now you decide which car we're gonna take."

Jenny Jonathan left her husband looking through his auto insurance files to come downstairs and start dinner. Jerry came into the kitchen furious.

"Why haven't you told Grandma and Aunt Tilly I'm gay?" he demanded. "You said I shouldn't tell them because you were gonna break it to them, but they've just spent the last half hour interrogating me about when I was going to get serious about finding a wife."

"Jerry, we have other problems right now."

"Fine, maybe I could help by coming out at the supper table. How's that? Maybe that'd take their minds off Jackie."

"Damn it, Jerry, if you really want to help, when we call 'em downstairs for supper you will put a roller skate on the stairs. But you will *not* tell them what you are, do you hear me? You will never tell them. This family is dealing with plenty enough shame right now as it is. Where are you going?"

"Out! This family doesn't deal with anything! You are all full of shit!" And he flounced out of the house.

Jenny was stunned. Not because he had never used that word to her before, but because it so elegantly solved the problem of that night's coronation.

After roast chicken, turnip greens, and mashed potatoes, dessert was served. Second helpings of fresh homemade brownies were pushed on Aunt Tilly and Grandma.

"I truly wish I could have some," Jim said, "but I can't have chocolate."

"Me neither," Jenny said. "I'm watching my weight."

"About time," grunted her mother. Some 45 minutes later, however, she was grunting in another room of the house for, you see, two boxes of Ex-Lax had found their unfortunate way into the brownies. Tilly was in another bathroom, equally noisome, equally purgative. The Coronation Pageant, sadly, was missed. But the inevitable disgrace had only been delayed. Both Jim and Jenny knew there was nothing that could save them from the parade the next morning.

When Jerry returned around midnight he found his mother sitting in the dark in the living room. "What's wrong with Tilly and Grandma?" asked Jerry.

Jenny rattled the ice at the bottom of her latest drink. "They're not quite as full of shit as they were," she said. "Where have you been?"

"Backstage at the coronation show. They needed some help with hair and makeup and all." He watched his mother finished her drink. "Are you OK?"

"Me? I'm just dandy. You know, all I've ever wanted was for Tilly and Mama and all the rest to treat me with a little respect. And to have friends of a certain class and station. Is that so much to ask? And I was so close. But by this time tomorrow it'll all be over."

At the ungodly hour of 7:15 A.M., cousins Earle and Jane and their three out-of-control boys arrived from Fayetteville. Jenny and Jim served them scrambled eggs, pork sausage, bacon, grits, and pancakes. Tilly and Grandma were fearful of eating anything Jenny cooked, so they made do with toast. Knowing the end was near, Jim sipped very Irish coffee from a quart-size mug. Jenny knocked back a screwdriver with only token orange juice. It helped take the edge off the caterwauling children, the glares from Grandma and Aunt Tilly, and their own imminent citywide humiliation come the parade, which would happen in a very few short hours.

After breakfast, Tilly and Grandma wedged themselves into Earle and Jane's van with their screaming spawn to take off for the parade downtown. Jim told them to go on ahead, he and Jenny would clean up a little and then join them on the bleachers. As soon as the van was gone, Jenny turned to Jim and wept. He led her into the house and put her to bed. Then he climbed in too and pulled the covers over his head.

A couple of hours later, Jim Jonathan woke up. In a perverse desire to witness the actual moment of disgrace, he reached for the remote and turned the bedroom TV on, keeping the sound on mute. There was the local coverage of the finale to this festive fiasco, the Azalea Parade in living color. He watched dully, waiting for the moment mortification would stab him, vaguely hoping it might be fatal.

Here came the float. Here was the pan shot of all the Azalea Queen's Court. And there was the missing place. And here was the Azalea Queen herself. Jim sat bolt upright in bed. There in white letters on the screen it read, "Jackie Jonathan, Azalea Queen." He boggled.

"Jenny! Jenny, wake up!"

"Whasit?"

"Look!"

Jenny barely opened her eyes, then jerked awake with a scream. "Sound! Sound!" Jim took the mute off and the commentator could be heard.

"…accident prior to the parade when Queen Sheri Zimmerman toppled off the float while trying to get up to her throne this morning, injuring her head. We understand she's in stable condition at New Hanover Memorial Hospital, but as you can see Jackie Jonathan is every bit as lovely, as the former First Princess takes over as Azalea Queen…"

Jim and Jenny were holding each other and whooping with joy! Then the camera went in for a close up of the new queen. Her velvet choker was not wide enough to hide the Adam's apple. Jim and Jenny froze in horror.

"Jesus, God, Mary, and Joseph!" Jim exploded. "My son is Azalea Queen!"

Because no one had seen Jackie since the Court had been announced earlier in the spring and all the other girls had been utterly absorbed in themselves anyway, no one had noticed the difference between Jackie and her twin brother in professional-quality drag. He had dressed and put on the makeup and wig at a friend's house, showing up at the parade ready to go. It had been just too, too unfortunate that his glove had slipped off as he was pulling poor Sheri Zimmerman onto the float in the staging area that morning. Down she went. Oh, well.

By the time Grandma and Aunt Tilly, plus Earle, Jane, and their hellions returned from the parade, Jim and Jenny were nervous wrecks. The humiliation they had anticipated earlier was nothing compared to what they steeled themselves for now as family members poured out of the van.

"She was so beautiful!" Aunt Tilly cried. "Jackie was positively regal!"

"I can't believe how much our Jackie's grown," said Grandma. "And such strong arms on that girl. Has she been working out?"

"Congratulations, you two," gushed Aunt Tilly.

"Oh, especially on that other girl splittin' her head wide open," added Grandma. "What a delightful stroke of luck!"

"You should have been there!" said Jane, swatting at her brats.

"We saw it on TV."

"I'll bet you were surprised, huh," Earle said, poking Jim with an elbow.

"You have no idea."

Jenny's family was thrilled to have been part of such a highly visible success in Jackie's ascension to the throne. Everyone was sad to have to leave for home, but they left wreathed in smiles and glory.

Jerry came home that evening. He sat his parents down and explained the deal. He would go quietly back to South Carolina, keeping it forever secret that this year's Azalea Queen had a Y chromosome and a penis—but it would cost them $115,000. Plus build-out expenses. Plus advertising.

So if you're ever in Myrtle Beach and need anything from a haircut to a makeover, simply everyone recommends Mr. Jerry's luxurious Azalea Beauty Salon. It's the one place in town where you can walk in a princess but go home a queen.

Confetti on My Heart

Marcello died on Halloween night. Larry, his life partner of 14 years, was too sick with an opportunistic infection to go out with him that night but insisted his lover enjoy the celebration. Marcello had been out on Santa Monica Boulevard in full Cruella De Vil drag with everyone else in the wild and wonderful crowd. He left a friend's party around 4:15 A.M., and on his way home a drunk driver hit him. He was pronounced dead at Cedars-Sinai hospital in an extravagant black-and-white gown, gloves, pumps, and enormous wig. He really knew how to attach a wig.

That was 11 months ago. He had been cremated and his remains were in a utilitarian urn in Larry's apartment. As the one-year anniversary approached, Larry became more and more agitated.

"I don't know what to do with him," he told me, a total stranger to him, at Revolver, a local gay bar. "I mean, we both figured I'd be the first to go. His family is in the Philippines, but they disowned him when he told them he was gay. I guess they figured his money was straight, though, because they cashed the checks he sent 'em every month. It's been almost a year since the checks stopped coming, and I haven't heard jack." He took a swig of Perrier and lime. "Marcello always said he had dependents but no family."

But there had been another family. That family of choice that gays have learned to forge so well. Their friends had called Larry often, sometimes practically kidnapping him for dinner. They had tried for months to get Larry to go with them, to get back to living. Skating dates at the beach had been broken. At the last minute he had backed out of a gay chartered bus trip to Yosemite with them. He couldn't bear to go when they invited him for gay night at Magic Mountain. Weeks ago someone mentioned that gay day at Disneyland was coming up soon, in October, but Larry only shook his head. The only thing that was on Larry's mind was what to do with Marcello's ashes.

Sometimes being a stranger is what people need, so I gave him my phone number. I'm glad I did; otherwise I would have missed this story. He called the first week of October, very upset. "I know it doesn't make sense, but I've got to find a place for him before Halloween. It's making me crazy. I should have gone to Yosemite."

"Did he like Yosemite?" I asked.

"He never went, but he might have liked it. He might have been happy there."

"Where was he most happy?"

"I guess in the kitchen, but I'm not pouring him down the disposal."

"I agree, that's out, but it's a start. Where else?"

"Um, at the movies. And Broadway. He loved *Beauty and the Beast* and *The Lion King.* Maybe I should take him to New York?"

"Will that make you happy?"

"I don't care. I want *him* to be happy." He started to cry. "Christ, why is this so hard? All I want is a place my Marcello can rest and be happy." He hung up. I called back but he wouldn't pick up.

That night, at precisely 4:15 A.M., Larry woke up wide-eyed. He jumped out of bed, dressed, and raced to the 24-hour Ralphs grocery. Once there he ran down the aisles with his cart, tossing in a value pack of quart-size Hefty One Zip plastic bags, two dozen eggs, milk, Bisquick, butter, syrup, two pounds of bacon, coffee, creamer, orange juice, fresh fruit, and Mumm champagne. Back home he hurriedly threw together a fresh fruit salad and whipped up pancake batter. He started in on the bacon next. By then it was around 6, so he started calling people. He called Stan first.

"Stan, this is Larry. Sorry it's so early, but you and George *have* to come over for breakfast today. Yes, I know what today is—that's why you have to stop here first. I even want to go with you, but it's really important to me that you do this, OK? Can I count on you guys? Thank you! You're the best! Eight o'clock? OK, 9. See you then." He then called Linda, Red, Luis and Tim, Peter, Sandy, Chris, Curtis, Beth and Donna, Raul, Harry—the rest of Marcello's and his family. By 9:30 Larry's apartment was full of bleary-eyed people in various kinds of red shirts, barely mollified by eggs, pancakes, pork, and mimosas. He called for attention and addressed them in front of the framed *Fantasia* poster in the kitchen.

"I wanted to tell the people who were closest to Marcello and me that I know the perfect resting place for him. The one place where he was always happy, from the minute we got there to the moment we left."

"And where's that?" someone asked.

"Where else?" Larry grinned. "The happiest place on earth!"

"Oh. My. God," Linda said. "Disneyland?"

"That's right," Larry said, opening a cabinet. He pulled out a tray with a dozen Hefty One Zip bags with about a cup and a half of Marcello's ashes in each of them. "It's going to be especially beautiful because you're all going to help." There was a palpable silence in the room.

Finally, from the back of the group, Curtis said, "Oh, what the hell. We're all going to gay day anyway." He came forward and picked up a bag. "I'll do it because I love you, Larry. But I'm going to need a few more mimosas before we leave."

The tension was broken. Friends reached out for bags. And champagne.

Larry rode to the park with Luis and Tim, beside himself with excitement. Boarding the parking lot tram, they could see a few regular families wondering what was going on, but mostly hundreds of smiling people in red shirts identifying them as Disneyland gay day participants. Larry was trembling by the time they bought their tickets. Just inside they gate he saw Chris emptying his bag in the flowers planted to look like Mickey Mouse. Chris looked up guiltily. "Is that all right?" he asked.

Larry was beaming with tears in his eyes. "It's perfect," he said, reaching out to touch the flowers. "They're pansies."

Everyone had agreed to meet back at 6 for dinner at the Carnation Café at the end of Main Street. Larry was too emotional to go on any of the rides, so he told Luis and Tim to go on and enjoy themselves. Larry was content just knowing that all was being taken care of. He stayed at the Carnation Café and spent the day reminiscing, nursing expensive decaf coffees, and watching the wildly varied crowd go by this one day of the year when queers take over and work their own spells on the Magic Kingdom. By the end of the afternoon, he had felt the magic himself. He was calm, peaceful.

Around 6 his friends began showing up with reports of how they had fulfilled their assignments. Beth and Donna had spread their portion of ashes on Tom Sawyer Island. Raul opened his bag on Space Mountain and let the roller coaster ride do the rest. Harry sprinkled his from his Doom Buggy all the way through the Haunted Mansion. "I thought he could play with the ghosts and really fuck with the tourists," he said.

Sandy said she emptied her bag at the top of the Matterhorn, "but it went in the faces of some straight people behind us."

"That's disgusting," Raul said. "What were straight people doing on that ride?"

As more friends arrived, the mood became rollicking. "We sprinkled ours in Honey, I Shrunk the Audience," said Tim, "with all those special effects, who would notice?"

"Even though I came out feeling like Honey, I Dumped the Body," added Luis.

"I wanted him to have company," explained Raul, "so I left half in Star Tours, where Paul Reubens plays the robot, and the rest in Innoventions, voiced by Nathan Lane."

"Mine's in the Indiana Jones Adventure," said Curtis, "Didn't mean to, but the damn ride jerks around so much I tore the bag."

Red ran up to join the group. "Sorry I'm late. I was at a bear jamboree."

"I thought they closed that," Larry said.

"Not Disney bears—these were from Ventura."

"So where did you scatter your Marcello?" Curtis asked.

"Oh, shit! I forgot!" And he ran off. Larry laughed, and his family laughed with him.

Chris and Peter came up together. "We scattered ashes in Toon Town," Chris announced. "And is it me or is it bad taste to have a sign that says GOOFY'S GAS by a public toilet?"

"I put mine in the water about the fourth time I did the Davy Crockett Canoes," Peter told them. "Those helmsmen are way hot!"

Stan and George had sprinkled their portion of ashes in Peter Pan's Flight. "After all," Stan said, "if that wasn't fairy dust, I don't know what is."

Linda, who had been sitting there very quietly, was now on the verge of tears. "Everyone else did such a good job. I let you down, Larry, I'm sorry. I was in It's a Small World and I had my packet over the edge of the boat, but I slipped and dropped the whole thing in the water."

"Wait a minute," Tim said. "We were in line for Small World when it broke down and they closed it around 4:30."

"Oh, no," Linda moaned even more upset. "It probably got sucked into the pump or the filtration system or something."

"Cool!" exclaimed Red, who had just returned. "Marcello fucked up It's a Small World!" Everyone high-fived and Linda felt much better.

But suddenly Larry was upset. "Oh, my God," he breathed, "oh, my God!" The group turned serious as they saw Larry start to cry. "I was so excited I forgot to keep some. I didn't mean to give him all away! I needed to keep some of him." He turned panicky. "I've got to get some back! Everybody go back! Go where you left him and try to get some."

"It's too late, Larry," Stan told him sadly. "It's all gone by now."

"I've got to have some back!" he shouted desperately.

"I just spread mine!" Red remembered. He grabbed Larry's wrist. "Come on!" Larry ran after Red, followed by Tim and Luis. They rushed to a side courtyard halfway down Main Street. There, 20 feet away, next to a flower bed, was a small, tidy pile of ashes on the asphalt.

"You call *that* spreading?" Tim remarked.

"I meant to get it in the flowers, but I dropped it," Red growled at him.

A look of horror crossed Larry's face. Luis yelled, "No-o-o!" A young sanitation employee had just swept the ashes into his portable dustbin. All four men descended on the poor kid, shouting and waving their hands. At last the frightened kid hollered, "Stop! I have a girlfriend!"

Tim couldn't help himself. "And you work at Disneyland?"

Red pulled out a $20 bill. "I'll give you this for what you have in that dustpan." The kid took the money warily but shook the contents of his dustpan into the plastic bag Red had kept. The ashes were there, but they were mixed with dirt, bits of popcorn, and a lot of bright confetti, probably from some parade or magic act. But the crisis had passed.

On the drive home, Luis asked Larry why this last bit of ashes was so important. "I needed it so I can be buried with Marcello," Larry explained. "After I die, I'll have this plastic bag in the left breast pocket of the suit I'm buried in."

They drove on in silence for a while. "It's a shame popcorn and all that paper got mixed in," Tim said. "Maybe you can sift it out."

"I don't think I will," Larry said. "It's kinda pretty. It reminds me of this day and the wonderful friends who helped Marcello and me. Friends—*family* I can't thank enough." He looked out the window at the passing lights, absently touching the lumpy plastic bag in his lap. "I will have Marcello and confetti on my heart."

And for the first time in almost a year, he was happy.

Aunt Marie's Christmas Present

People love nice, happy Christmas stories, tales that melt our thick cynicism and open us up to feel the joyous wonder of the season. Well, too bad, 'cause this ain't one of 'em.

Ricky lived down the street from me in Wilmington, N.C. He was my age, and we both pined for Christmas the way winos lust after Night Train. At my house, the decorations and carols on the stereo were forbidden until after Thanksgiving. I'm sure that was in response to yuletide displays and decorations going up in stores like Sears the second week of November, a jump on the holiday that was then considered outrageously early. Seeing glistening snow and reindeer displays in stores while being denied them at home made me crazy with desire for them. Ricky's parents, however, both worked and were never home, so I easily talked him into dragging the boxes his dad had labeled "Christmas Crap" out of his attic the day after Halloween. Ha! Take that, Sears!

In their never-used living room we set up their genuine aluminum tree with the exciting and very glamorous electric rotating tricolor wheel. We were too young to know what kitsch was; we only knew it was dazzlingly shiny and electric and therefore on the cutting edge of Christmas technology. With Doris Day, the New Christy Minstrels, and still-straight Johnny Mathis singing away at a volume far past the "Too Loud" mark Rick's parents had notched into the dial, we hung the dozen boxes or so of identical red balls on the tree, each one's placement as carefully considered as a ruby on a Fabergé egg. Then we'd turn out the overhead light, plug in the tricolor wheel, and sit in awe on the plastic-covered sofa to behold the beauty. The carols were turned down to the "Acceptable" notch so we could talk now, naturally about Christmas.

And naturally about presents. Rick told me about the gifts he always seemed to get from his Aunt Marie since he could remember. Every year she'd spend the week of Christmas with them. She'd arrive with three wrapped packages, a small one for Rick's dad, another small one for his mom, and a large, heavy, TV-size gift for Rick that she'd put under the silver Christmas tree with great fanfare. All week long, Aunt Marie would drop nonsubtle hints that he was getting something wonderful. Obviously this was a big, expensive item from Aunt Marie, and if Christmas had taught Rick anything, it was that there must be gift parity. Succumbing to panic, he would scrape together his allowance so he could get her a gift of what he guessed to be approximately similar value, blowing his entire savings every time. When he was eight he collected his pennies to buy her a nice towel set from Belk's department store. The gift he got from her that year was a clip-on tie, disguised by the enormous box. See, every year she did that sort of thing just to fool Ricky. He'd open his gift on Christmas morning with wild expectations only to discover she had tricked him again. When she saw little Ricky's crestfallen face, she'd rock back and forth with laughter, saying, "Gotcha!" And laugh some more.

Being a child, Ricky simply couldn't believe she would do such a thing again, not his aunt who loved him, not on his beloved Christmas. But she would. And every year, by the end of the week's visit, he fell for it. When he was 9, he bought her a desk set with Crane stationery embossed with her initials. He got a lousy

Matchbox car in a box weighted with a brick. "Ha, ha, ha, ha, ha!" cackled Aunt Marie clutching her bony knees. "Gotcha! Ha, ha, ha, ha, ha!"

When Ricky was 11, he bought her one of the new vanity mirrors that adjusted for sunlight, evening, and indoor lighting. He unwrapped his present to find…a deluxe wood-burning set! Cool! Wait, no, it was a deluxe wood-burning set *box* with a copy of Louisa May Alcott's *Little Men* inside. Paperback. Oh, how Aunt Marie rocked with hilarity that year. "Ha, ha, ha, ha! *Double* gotcha!"

Well, Ricky grew up to be gay, a fact that took everyone in his family by surprise. I guess no one had been paying attention when this preteen Christmas queen was giving such obvious gifts as bath linens, personalized stationery, and a makeup mirror. He was a deep disappointment to his family, especially to Aunt Marie because she was such a devout Christian.

Ricky moved the hell away from home to Atlanta, where he ran a very successful business pumping concrete. Despite holiday and birthday cards, he sent to his family, the only thing he ever got in return was a single Christmas card from Aunt Marie every year filled with religious pamphlets about how homosexuals were abominations on the fast track to a loving God's fiery hell. "Merry Christmas, your Aunt Marie."

After enduring many years of this, Ricky decided he needed to respond. So he sent Aunt Marie an enormous, heavy box wrapped and decorated to look like something Ari Onassis would have given Jackie. Ricky knew full well that Aunt Marie would follow tradition and not think of opening it until Christmas morning with the family. When the package arrived, she saw the thing and it was her turn to panic. Thinking her religious tracts must have done their work, she rushed out, bought, and sent back to Ricky a beautiful, large, sumptuous, and—most important—very expensive quilt.

On Christmas morning in Wilmington, she and Ricky's estranged parents gathered before the now-dull, tired metal tree. Ravenous with anticipation, she tore into the gift from her nephew.

Inside she found a single cinder block with a stack of her religious pamphlets torn in half and lashed to it with crude #3 baling wire. Also attached was a large red tag. Scrawled across it in black Magic Marker were the words "Gotcha back, bitch."

Well, at least it stopped the yearly pamphlets. And in case you were wondering, Ricky snuggles down into his warm bed and sleeps very well under his lovely quilt, thank you.

A Funeral and a Wake—Dinner and a Show

I have attended plays, musicals, concerts, and dance performances, but I missed the best show this year. It took place in a sandy, marshy county in northeastern North Carolina at a funeral my brother the preacher attended.

Wade Futrell and his wife, née Lilah Futch, had a double-wide trailer home. Wade had been under it, adjusting the cinder blocks to make the back half level with the front. A slight, however important, miscalculation caused the entire back half to fall on Wade, crushing him not unlike the Wicked Witch of the West. When Lilah got back from her shift at the chicken processing plant, it was dark. She got the mail and walked into the house, flipping through the Wal-Mart circular. Engrossed in fantasies of redwood patio furniture at 25% off, she stepped into the kitchen, which, now on a severe and unexpected angle, caused her to fall on the slanted linoleum. The Futch women run large, so Lilah slid with great force down the floor, crashing through the many legs of the pine dinette set and into the cabinetry below the sink, completely shearing the U-joint. She cracked her jaw, broke a leg, and dislocated a hip. Using only her arms, she had to pull herself up the inclined floor and into the living room to dial 911. It was one of the paramedics who, unable to negotiate a tilted bathroom, went out back to pee and discovered Wade.

Now, when Wade was a boy, his family was so poor they shared a small house with the equally impoverished Reverend Symms and his family. Reverend Symms's son, Delbert, who also grew up to be a preacher, had been Wade's closest and best friend from boyhood. For the funeral, the Futrells asked Delbert to deliver the graveside eulogy. Although he was now serving the Lord in the relative metropolis of Climax, N.C., Delbert agreed to attend but, stricken at the loss of his friend, was unsure he could get through it alone, so he got his elderly father, Reverend Symms, from the Elks Retirement Home to stand by as backup.

By the open grave were Wade's parents and the recently released and still woozy Lilah, covered in fresh plaster and propped up in a wheelchair. Sure enough, Delbert collapsed into his metal folding chair where he wept and was comforted by his wife, Naomi, who was regarded with deep suspicion, being a Yankee from Boston. So Reverend Symms Sr. took over the sermon. Since he was of the old school, it naturally involved the winepress of God's wrath and lambs breaking apocalyptic seals. And since he was also quite elderly and out of practice, the sermon also sounded like something out of Monty Python. At the close of the final prayer, there was a moment of stillness. Then Beulah Futch, Lilah's mama, stood up and wailed, "I don't care what anybody says! I always loved Wade!" Shocked silence fell, because everybody knew the Futches were an unpleasant, spiteful bunch.

Finally, Wade's uncle, Unc, stood and faced her. "Then why didn't you show it when he was alive?" he shouted. "You slut bitch!"

Beulah yelled back, "I don't have to answer to you—the Lord knows my heart!" and she started bellowing the old hymn "It Is Well With My Soul."

Someone from a group of disturbingly look-alike cousins said the Futches were "just a buncha asshole bastards" anyway. That was it. Stand back, folks, fistfight at the graveside.

At last Mr. Futrell took out his .45 and shot it into the air. Everything stopped. "You will show some fucking respect!" he shouted. Shamed, everyone sat down. "Now if y'all can behave, the wake is at Wade and Lilah's."

The Futrells, being hosts, hurried to get to the wake first. Lilah, in her wheelchair, bounced the whole way in the back of her brother Rip's pickup truck, holding on for dear life. Rip and his buddy Ray carried her into the living room, which was already crowded with mourners eating collards, green bean casseroles, cake, cobbler, and other Southern death foods. It was crowded moreover because the back half of the house remained on a dramatic slant, rendering it inhospitable.

Delbert and Naomi paid their respects to Lilah and jostled their way over to my brother to say hello. "I understand you're from Boston?" my brother asked.

"Yes," Naomi answered. "Our family owns a jewelry store downtown. Steins."

"That's funny," said one of the cousin boys, blood still on his shirt, "isn't that a Jew name?" There fell a hush of gasps and stares.

"Delbert married a Yankee Jew!" breathed Uncle Unc. "And him a preacher!"

Delbert turned to him saying, "Give it a rest, Unc. She converted."

Unc was not mollified and started to get belligerent. "How do you convert from being a *Yankee*?" My brother stepped between then and said there was a little-known ritual but it had to be performed by a priest. Unc's ire was defused, and he was even impressed. "Those Catholics got mumbo-jumbo for ever thing." Reverend Symms Sr. called Unc outside to corral his kids, who had been caught letting air out of the Futches' tires.

Naomi was plenty ready to leave at this point. "Del, dear," she said, "if you want to say goodbye to Rip, now's the time." Delbert nodded and edged through the crowd.

"I didn't know Delbert knew Rip," said Beulah who had come over to look at a Jew.

"Oh, Rip was Delbert's first," Naomi said, "after Wade, of course."

Beulah's mouth fell open exposing chicken salad. "Delbert's first *what*?"

"Oh, you know. Lots of boys go through that." Across the room Rip was hugging Delbert.

"No, I do not know!" Beulah hollered with her mouth full, and she turned to see Rip introduce Delbert to his friend Ray, who also hugged him most familiarly. Beulah gulped for air, sucking a sizable piece of chicken down her windpipe. There was much sudden commotion around her until they located someone with big enough arms to perform the Heimlich maneuver. By this time everyone had gathered around Beulah, who lay wheezing, coughing, and sweating on the floor. Delbert, in their midst, asked his wife what happened.

"I just mentioned that phase before we met," she whispered, "when you and your friends experimented with homosexuality." All eyes that had been on Beulah suddenly shifted.

"Damn it, Naomi. That was in the privacy of our therapy!" Delbert felt the stares and looked around. The parents, aunts, uncles, and cousins of two families looked back, their eyes wide and mouths as open and round as Krispy Kreme donuts.

"Shameful! My God!" cried Reverend Symms. "Shameful, shameful! My son has had *therapy*!"

At this point my brother decided to depart unnoticed. Driving home he resisted the temptation to thank God that Wade's relatives were only "paper members" of his church and not in active attendance. It was a small community and he would, after all, see them around town. There was a bright spot, though: When his brother came to visit from West Hollywood, he'd have someone to talk to now.

Love Story

It was far too early in the morning on Valentine's Day in Los Angeles for my vintage powder-blue Princess phone to ring, but it did. I stirred under my Polo sheets and fumbled for it. The instant I picked it up, my friend Harold began screaming on the other end.

"Have you heard! Can you believe it? Could you just die!"

I rolled my still sleepy eyes. "What, Harold?"

"What do you mean 'what?' It's only the apocalypse! Matt Damon and Ben Affleck have broken up!"

I sat bolt upright, completely awake. "You are lying!" I shouted at him. "You have no right to do this to me!"

"It's true! I was at Matt LeBlanc's monthly sex party when Keanu asked Joaquin how they were doing because usually they're always there, you know, getting things started with that thing they do with the double dildo?"

"Keanu and Joaquin?"

"Matt and Ben! Please, you couldn't fit a pencil in those other lightweights. Anyway, Tobey Maguire overheard them and suddenly burst into tears. It took both Cuba Gooding Jr. and Casper Van Dien to calm him down. Needless to say, everything came to a complete stop. Well, except for those Bridges boys—nothing stops them. Honestly, it's a wonder Jeff and Beau ever leave the house."

"Focus, Harold, focus."

"Well, I'm upset! But that's when it comes out that Tobey and Dylan McDermott, who's a little old for him if you ask me, but I make no judgments, were double-dating with Matt and Ben at Cobalt Cantina earlier in the evening. The atmosphere was very tense, and Dylan was trying to lighten things up with that tired old story of how he and Billy Campbell took advantage of Matthew Perry while driving him to rehab, when in walks John Leguizamo and Freddie Prinze Jr."

"When did they get back together?"

"Do you want to hear this or not?"

"Sorry."

"So Freddie comes right up to the table and says, 'Last weekend was great, Bottom Boy Ben. Give me a call when Monotonous Matt's on location again.' Matt shouts, 'Fuck you, Prinze!' and Freddie says, 'Not for money! And don't blame me if he likes 'em big and uncut and you're neither,' then snaps his fingers and walks away. Huge argument at the table. Matt walks out, and that's it. It's all over!"

"That's terrible! What is John Leguizamo doing with an abusive shit like Freddie?"

"Don't ask me, that's his damage. I mean, remember that ugly daddy thing he had with David Soul? The important thing is, What are you and I going to do?"

Half an hour later I pulled up at Harold's place and honked the horn. His front door opened, he soul-kissed his tall, handsome lover goodbye on the porch and got in the car.

"It's nice to see you and Denzel settling down," I said as we sped off.

Herman nodded in agreement. "Yeah, he says I've really helped him get over that dysfunctional thing he and Clooney had. Where are we going?"

"Where else? Gus Van Sant's." Gus directed Ben and Matt's first film, *Good Will Hunting*. It was on that shoot that Ben and Matt finally realized they were much, much more than friends and cowriters. Gus would know what to do.

We rushed up to the door and beat on it. Nothing. Gus's bright lavender '64 Mustang convertible was in the drive, so we knew he was home. Harold went around to the bedroom window and shouted until Gus finally stuck his head and bare upper torso out.

"Damn it, Harold!" he called down in irritation, "I'm right in the middle of Andy Garcia!" Harold told him the news. "Oh, my God! I'll be right down."

We were let in moments later. Gus and Andy were in matching pink bathrobes. Andy's fell open, showing much matted chest hair, and he kept smiling at me, the shallow bastard. Didn't he realize how serious this was?

"I know these boys," Gus said, pacing in distress. "Biblically. But I know them as great friends too. Hurry, there's not a moment to lose!" Still in his robe he herded Harold and me into his Mustang. As he threw the car into gear, he called over to Andy on the porch that his 3 o'clock, Vince Vaughn, was due any minute and Andy could have him to himself this week. "I've got more important things to do right now!" he shouted as he sped down the drive and onto the main road.

Passing cars left and right, Gus explained. "When *Rounders* tanked, Matt needed a father figure. I took him to Sam Elliott's men's spa in Palm Springs, where Matt ran into Tom Selleck. They started talking and really got into each other. Literally. Matt felt bad about it, like he had cheated on Ben, so Tom had to explain to him the difference between sex and love." He took a sharp turn off Sunset into Beverly Hills that I thought was going to roll the car. Gus never missed a beat. "Meanwhile Ben was at Johnny Depp and Brendan Fraser's commitment ceremony. Did you go to that?"

We nodded. Harold and I had gone in together on their gift: a sling from Mister S. Leathers. Three years and still no thank-you note. Gus continued. "Well, Ben was feeling he'd let Matt down and was crying on David Boreanaz's shoulder next to the open bar."

"I wondered what that was about," Harold said.

"He was needing a friend, but David was only interested in getting together a four-gy with him, Ving, and Benicio. Ben left feeling miserable just as Matt showed up in the parking lot. They had a tearful reunion and were closer than ever. What we need to do is get them together in the same room and I'm sure we can work this out." Gus stomped on the breaks in front of a grossly expensive tacky faux Tudor home. He leaped out of the car and ran up to the door. By the time we had scrambled up behind him, two handsome men in tight jeans, flashy shirts, and cowboy hats were letting us all in. "Harold, Joel," Gus said making quick introductions in the foyer, "this is Brooks and Dunn."

As Gus told them why we were there, I whispered to Harold, "Which one is which?"

"I don't know; I can't tell," he said. "But that's what happens to long-term couples."

Brooks or Dunn said they were well aware of the situation. In fact, Ben was upstairs now, watching Sally Jessy and stuffing himself with Toblerone. "This is great!" I said. "Now all we need to do is call Tom Selleck and see if Ben is there."

"We don't know Tom's number," the other of the Brooks or Dunn said.

"Well, girls, that's why God made speed dial," said Gus, pulling a cell phone from a pocket in his pink bathrobe. "Hello, Tom—oh. Well, who is this?" Gus covered the receiver. "Should I call him LL or Mr. Cool J?"

Harold yanked the phone from him. "Listen, Miss Thing," he yelled into it. "This is Harold and you owe me one Vera Wang knockoff. Uh-huh, I know why you never returned it. Ryan Phillippe told me he saw you in it at Numbers and you had stretched that dress out worse than you stretched out Ben Stiller. Now shut up and tell me if Matt Damon is there. That's better. OK, you do that." He handed the phone back to Gus. "Girlfriend says he's out by the pool with Tom."

So as not to call either by the wrong name, I asked both Brooks and Dunn to show me upstairs to Ben's room. There I found him with tears and dark chocolate on his face. He threw himself on me, weeping. "Oh, Joel, he doesn't love me!"

"Of course he does, Ben" I said, trying to keep the stickiest parts off my Hermès sweater. "He only did that bitch Freddie on a whim," I reassured him.

"A whim? Oh, God, that makes it worse!"

Mercifully, Harold came upstairs. "They're on their way," he said.

Ben turned his drama on him. "Nobody's going to love me!" he wailed. "I'm the girly little wimpy one!"

Harold smacked him hard across the face. "Get a grip!"

Ben cowered in the corner but stopped sniveling. Brooks and Dunn took him downstairs for some coffee and a face wash, giving me a chance to catch my breath and wonder aloud, "Why Brooks and Dunn?"

"Who do you think taught them that double dildo thing?"

Tom and LL pulled up with Matt in tow. "Where's Ben?" Tom asked as they hustled Matt inside.

"In the den," Brooks and Dunn said in perfect unison.

Tom turned Matt around and spoke directly to him, like father to son. "Remember what I told you about the difference between sex and love when you cheated? It's the same thing with him. So just forget that whore Freddie Prinze—in this town only the Santa Anas have blown more people."

"Yo, yo, yo, that's right," LL added. "You just remember what's important and you'll be cool, know what I'm saying?"

Matt nodded and went into the den where Ben was waiting. We all wanted to see how it went, but Gus shut the door softly. "They need to do their healing alone," he said.

"Is that my bathrobe?" Tom asked him. "I know I had two that color."

That evening I turned on *Entertainment Tonight,* where Leeza Gibbons was reporting. "Rumors of a split between Matt Damon and Ben Affleck have proved false! The beautiful boys were seen laughing and dancing into the night at Rage. As this footage shows, all is well with this most enduring of Hollywood love stories. Whoa! Tonsil hockey anyone?" I clicked it off and turned in early, secure in the knowledge that love as well as a few concerned, caring, well-connected friends, had prevailed on this most tumultuous of Valentine's Days.

Urban Myths and Legends

WARNING: None of what you're about to read is true. Not one damn thing. You know, however, that this fact won't keep some loser freak from believing and repeating it as the gospel truth. And that is just fine with me.

Urban legends are made of a curious blend of deep-seated fears, exploited psychoses, absurd circumstances, unlikely events, and an element of credible horror. I don't know about you, but that's my definition of a good night out. The stories are grim, totally unnecessary, politically incorrect and hateful. I love 'em.

You've heard them all before, but what you don't know is they actually started out gay and were co-opted by straights who were too dull to come up with their own neuroses-revealing stories. (It's true, a friend of my dentist's ex-lover's dog walker told me.) As a public service, I give you the real honest-to-God fake stories, in their original fag form.

THE HOOK ON THE DOOR HANDLE

Two guys—I'll call them Bill and Ted just to keep them, uh, straight—were making out in a car on Lover's Lane. Bill had gotten

Ted's pants unzipped and was giving him a blow job when an announcement came over the radio:

"We interrupt this program for an important bulletin! A criminally insane person has just escaped from a conveniently nearby loony bin. He is a known murderer, has a hook instead of a right hand, and lurks around places called Lover's Lane where he likes to kill people. We now return to our regular playlist with Christina Fucking Aguilera."

Ted pushed Bill's face away from his crotch. "Oh, Bill, I'm frightened!"

"Don't worry," Bill consoled him, "she won't last."

"No," said Ned, "I mean about the madman with the hook. Maybe we should go home."

"Oh, forget about it. I'm sure they don't mean this Lover's Lane. Now sit still and get ready for heaven," Bill said as he clamped back down over Ned's dick. Ned's eyes rolled back into his head and he leaned back.

A few moments later, though, there came a scraping noise, which sounded frighteningly like metal against the car bumper. Ned sat up, alarmed. "I think I heard something!"

"Damn it, Ned, are you going to let me get you off or what?"

"I think we should leave, now! I'm really scared, Bill."

"Oh, yeah? Then why is this still hard?" Bill smirked and went back to work with a vengeance. Ned immediately moaned in ecstasy and relaxed. Bill's rhythm was working its magic. Ned started breathing heavily. His right leg twitched slightly as his torso became tense with a need for release. Bill knew it would be only a matter of seconds. Suddenly there was a sharp metallic scrape against the door nearest Ned. He jerked himself away from Bill, looking all around the darkness outside in terror.

"What was that?" he yelled, horrified, as he scrambled over Bill to the other side of the car.

"Shit! I almost had you! You were this close!"

"It's the madman, I know it! Drive away! Drive away!"

Instead, Bill angrily opened the door and stepped out. There on the door handle was a hook! He heard an insane-sounding laugh off to the side and whipped around to see the blood-crazed lunatic charging toward him. Bill reached inside the car, opened the glove compartment, took out a SIG-Sauer P228 handgun and shot the bastard dead.

"*No* one," Bill whispered hoarsely at the corpse, "fucks up one of *my* blow jobs!"

ORGAN HARVESTING

A man spent the night in a hotel with an expensive escort. The next morning he woke up alone, groggy, and naked in the bathtub covered in ice. There was a note that read, "Call 911 immediately." He staggered to the phone and did so. He explained his circumstances to the operator. The operator gasped, then asked if he had two incisions in his back, because there had been a rash of black-market kidney harvestings.

Terrified, he raced to the mirror to see. "No," he said, "I still have my kidneys, but oh, my God! My balls are gone! What sick person would harvest someone's testicles? They can't be transplanted!"

"Stay where you are," the operator told him. "I'm sending an EMT unit immediately."

"Uh, no. Don't bother," the man said. "I'm OK. I found my balls, and…um, they're where they're supposed to be."

The operator was very angry with him. "How the hell could you think you'd lost your balls?" she demanded.

"I *was* packed in ice, hel-*lo*?"

"Moron!"

"Bitch!" He hung up and life went on.

SATAN WORSHIP

In the late '80s, there was a story of how the CEO of Procter & Gamble was on an episode of *Donahue* in which Phil questioned him harshly about the suspicious moon and stars that made up the Procter & Gamble logo. According to urban myth, the CEO said he worshiped Satan and that a large portion of his profits went to support the Church of Satan! This caused a backlash against the company that lasted for years. Finally, the CEO was forced to go on *Oprah* to explain that it was all false. "In reality," he said, "I worship Britney, Xena, and Colt model Carl Hardwick when he doesn't shave, and a large portion of my profits goes to support Catalina Videos."

A PAIR OF SHOES

An attractive senior from the local college brought her cute, hunky boyfriend home with her to meet the family. The young man was a star track athlete, but a bit too pretty and stylish to be totally straight. He was very proud of his new shoes, showing off a pair of those one-of-a-kind cross-trainers you have to custom order over the Internet. The girl's brother, who was gay, became so hot and bothered by his sister's hunky, if slightly effeminate, boyfriend that he decided he needed to get out of the house after dinner. So he drove to a nearby rest stop to relieve his tension. He took a position in one of the stalls and waited. After about half an hour, a man entered the stall next to him. The young man stuck his finger inside the glory hole in the wall as an invitation. In response, a good-sized, semierect, cut cock came through the opening. It was beautiful, and the young man pulled on it for several minutes to get it fully hard. Then he took it in his soft, warm mouth. In very little time, the man in the other stall came. The scene was so hot that the young man also shot, some of his semen dribbling onto the shoes of the other man. When he looked down, he couldn't believe his eyes. *It was the one-of-a-kind shoes!* But the pants were quickly zipped up and the man was gone.

The brother returned home, smug in the knowledge that he'd just had his sister's boyfriend. When he came inside, there was the boyfriend washing off one of his shoes in the sink.

"Whatcha doin'?" he asked the boyfriend, with a sly smile.

"Just taking care of a little stain," he said.

"Uh-huh," the brother smirked. He noticed the boyfriend was wearing a pair of Doc Martens boots. "I see you changed into more butch footwear for the late evening."

"Nah, I've had these on since after dinner.

"Oh, yeah?" the brother smiled knowingly, inches away from the boyfriend's handsome face. "Then where have those cross-trainers been?

"I dunno," he said. " I loaned 'em to your dad. Ask him."

LITTLE MIKEY

You probably heard how Little Mikey, the kid in the old Life cereal commercial, died. He ate too much Pop Rocks candy followed by soda and it caused his stomach to explode! That's nothing. One of the other kids in the commercial grew up to be gay and recently died on the toilet from a similarly horrible medical reaction: Xenical and stuffed-crust pizza!

THE KILLER UPSTAIRS

There was a young man hired as a baby-sitter in a two-story house. He had put the children to bed and was downstairs watching a *Buffy the Vampire Slayer* after-midnight marathon and eating Marshmallow Fluff right out of the jar because he was alone and no one could see him. Then the telephone rang.

"Hello?"

There came a gravelly laugh on the other end, followed by "I'm going to tie you down and torture you horribly!"

The young man rolled his eyes and hung up. *Talk about a lame crank call,* he thought as he went back to *Buffy.* About 20 minutes later, while he was lusting after Angel, wondering what Vampire Watchers got paid and if the undead were uncut, the phone rang again.

"Hello?"

Again came the low, grating laugh. And again the frightening threat: "I'm going to tie you down and torture you horribly!"

The young man quickly hung up, unnerved that it had happened again and that it had caused him to miss the scene with Xander in a clingy tank top. He decided to call the operator.

"Yeah, hello. I'm all alone in a house where I'm baby-sitting innocent children upstairs and a creepy guy keeps calling and threatening to torture me."

"Wow, this sounds familiar," the operator said. "The next time he calls, try to stay on the line and I'll trace the call."

The young man went back to watching TV, wondering if Oz had red fur on his balls and if Giles would make a good Daddy. Then the phone rang.

"Hello?"

There was the hideous laugh again. "I'm going to tie you down and torture you horribly!"

The young man knew he had to keep the evil caller on the line. "OK, like, I'm taking nursing in college? But what I really want to do is stand-up, because that's how you get a TV show. Meanwhile my parents are on my case to go for premed. What do you think?"

"When I'm done with you," the cruel voice said, "I don't think it's going to matter."

"Well, it matters to me. I mean, my sister dropped out in her junior year and went to business college and my parents didn't say a thing, but it really put the pressure on me to perform, you know? Do you know what that's like?"

"Shut *up*!"

"Why should I have to be the college grad and make the family proud when, like, they never even asked me what I wanted, you know? I mean, don't I get a dream? Well, I have one and it's to move to New York or L.A. and get a really killer 20-minute set."

"*Stop talking!*"

" 'Cause I figure then all I'd need is to go to the right parties and meet the right people and in no time I'll be...hello? Hello?" He shrugged and hung up. Immediately the phone rang again.

"Yes?"

It was the operator. "I traced the call! It's coming from inside the house! It's the upstairs extension! Get out of the house! *Get out of the house!*"

Instead, the young man raced up the stairs to check on the children. Sure enough, there was a large, hulking figure dressed in black in the darkened hallway who roughly grabbed the young man by the hair and, in no time, had him tied up and helpless! The fearsome, deep laugh filled the house.

"Now," the intruder growled, "I'm going to torture you horribly!" And from a black bag he pulled nipple clamps, clothespins, and candles for hot wax. There was spanking, C&BT, and heavy ass play. It went on for hours, and it all happened right there in front of the children because it's my story and I'm just that fucked. The young man took it all as entire new worlds were opened up to him. But he wasn't satisfied.

"You call this bondage?" he taunted his captor. "Look at this, I can move all over the place. And where's the humiliation? Don't you think you should have at least peed on me by now? I mean, really!"

Finally the large man in black leather could stand it no more. He dragged the young man to the stairs and threw him down, killing him with a snap of the spine. He hadn't gone to the house to kill anyone, but *no one likes a pushy bottom!*

OK, enough of this foolishness. Get out there and start spreading this tommyrot to your friends. Sure, the stories are 100% bullshit, but don't let that stop you from adding to a bleak world's swirling chaos. It's great fun when you hear some ridiculous lie you concocted repeated back to you months later as the truth. I know, because at a reception several years ago at the Hotel Roosevelt in Hollywood, Richard Gere snubbed me, so I came up with that lunacy about the gerbils.

Yeah, that was me. Tell your friends.

Birth Day

Cyrus Tingle lived outside of Lumberton, N.C., where he worked on his father's tobacco farm. He hadn't counted on attending Coastal Carolina Community College when he graduated from high school, but he could play flute and, more important, march at the same time, which was what CCCC needed in its new marching band. Cyrus treasured the music scholarship he was awarded because it finally made his father stop asking, "Why couldn't you play something manly, like drums or tuba?" As it was, he couldn't practice Debussy or Satie when his father was in the house, only the muscular sousa marches and 4/4 renditions of rousing overblown pop songs like Neil Diamond's "America."

Cyrus's college band teacher, Dr. Hurlahee, convinced the dean that what they needed to do to put dear old Quadruple C on the map was to march in the Pasadena Tournament of Roses Parade and be seen on national television. Unfortunately, funds had already been earmarked for improvements to the gym, and the dean could only offer Dr. Hurlahee enthusiastic encouragement, no money. So for the past two years, Cyrus had helped band members hold car washes, spaghetti dinners, silent auctions, Halloween carnivals, spring flings, and a pig picking. Dr. Hurlahee had seen to it that the Rose Parade Committee invited them, and by the end of the second year, they had just enough money to make it. The band was ecstatic to be going to Pasadena.

The only other cities Cyrus had ever been to were Durham several times with his dad to sell tobacco, and Washington, D.C., once for a senior high school field trip. Everyone in Lumberton talked as if going to a big city was as remote and idiotic as traveling to China. Every news story from New York or Atlanta was another reason to fear cities. "We belong where God puts us," his Aunt Lulah would say. And Los Angeles? Well! Folks would roll their eyes and that was considered 'nuff said. In fact, Cyrus could recall only one time he'd ever been encouraged to go to a big city. It was after he'd bought the cast album of *A Chorus Line*. He played it over and over until his father, driven to distraction by hearing "At the Ballet" five times in a row, stormed into Cyrus's bedroom. Cyrus looked up, enraptured and oblivious to his father's ire, sighing, "Oh, Daddy, I wish I could see it on Broadway."

"I wish you and that goddamn record were there right now!" he yelled.

"Daddy?"

"You play that faggot song one more time, I will smash it with your mother's skillet."

At least Cyrus had been able to convince Dr. Hurlahee they should perform "What I Did for Love" when they marched down Colorado Boulevard in Pasadena. Most of the other band members had taken convincing. Honestly, sometimes it felt like he was the only person in four counties who had any musical sensibility. Being the odd one out like that didn't particularly bother Cyrus. It was just the way things had always been. He assumed his life would always be like this and that things were pretty much the same the rest of the world over.

Then he came to Los Angeles.

When the plane touched down a little after two in the afternoon on December 31, the 75 members of the CCCC marching band cheered wildly. For many it was their first time outside of North Carolina. On the bus from the airport, the band members pressed their faces against the tinted glass, their eyes devouring every strange and new sight of this city that just went on and on. When they got to the Hyatt on famous Sunset Boulevard, the lobby was filled with the chatter of their excitement. Cyrus was assigned a room with Robbie Poovey (trombone), Big Ed Stowe (bass drum), and Lee Hinkley (trumpet), all of whom threw their stuff on the floor of their 11th-floor room and took off for their girlfriends in rooms down the hall.

Cyrus sat on the bed quietly looking out over the city, recalling the fearful warnings of his family and friends about dangerous, cold, sin-filled cities. But there was also an insistent and growing tug of adventure that would not be ignored. Dr. Hurlahee had warned them all to stay in the hotel on threat of expulsion, but the world-famous Comedy Store was right next door. Surely that would be OK. He hung up his uniform in its zip bag and took the elevator down. None of the band members were in the lobby, so he scurried out and over to the Comedy Store. It was beginning to get dark but still only 4:30, so the Comedy Store wasn't open yet. He saw a convenience store on the other side of it, so he walked a little farther over, went in, and bought a Coke in a medium cup. Back on the street, he sauntered another few dozen steps so he could look down La Cienega Boulevard, the street that plunges down the hill from Sunset.

The sight took his breath away. The city seemed to be lighting up just for him. and he had a grand view of the L.A. basin below, already a grid of light like living jewels. It was too enticing. He had to walk down that hill.

Two blocks down, the road flattened out at Santa Monica Boulevard where Cyrus turned right. There was a something important in the air. It wasn't fear, because he felt perfectly safe. Indeed, two men he passed had smiled at him. As he walked farther west his senses heightened. Why did this place he'd never been within 2,500 miles of seem to be familiar, as if it had been waiting for him? He didn't feel he was walking so much as being drawn onward, pulled by something inside his chest. He continued past the Ramada Inn, the huge gym across the street, the car wash. Suddenly he stopped short.

Coming toward him were two men holding hands. They were talking and laughing and they walked right past him like it was nothing. They were homosexuals! Right there on the street. He turned to watch them walking away. Then he realized that almost everyone on the street was male. There was a bookstore up ahead. It was a bookstore for homosexuals. Couples passed, and they were almost always two men. Homosexual men. And they were happy. Well, some were angry or distracted or aloof, but they weren't sad. And they were all so animated. So loud. So big. Open. Familiar. Waiting. Possible. And *alive.* That was what had felt important, it felt alive. *He* felt alive. The pieces all fell into place and he was terrified. The awareness of how dead he had been seemed to crush him. Too weak to stand, he sat on the West Hollywood sidewalk and sobbed.

After several minutes he caught his breath. He picked up his medium Coke cup to find passersby had dropped change in it while he'd been crying. There was $1.30 among the last of his ice. He laughed. People were generous here. He got up and walked farther down the street. Why had he been taught to fear a city? Why had he been taught to fear everything? Questions and emotions were whizzing through him, all of them new, each one clamoring for attention as he continued walking in a daze.

There was a motor's roar. He was hit and knocked to the rough pavement. Cars in the intersection screeched to a stop. A man in a leather jacket and motorcycle helmet was helping him up.

"Are you OK?" the man asked. "You just walked in the road, man. Are you tweaking?"

"What?" Cyrus asked confused. "I don't live here."

The man lifted the visor on his helmet. He looked to be about 25, with amazingly golden-brown skin and beautiful black eyes. "I think I just grazed you, but Jesus, you gave me a scare." The man walked Cyrus to the curb. "Are you sure you're OK? Can you tell me what today is? Your name?"

"Tingle."

"Oh, shit. Where?"

"My name. Cyrus Tingle. I'm fine."

"Thank God. Ryan Ramirez." He shook Cyrus's hand. "Let me buy you a drink. God knows I could use one." He rolled his motorcycle onto the sidewalk. "Come on." About 15 feet away he parked it, and motioned for Cyrus to follow him into the pounding music coming out of a club called Rage.

Inside there were men who were dancing with other men. Another man was leaning over the bar to kiss the bartender. On the mouth. Like it was nothing. And the bartender looked just like a model. Most of the men here looked like models. Ryan took off his helmet and shook his short, wavy hair, so black it looked almost blue. Was Ryan a model too?

"What is this place?" he asked Ryan.

"Gay bar, so I hope you're not straight. What'll ya have?"

Cyrus was 20 years old, but his adrenaline was pumping and he felt strangely fearless. "I would like a beer, please."

Ryan caught the bartender's attention. "*Dos* Coronas." He looked hard at Cyrus's pupils. "Your eyes look OK. I thought you might have been high or something."

"No, I'm just from out of town." Cyrus told Ryan about coming from North Carolina to march in the Rose Parade. He told him about how it felt to be in Los Angeles, and that he'd never expected it to be so big. He didn't tell him about walking down Santa Monica or how he wanted to touch the back of Ryan's hand or bury his face in Ryan's wavy blue-black hair and inhale.

"Well, shit," Ryan finally said. "I need to take you to an honest-to-God celebrity party, don't I?"

"You mean like movie stars?"

"Drink up."

Outside Ryan straddled his motorcycle and put his helmet on. "You ever ridden one of these?"

"No."

"Well, just climb on and hold tight." Cyrus felt awkward and nervous clambering onto the seat. He needed to be getting back to the hotel, but he needed to be sitting close to Ryan even more. Afraid of where to put his hands, he hooked his index fingers in Ryan's belt loop. "That ain't gonna work," Ryan said. He pulled Cyrus's hands firmly around his stomach, kick started the motorcycle, and took off. Cyrus held on for dear life, scared of traveling so fast on two wheels, and of being seen hugging Ryan, even if it was on the back of a motorbike. The roar of the motor mercifully covered the sound of his pounding heart.

They went uphill for a long time and then turned onto a high road that seemed crazy with twists and turns. There were glimpses of vistas that were fantasies of light falling away into the distance. Suddenly Ryan took a road that plunged downward. A few hundred feet below the turnoff, there was a wide area where Jaguars, Mercedes, and limos were jammed in rows. Ryan parked the motorcycle by the catering truck and led Cyrus around to the side where they entered an enormous kitchen. To Cyrus it was whirling with activity. A dozen Spanish-speaking men in white uniforms were quickly and expertly loading large trays with exotic food and champagne. Others were cooking like mad on huge stoves. Ryan waved at a busy man wearing a chef's hat who waved back. "My cousin," Ryan told Cyrus.

A beautiful young Asian man came through the double doors. He was wearing a grass skirt and clearly nothing else. "Need more satay, *por favor.*" He was handed a platter of flat, grilled chicken pierced by long toothpicks and exited back into the party.

"Come on," Ryan said, taking Cyrus by the hand and steering him toward the double doors. Cyrus balked.

"I don't know these people."

"They don't know that. Just act like this place is a dump," and he pushed Cyrus into the party. There was a wide expanse of plush pale yellow carpet that stopped at glass walls overlooking the light grid of Los Angeles below. Half a dozen more of the beautiful men in grass skirts were maneuvering through and around a crowd of men who looked impossibly, casually perfect. There were two intermingling camps: plain but expensively dressed men in their 30s and 40s; and men Cyrus's age who looked like they lived in fashion advertisements.

An older man with a bright and sinister smile stepped in front of them. "Hello, I'm Philip. I don't believe I know you."

Ryan stopped a passing Polynesian for a flute of champagne before he bothered to respond. Then, without looking at his host, he said, "We're David's boys."

Instantly the old man's demeanor changed. "David's coming? David Geffen at my party?"

Ryan shrugged. "He said to meet him here." He pointed at a particular waiter on the other side of the room. "He's cute. Could you have him get us some satay?"

"Certainly," said the excited host. "Enjoy the party and happy New Year!" He bustled away on his errand.

"I thought for sure we were going to be thrown out," Cyrus said.

"Oh, we will be. Eventually, one day we'll die too. Drink up while you can."

The indicated waiter appeared with savory smelling satay and a smirk. "Hello, Ryan. What kind of crap did you feed Philip?"

"Nice to see you again too, Noel. This is Cyrus. He's visiting from another country."

"So I see. One where they don't have Clinique. Ryan, don't think I've forgotten you still owe me $1,400 and change."

"Oh, my God," said Cyrus. "Are you into drugs?"

"Only AZT. Noel blames me for having my car stolen with his negatives, head shots, and résumés inside at the time. You know, Noel, you could substitute shots from your movie career."

"Are you famous?" asked Cyrus.

"Yeah, that's why I'm in a grass skirt with my dick hanging out at someone else's New Year's party."

"Noel's movie career depends on his dick hanging out."

"Fuck you, Ryan," he said, and huffed away.

Cyrus felt uneasy. "Are we in trouble?"

"It's possible. Let's mingle."

An awestruck Cyrus met a supporting player in his favorite cop drama plus his lover. He also spoke with a Broadway and movie star, a sitcom star with three young men hanging on him, a director, something called a show runner, several producers, and a woman with the biggest Adam's apple he'd ever seen. It was close to 11 when there was a happy commotion in the foyer. A well-dressed but nondescript man in his early 30s was the center of attention. An entourage of half a dozen gorgeous young men wearing designer fashions and an abundance of attitude followed him.

"OK, party's over," Ryan said.

"Why?" Cyrus asked.

Ryan nodded at the man Philip was fawning over. "That's David Geffen." Philip pointed across the room toward Cyrus and Ryan. The man shook his head. Philip's smile fell as he glared at them.

Noel slunk by. "I'm only telling you this because we're friends," he said, "but I hid one of the Baccarat figurines from the piano and reported it missing to the host. It may have slipped out that I'd noticed you two lingering suspiciously near it."

"It's nice to know you don't limit your fucking people to video, Noel." Philip was advancing toward them with a very large man with scary muscles right behind. "Cyrus, I think you should get ready to run like hell."

"What? When?"

"Now!" Ryan grabbed Cyrus's hand and bolted for the kitchen, knocking a waiter on his grassy ass and sending his tray of champagne filled glasses flying.

"What the fuck?" exclaimed Ryan's cousin.

"Could use a little help, cuz!" Ryan shouted at him as they leaped over the catering staff and out the back door. "This way!" Cyrus found himself yanked into thick shrubbery by the trash bins.

The scary man and Ryan's cousin appeared at the kitchen door. His cousin pointed off to the right and the large guy took off that way.

"Jesus Christ, Ryan," Cyrus breathed, his chest heaving for air in the cramped prickly space. Ryan was facing him, gasping just as hard. Cyrus could feel the hot breath on his lips, could smell the champagne. He looked into Ryan's eyes. Ryan leaned forward and kissed him lightly on the lips. Cyrus stopped breathing, in shock. He tried to say…what? He didn't know. And he didn't get time to think because Ryan was kissing him again. Cyrus kept his mouth closed, not knowing how to respond.

"I've been wanting to do that since we got here," Ryan said.

The scary man strode by, his large shoes crunching on the ground inches from where they lay. He was on a walkie-talkie. "I lost 'em. Take J.J. and check out the north side. I gotta report, then I'll join you," and he disappeared into the kitchen.

"Time to go," Ryan said and started to move. Cyrus pulled him back for a real kiss. This time he opened up and let it happen. His hands come up to embrace Ryan's face and he felt Ryan pull his body closer. When it was over he was breathing even harder than before, and trembling. Ryan smiled at him. "We gotta get outta here."

They tiptoed among the cars to Ryan's motorcycle and soon Cyrus found himself hurtling down a canyon road. He didn't care who saw him hugging Ryan now. He leaned his head against Ryan's shoulder, lost in delight at the surprise of how right this felt.

After some time on flat, straight streets, they pulled into a dark neighborhood of houses and light industry. Ryan parked on the street and they joined an intermittent stream of men in black, all walking in the same direction. They turned in between some buildings and found a line of men waiting to get into an otherwise hidden bar. "How Soon Is Now" by the Smiths came thumping from inside. Cyrus eyed the line of men with deep apprehension. They had on leather chaps with no pants, shirts that looked like they were made of black rubber, leather pants, and shirts with metal studs and spikes. One man had his hands tied together and a leash around his neck. The night air was cold. He could see his breath and there was a different kind of trembling in his gut.

"Where are we?"

"Outside," Ryan said, frowning, considering their next move. "The trick is gonna be getting your underage ass inside. Come on." He led Cyrus around to the back, by the Dumpster. There he took a piece of cardboard from the trash and leaned it next to the back door where they were positioned. "Kiss me," he said and pulled Cyrus to him. Suddenly, Cyrus didn't mind the cold.

The back door opened as a bar back brought out a case of empty beer bottles. With a friendly grunt he noted the two young men making out by the door. He set his load down on a stack of other bottles and went back inside. Ryan pulled away from Cyrus, grabbed the cardboard piece, and stuck it in the door, blocking the latch from closing. He waited a moment, then peeked in the door. "Let's go," he whispered and pulled Cyrus inside after him.

The bar was filled wall to wall with masculine flesh, much of it exposed. The air was hot and the music intense. Moving through the loud, dense crowd was an experience in getting groped.

"Are you OK?" Ryan yelled above the din.

"People are touching me."

"Touch 'em back!" He glanced down at Cyrus's crotch. "You seem to be enjoying it," he smiled.

They made their way to the room with the most people. Inside, the crowd was facing the same direction and in a regular rhythm, everyone would shout, "Yeah!" Cyrus craned his neck to see what was going on. "Yeah!" the men shouted again. He and Ryan pressed into the wall of leather and sweaty men. "Yeah!" Standing on tiptoe he got a shocking view of the inner area. There was a naked man chained facedown to an X-shaped wooden cross. His back, buttocks and legs were deeply red. "Yeah!" There were two men, one wearing leather pants, no shirt, and a leather hood, the other in a full highway patrolman's uniform, taking turns flogging the man on the cross. "*Yeah!*" An earsplitting announcement came over the bar PA, "It's 10 seconds to midnight!" The patrolman and the man in the hood coordinated their strokes as the bar patrons counted down the seconds. "Seven! Six! Five!" With each stroke Cyrus could hear the man on the cross screaming with the pain as his tormentors put their backs into it. "Four! Three! Two! One!" The bar erupted in a deafening roar. Strangers were kissing him roughly. The groping turned aggressive. He couldn't get away. He couldn't find Ryan. Through the action he saw the patrolman and hooded man had released the guy from the cross. They were caressing him tenderly while he clung to them. It made no sense. And where was Ryan? He had no idea where he was or how to get back to his hotel. "Ryan!" He began to panic. "Ryan!"

"Over here!" Ryan strained to reach toward him.

"Ryan!" Cyrus desperately fought through the melee.

"I'm right here! It's OK!" He grasped Cyrus's hand and pulled him out of the thick of it.

Cyrus was shaking. "I gotta get out. I gotta get out now."

A few moments later, outside, Cyrus still hadn't recovered. "What the fuck was that?"

"I'm sorry," said Ryan. "I wanted to show you something, you know, different. Exciting. I didn't mean to upset you." He watched Cyrus pace back and forth by the motorcycle, shaking his head. "It was too much. I'm sorry."

"But what the hell was going on in there? Christ, whips?"

"Just a scene, let it go. I'm really sorry, Cyrus." He breathed a deep sigh. "I'll take you back where you're staying."

Cyrus stopped pacing and looked down. He put his hands on his hips, facing away from Ryan, working hard to assimilate what he had seen this evening. He inhaled sharp, cold air. He looked up at the low clouds eerily lit from below by the city. He turned around. "I think I'd rather go where you're staying."

"Really?"

"Yeah."

Ryan smiled at him broadly. *Damn,* thought Cyrus, *just like a model.*

They arrived at an old, tall apartment building north of Santa Monica Boulevard. "We're close to the Hyatt, so you can get back before the parade," Ryan told him as he parked the motorcycle in the garage in the back. The elevator creaked as they went up to the

10th floor. They padded down a dim, carpeted hallway to a paneled door. As Ryan was unlocking the door, it was opened wide by a thin man in his late 40s with a trim salt-and-pepper beard and bright blue eyes.

"For *moi*?" the man said with a jolly leer at Cyrus. "He's adorable, but a little young, even for me."

"Good," Ryan said, pushing him aside, "because he's mine. Cyrus, this is Trevor, Trevor Zendt."

Trevor shook Cyrus's hand. "Happy New Year. Come on in."

"I thought you'd be asleep, Trev."

"With Glenn Close boiling a rabbit on HBO? You must be mad."

"You eat dinner?"

Trevor shrugged. "Most of it."

Ryan ran his hand through Trevor's thinning hair. "OK, sport. We'll be in my room." He led Cyrus down the hall to a bedroom just large enough for a bed and a small dresser.

"Is he sick?" Cyrus asked.

"It comes and goes with the meds," Ryan said, unbuttoning Cyrus's shirt.

"But are you two…together?"

"Relax, no. When my parents threw me out, well, he was the uncle I never had." Ryan removed Cyrus's shirt, then pulled the undershirt over his head too. Cyrus started to ask another question, but Ryan kissed him. "No more talk." He put his lips on Cyrus's nipple and gently gnawed.

"Oh, God," Cyrus whispered.

An hour and a half later, Ryan was snoring softly, his arm and leg draped over Cyrus, who was wide-awake. He carefully disentangled himself and put on a pair of pants to go to the bathroom. Trevor was still watching TV and gave him a knowing smile as he passed. He finished peeing and caught sight of himself in the mirror. Suddenly he was overwhelmed and began to quiver, then weep. Helpless, body-wracking sobs. He slid to the floor. Trevor knocked on the door. "You OK in there?" Cyrus couldn't catch his breath to answer. Trevor opened the door. He lifted Cyrus and gently led him into the living room. He held Cyrus, stroking his hair for a good 20 minutes until the crying subsided. He held him for several minutes more, gently rocking him. At least Trevor held him at arm's length. "Girlfriend, that must have been some mighty good sex."

Cyrus managed a confused and embarrassed smile. "I don't know what just happened," he said wiping his nose. "Jesus, I don't think I know anything."

Trevor went to the kitchen and poured vodka from the freezer into a glass. "Here," he said returning, "take this and tell Auntie Trevor all about it."

And he did. There was a kindness about Trevor that made Cyrus tell him all about his life in North Carolina, the marching band, coming to Los Angeles, all the astonishing things that had happened to him that evening. "But I don't know why I lost it in the bathroom."

"Sounds like it's the first chance you've had to stop since you fell down the rabbit hole, Alice."

"What?"

Trevor looked directly into his eyes. "Everything you were died tonight, darling. That's why you had your little crying jag. You can't go back."

"I have to go back. We're flying out tomorrow night right after the parade."

"Not literally, you lunkhead. Get a clue. The person going back is not the same person who left. Which means you've got a lot of work ahead of you figuring out what you're gonna do about that in dear old Dixie." Cyrus screwed his forehead up even more. "You know, how do I come out to Dad? How do I tell my friends?"

"I could never tell them. They can't ever know."

"You and Ryan just fucked your brains out. You had your cherry popped by a hot man. How are you gonna put that genie back in the closet?

"They can't know," he repeated.

"Then your job is going to be learning how to live half a life," Trevor shrugged. "Plenty of people do it. I don't know how, but they do. I couldn't live knowing I was magic but never using it."

"I'm not magic."

Trevor laughed big and hearty. "Oh, honey! Yes, you are. You have amazing shit in you that you haven't even dreamed of."

"I don't think so," Cyrus scoffed.

"Ah, then let me tell you a thing or two, grasshopper." Trevor began by teaching him how being shunned for being different had created in Cyrus a wondrous capacity for empathy as well as survival. How the deep and private joys Cyrus quietly delighted in was a gift of being outside the company of the majority. How being thrust outside of the norm forced him into self-examination, opening him up to discoveries that were his and his alone. How this had made him able to see things in ways not available to most people, and how badly those people needed that insight. He told Cyrus what being two-spirited meant, and how he carried both masculine and feminine within. How this was a gift that ancient cultures recognized and revered, even if this one didn't. How not falling into the rigidly narrow paradigm of only one kind of allowable sexuality was powerful because it freed not only himself but others by showing the world that other options do exist. "You're a great gentle flute-blowing, cocksucking elf, my friend, full of wisdom, magic, and power. You need to know that, and you need to learn to trust it."

By sunup, Trevor's fire had excited yet confused Cyrus, whose mind was reeling. It was too much to absorb. Certainly not to be believed. It had to be the medicines Trevor was taking, Cyrus thought. At the very least, these wonderful things Trevor was saying were, well, if not impossible, certainly impossible for him. "I know you mean well," Cyrus said, "but that isn't me."

Trevor laughed at him with affection. "We'll see, you little homo hobbit, we'll just see!"

Ryan stumbled into the room naked. "Could you keep it down? It's New Year's, for chrissake."

"New Year's!" Cyrus was suddenly seized with panic. "Oh, my God! I've got to get back to the hotel! We're marching in the parade! How could I do this? I'll lose my scholarship!" He and

Ryan threw on clothes and jumped on the motorcycle. They raced down a nearly deserted Santa Monica Boulevard and up La Cienega to the Hyatt on Sunset.

"They left an hour ago," the desk clerk told them. Cyrus ran up to his room, grabbing his flute and the zip bag with his uniform. Downstairs Ryan had the motorcycle ready for him, and as soon as Cyrus was behind him, he gunned it and they tore off for Pasadena.

At the parade route, the motorcycle proved the best possible way to thread through the blocks and blocks of jammed cars. Cyrus shouted urgently at any parade official they passed, "Where's the staging area?" When they found it there were still dozens of giant flowered floats, marching bands, horses, and personnel to elbow through. Music played and a cheer went up from the spectators in the distance.

"It's started!" cried Cyrus. "Where are they? Sweet Jesus, where are they?"

"Tingle!" shouted an angry, familiar voice. Cyrus turned and saw Dr. Hurlahee. "You are in deep, deep shit with me, boy. You get on that bus, get in that uniform, and get back here in five minutes ready to go or so help me, God, I will send your ass back to North Carolina in a #10 can now!"

Other band members in their sparkling red and gold uniforms watched, sniggering, as he got off Ryan's motorcycle and made his way through them onto the bus. He found a paper grocery bag to put his street clothes in and pulled on what felt like a foreign costume. Trousers, tunic, boots, hat with chin strap and golden plume. He emerged from the bus as the rest of the band assembled awaiting the imminent sign to march.

Ryan was leaning against his motorcycle, his arms crossed. "I do love a man in uniform," he grinned.

"Tingle, we're up!" shouted Dr. Hurlahee.

Cyrus ran over to Ryan. "I can't say goodbye like this. Will you wait?" Ryan nodded and hugged him. Then Ryan did the most natural thing in the world. He kissed Cyrus on the mouth, which, naturally, made Cyrus kiss him back.

"Tingle!"

He whipped around to see 75 band members, baton twirlers, and majorettes gawking openmouthed. Horrified, he stumbled toward them, but he was so upset he dropped his flute. In the lunge to catch it he fumbled, it hit the asphalt, and he stepped on it, crushing the instrument.

The signal was given for the band to march, and the formation started forward around and past him, bent over his ruined flute. Dr. Hurlahee yanked him upright. "Take your place!"

"But my flute…"

"I don't give a good goddamn! Everyone back home is watching this parade and they are gonna see my band looking as it should! You get your faggot ass in line and you'd better by God look like you're playing!"

Cyrus scurried into line. He marched in this blaring, floral nightmare, miming his part. His head swam. Everyone knew. How could he have done that? What about his scholarship? Christ, what had happened to him in this terrible town? And what would happen back home? When his father heard the whispers? How could any of this have happened?

Nothing had made sense from the moment the plane touched down. God, he wished he'd stayed in the hotel. He'd never have seen a town full of homosexuals. People like Mr. Bruce, his Aunt Lulah's hairdresser who people made fun of and cheated, who'd turned bitter and grim. If that's what homosexuals are, then he was nothing like that. He wished Ryan had run him down and kept on going. What on earth had made him get on a motorcycle and go off with a total stranger? *Stupid, stupid!* Concentrate on the marching, that's all he had to do now. But the big celebrities he had met weren't at all like Mr. Bruce. They were successful, many of them stars. True, some of them were assholes. But he knew assholes in Lumberton who were only successful at being assholes. And who knew what these Hollywood types were really like? Aunt Lulah had warned him the cities were filled with sin. And he'd seen it with his own eyes. Jesus Christ, the man those other men were whipping in that awful place.

That awful place that terrified him. That had him hard the whole time he was in there. What was that? And the hands groping him in the sweaty closeness, each pressing touch a thrilling dark promise of sex with men. Men who did not look anything like sad or bitter. But the devil is clever, that's what the preacher always said. Keep marching. He confuses you. Like with Trevor and his honeyed words, even if he had been so gentle and well-meaning. He told seductive and pleasing lies. But sharing his body with Ryan was not a lie. No, that burned true. It stripped away everything he had pretended to be or thought he was and left him raw, exposed, and drunk with hope and possibility. It was like listening to *A Chorus Line*, only instead of from other people, the singing was coming from inside him. Everyone but Cyrus was playing "What I Did For Love" as he struggled to keep putting one foot in front of the other and find some sense in overwhelming events. Could everything he knew be false? Who can tell where the real lies are? Whose lie is the right lie? Or is everything lies? Keep marching, keep marching.

They turned down Colorado Boulevard, where the cameras were. People, so many people watching him, thinking he was normal. Thinking he was playing a flute. Passing. His family, teachers, friends, and schoolmates watching on TV. Not knowing the flute was broken. Not knowing his life was over. But they would, they would hear. And that would be the end. But keep marching now. Keep "playing." Keep playing at playing. The music faded in his head until he could only feel the throb of the bass drum in his chest, a beat that matched his heart on what felt like a death march that would not end.

There was an enormous mass of people milling about at the end of the parade route. Only when he ran into the trombone player in front of him did Cyrus realize the parade was over. Band members were murmuring to each other and starting at him. Numbly, he trailed behind them as they made their way back to the bus rendezvous point. There stood Dr. Hurlahee.

"Tingle, your disruption of this trip in inexcusable. You broke curfew, you went off limits, and your behavior was irresponsible.

Good God, boy, we had the LAPD looking for you! You disobeyed your chaperones, and more important, you disobeyed me." His schoolmates were all watching Hurlahee's practiced harangue and his own humiliation like it was an entertainment, some of them hanging out of the bus smiling. "I am hereby withdrawing your scholarship to Coastal Carolina, and when we get back, you just see if I don't have you expelled by Monday. But starting immediately, you are out of this band, you understand me? And you can start by turning in your uniform. Now, mister."

Cyrus got on the bus in a daze. As soon as he entered, the others pointedly left. He changed out of his fine red and gold tunic and boots and pants. He carefully wrapped the splendid hat in its proper plastic and closed the zip bag for the last time. He looked for the paper grocery bag with his clothes. He couldn't find it. He looked frantically all over the bus.

"Dr. Hurlahee," he called from the door of the bus trying to hide the fact he had only his pale blue boxers on. "My clothes have been stolen."

"Jesus Christ, Tingle, what now?"

"And my wallet, all my money, my plane ticket. My shoes, keys, everything!"

"Well, you're just up shit creek, aren't you? Everybody on the bus! We've got a plane to catch in two hours!"

"But what do I do?"

"Please shut up, Tingle. You've caused enough trouble. We'll deal with it at the airport."

Tears streamed down his face. The students boarded the bus, snickering at him in the doorway in just his boxer shorts as they passed.

"What do I do?" he whispered to himself, trembling and crying. "What do I do?"

Ryan appeared at the bus door. "Are you gonna be all right?"

"What do I do?" Ryan pulled him down and hugged him. Cyrus saw the students staring at them. He began to panic and squirm away. "No, no!"

Ryan glanced up at them for only a second. "Fuck 'em," he said. He held Cyrus again, kissing the tears on both cheeks. "Goodbye, Cyrus. I'm so sorry about everything. And I wish you didn't have to go back."

Cyrus sniffed back snot. "I don't even have any clothes."

"Actually I kind of prefer you that way."

Cyrus smiled a little. "I've got no scholarship. No school."

"No flute."

"No plane ticket."

"Tingle! You board this bus *now*!"

"Fuck you!" Ryan shouted back at him. He noticed Cyrus's reaction of horror. "Oh, please. What can he do? Have you expelled?"

With that, the freedom of the situation broke through to Cyrus. In a world where he had lost everything, the awesome power of possibility rose in him. With it came terrifying fear, but also a hope that made him feel giddy and alive. He starred into Ryan's beautiful eyes, seeing a man who understood what this was like. He grinned. They both laughed. Ryan nodded toward the motorcycle parked off to the side. "Yeah," was all Cyrus said. He took Ryan's hand and walked toward it.

"Tingle!" Dr. Hurlahee was leaning out of the bus door, his face a furious red. "Are you getting on this bus this instant, or am I going to have to haul your sorry ass up here myself? Answer me!"

Cyrus turned his sorry ass to his former teacher and dropped his boxers, mooning everyone on the bus. There was a most satisfactory whoop of amazement from them. So encouraging was it that he stepped out of his shorts and flung them at Dr. Hurlahee. Ryan kick-started the motorcycle, a completely naked Cyrus got on, and they roared away through the milling parade crowd.

"That was my New Year's, 1988," Cyrus told me at a New Year's party for a young millennium. "The year I began living my life." There was still a hint of an accent in his voice, and a graying at his temples that was very becoming. Cyrus is the manager of a hardware store in Hollywood now and plays the flute in the West Hollywood Orchestra. By the early '90s he and Ryan had nursed Trevor through dementia, blindness, several severe bleeds, and finally pneumonia. A year after that, Ryan was struck and killed on his motorcycle. But I saw no signs of regret from Cyrus. "You know, in medieval times people didn't mark their age by their birthday, but by the beginning of the new year. On the first of the year, everyone 'became' one year older. I mark my birthday the same way now." He took a sip of champagne. "By my count, I'm turning 14 tonight."

"Happy birthday," I told him.

He raised his glass. "Happy New Year."

A Final Thought

We're Here, We're Queer...Now What?

We all know that Pride is a series of steps on a long journey. Step 1 was coming out to yourself. It was when you realized you liked church sleepovers for none of the right reasons or, later, that you had married for all of the wrong reasons. Step 2 was coming out to others. You gathered your courage and told them, because the baggage of this secret made a truly rotten accessory that didn't go with a thing you owned. Step 3 was sifting through all the bullshit to get to a place you can live your truth with integrity. You remember that part. It started when you first said, "Since I know I'm not scum after all, I'll march right up to that cute guy (or gal), tell 'em I'm queer, and if they don't like it, they can kiss my ass." OK, so you said that in a gay bar, the point is you were making a start. And if you got really lucky, they did kiss your ass—long, slow, and deep. Step 4 was finding and claiming pride in yourself and your accomplishments. That's what we celebrate at pride festivals and it's great, even if you're only there for the eye candy or shopping for crap covered in rainbows. But after a few pride festivals, you start wondering about things. Like, "Who told some of these people that taking their shirts off was a good idea?" And, "Did we really need a remake of 'Lady Marmalade'?" Eventually, an even more important question arises: "OK, what's beyond pride?" And I'd like to answer that for you.

But I can't. Hey, I'm just a humor writer. Alleged humor at that. I suspect, though, that the answer to that question is tied to another. That being: Why are there so many of us *now*? Only 40 years ago, a pride event was Rock Hudson at your pool party. Today, so many of us have taken steps 1 through 4 that in Los Angeles alone pride shuts down West Hollywood and the damn thing costs 15 bucks to get into, which I suppose is progress of a sort.

It's a big question that can be asked in a number of ways. If you believe in evolution, it could be worded, "Why, at *this* point in the evolution of humankind, are there so many visible GLBTs?" I mean, if we really are "biological errors," why would nature create—and continue to create for millennia—a population that (generally) does not reproduce unless that population served an important purpose to that species other than Sondheim musicals? Don't forget that this phenomenal emergence has taken place in roughly a mere half century and, like karaoke, it refuses to die. *Something* seems to be happening.

If you believe in reincarnation, it's "Why did so many gay souls choose *now* to incarnate?" I think I chose now because it took humankind this long to perfect air conditioning and takeout. But what about you? Surely it wasn't the free condoms. Which brings up another point: With AIDS we've gone through a helluva lot of souls lately, yet the queer souls continue to incarnate like mad, arriving by the busload. Watch a pride parade. Despite the plague, we just keep going and going and going. (Now you know why the Energizer bunny is pink.) These are some pretty awesome numbers here. Why did we all decide to have a party *now*?

If you believe in God, the question becomes, "What is the action of the Holy Spirit in the radical emergence of gay people in our time?" I mean, the church already had those fabulous dresses for men centuries ago, why would God want more queers now? God knows, most churches don't want us, yet it certainly seems to please God to create us in such numbers. Surely there's a purpose to that, beyond God just wanting to piss off Jerry Falwell. Maybe it's time we started looking around for the reason.

Could it be happening because of the gifts we have that the world needs now? I know that may seem like an odd concept. The first time I heard it I thought, *Gifts to the world? I don't even know the world was registered.* But we do have gifts. For instance, by our being different yet thriving and having fun doing it, we give others permission to be different and do the same. We do that. What, you think Dame Edna happened on her own?

Another gift we exemplify, for those willing to learn from it, is that despite living in a culture that spends a lot of energy trying to tell people what role to be, we shrug it off and make up our own roles. "A man must be gruff and tough." Wrong! Catch me in my butch leather pants and manly denim shirt during the second act of *Into the Woods,* and I'm such a blubbering mess you could miss the final number for the floor drains gurgling. "A woman needs a man to be complete and to make babies." Bullshit! How do you think Heather got two mommies? When other people see us bursting through those walls, it's dynamic, powerful stuff.

That is our gift of freedom. Because we are outside the established norm, we can be whatever we want. That's why you'll see people in black leather, feather boas, cowboy hats, glitter, chains, *and* rubber at pride events. When you see them at Holiday Inn you'll know the struggle is over and we won. But our example shows others that this kind of liberation is available for the claiming.

And beyond merely being different, we are exemplars of how it can be done. You know damn well that Eddie Izzard was forced to catalog-order from the British equivalent of JCPenney until one day he saw a drag queen walking bold as day into Lane Bryant. Likewise, if some straight person is dying to try a little S/M, all they have to do is walk up to the guys on the Avatar float and ask. He or she will get good information and very possibly a friendly grope and phone number. We are an incredible and highly available resource.

We also offer enormous amounts of empathy and care. Just look at all the fags and dykes in nursing and the clergy. When I go to visit a friend in the hospital it's like old home week before I even get to the room. Despite all the antigay rhetoric of various churches, our urge to care for others fills pulpits like Leo DiCaprio is filling out his Calvins these days. I'm not saying heterosexuals don't do this, too, but gays are as overrepresented in these fields as we are at Home Depot and Disneyland.

Do you believe we think like straight people do? No, my sisters and other sisters, we do not. If we did, do you think the windows at Saks would look so fabulous? We offer an alternative thought structure. Einstein said that you can't solve a problem with the same kind of thinking that created it. The world is kind of a mess. Straight people could really use a hand cleaning up a few things and it's exciting to think we could help do that. I like to think of myself as Mr. Clean. Well, before he got his gym membership.

These are only a few of the gifts we offer. If you think about it for five minutes, you can come up with half a dozen more on your own—that is, if you can keep your mind off sex for that long. As a man, I know how unlikely that is for me; therefore I'll be relying on you lesbians. Again.

So if this many of us have come out, and done it at this moment in history, what *are* we here for? I mean other than the $9 sour-apple martinis? I don't know, but the clues are worth considering and talking about. It's certainly a more interesting topic for an ice-breaker than, "Got any Tina?" Through emphasizing our differences from heterosexuals, we could become a mirror that will allow straights to see their culture and themselves in ways they never could before. Who knows where that could lead? A healthier society, perhaps? Equal rights? Jack and Karen getting their own show? Wherever events may take us, these are ideas we need to explore.

I wish I could claim any one of these ideas as my own, but the truth is, I'm not that smart. I can't even get on *Jeopardy!* and I've tried three times. Fortunately, I have friends who are brilliant. How brilliant? Well, they hang around me, and that's points in their favor. They also write and have degrees in things I didn't know existed, like theopneustic semiology and canonical hermeneutics. I'm automatically impressed by people who have studied things I can't even pronounce. But they're the ones who sit around and come up with this stuff. Or I read it. I just try to digest it and pass it along. Basically I'm performing the same job as the colon.

And as we leave the colon (note to self: Find a better metaphor), there can be but one conclusion: Something is afoot. I don't know what it is yet, but there's evidence it could benefit the rest of the world far beyond the return of pastels and earth tones. So in taking the next step beyond pride and moving past "We're here, we're queer, get used to it," I propose a new slogan, not meant to be funny but to be investigated. It's one that speaks to our community as well as the dominant culture:

"We're here. We're queer. How 'bout we explore this together?"